Wonder House

(An imprint of Prakash Books)

contact@wonderhousebooks.com

ISBN : 9789354404351

Table of Contents

Force and Movements

Future Science & Technology

Light and Energy

Living Things

CHEMISTRY & ELEMENTS

THE BASIS OF ALL THINGS

When you hear the word 'chemical', do you think of coloured liquid sloshing around in a glass flask in a laboratory or of large tankers with 'Hazardous' written on the side?

Yet, did you realise that you too are made of chemicals—proteins, carbohydrates, lipids, nucleic acids, and water? Or that all our food is chemical? Indeed, all matter in the Universe is made of chemicals, as long as it is made of atoms, molecules, or ions. Apart from some stars that are made of subatomic particles, everything in our Universe is made of different combinations of about 100 elements that came into being the day the Universe itself did, with the Big Bang.

Once upon a time, alchemy was popular all over the world, as humans tried to find out the secrets of the material world and turn everyday things into gold. They finally found that it was impossible to do so, but in the process, they discovered various other useful things—how to purify materials, the nature of chemical reactions, the uses of petroleum, and even the chemical basis of life. And that became the modern science of chemistry.

▼ Modern chemistry owes its origins to ancient alchemists' quest for gold

What Makes Up Matter

In the past, people thought that the Universe was made of five elements: earth, water, fire, air, and ether. Today, we know that none of these are elements. Air is a mixture of gases, and earth is a complicated mixture of solids, liquids, and gases. Water and ether are compounds, while fire is simply the light emitted when a compound is **oxidised** at high temperature. Let's read on to find out what these words mean.

Element

An element is anything that cannot be broken down into simpler things by ordinary **chemical reactions**. So far, we know of 118 elements, of which about 20 are artificial elements made in nuclear laboratories. The rest all occur naturally. The most common elements on our planet are nitrogen—which encompasses most of our atmosphere—oxygen, silicon, aluminium, and iron in the Earth's crust. The core of our planet is made of a molten mix of iron and nickel, and deep inside is a ball of solid iron.

Chemists use one or two letters which represent elements when writing down chemical reactions. These letters are known as chemical symbols that are based on the elements' names.

For most elements, the first letter of their English name, such as C (carbon) or O (oxygen) is their symbol. Some elements have two letters, like Cl for chlorine. Elements known to science before the year 1800 have different names in different languages. Therefore, scientists use symbols based on their Latin names, such as K for potassium which is *kalium* in Latin, or Na for sodium which is *natrium* in Latin. Most metals and elements discovered recently have names ending in -ium—such as sodium or rutherfordium, while non-metals have names ending in -on, -gen, etc.—such as argon or nitrogen.

▼ *A lump of pure silicon, an element that is represented with the chemical symbol Si*

▼ *There are just 118 elements, but millions of different chemical compounds*

Compound

A compound is a substance made of two or more elements that can be broken down into its constituent elements by ordinary chemical reactions. Some compounds, such as deoxyribonucleic acid (DNA), can be very complicated and made of billions of atoms of different elements. A compound is written using the symbols of the elements in it, and numbers which depict the ratio these elements are found in. (The numbers are written in subscript after the symbol of each element in a compound).

For example, common salt is made of sodium (Na) and chloride (Cl) in equal proportions, so it is written as NaCl. Water is made of two parts hydrogen (H) and one part oxygen (O), so it is written as H_2O.

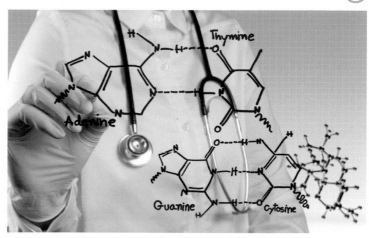

▲ DNA is a complicated chemical compound made of carbon (C), hydrogen (H), oxygen (O), nitrogen (N), and phosphorus (P)

Atom

Every element has a number of traits by which it can be distinguished. These are called its chemical properties, which include things such as mass, reactivity, density, and hardness. All of these in turn depend on the atoms that make it up. An atom is the smallest thing in the Universe that exists by itself at ordinary temperatures. In turn, an atom is made of three things called subatomic particles:

1. Electrons, which weigh almost zero, have a tiny negative electric charge and revolve around the **nucleus** (like the Earth revolves around the Sun).
2. Protons, which have a tiny positive electric charge.
3. Neutrons, with no charge. Protons and neutrons live in the centre of the atom, forming its nucleus.

An atom of an element always has the same number of protons and electrons, while atoms of different elements have different numbers of protons (and electrons). So helium has two protons and two electrons, while helium and lithium have two and three protons and electrons respectively.

▲ Model of a helium atom, which has two protons, neutrons, and electrons

Molecule

A molecule is made of two or more atoms that have come together in a chemical reaction. A molecule may be made of atoms of the same element or different elements. Some elements—such as nitrogen, oxygen, or chlorine—can exist in nature only as molecules.

▶ A water molecule is made of hydrogen and oxygen atoms that have come together in a chemical reaction

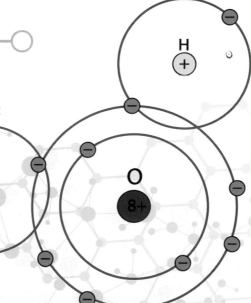

The Periodic Table

All atoms are made of electrons, protons, and neutrons. The number of protons in an atom—called its atomic number—decide which element it belongs to. For example, if there is only one proton in an atom, then it is an atom of hydrogen; if it has six protons, then it is an atom of carbon, and so on. The number of protons and neutrons together make up an element's atomic mass. Atoms of the same element may have one or more additional neutrons, which increase its atomic mass, but not its atomic number. Such atoms are called isotopes of the element.

Elements can be lined up based on their increasing atomic number. Scientists originally discovered that the chemical properties of elements were similar in periods of eight, so lithium, sodium, and potassium are similar to each other as highly reactive metals, while helium, neon, and argon are similar to each other as unreactive gases. This is now known as the periodic law, and the table is called the periodic table.

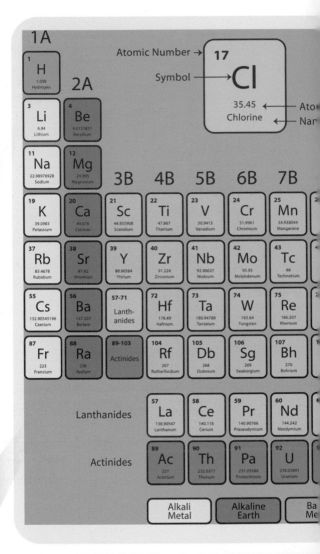

Hydrogen
Hydrogen (H) is the simplest element made of one proton and electron and no neutron. This element is abundantly available in the Universe and is known as the mother of all elements.

Alkali Metals
These are some of the most reactive elements in nature. They do not exist in their pure state, but are always found as compounds known as salts.

Alkaline Earth Metals
After alkali metals, these are the most reactive elements. Magnesium (Mg) is needed for photosynthesis, and calcium (Ca) is needed for our bone formation.

Transition Metals
These make up the biggest section of the periodic table. They have chemical properties between alkali metals and non-metals, so they behave like metals sometimes and like non-metals at other times. They form some of the most industrially useful chemicals, such as copper, iron, and manganese.

⊛ Incredible Individuals

The Russian scientist Dmitri Mendeleev (1834–1907) created the periodic table in 1869, after studying the properties of all the elements known in his time. He even predicted the chemical properties of elements that were unknown at the time, such as gallium. When gallium was discovered in 1875, it had the same properties Mendeleev had predicted for it!

▲ In 1969, Russia printed a stamp honouring Dmitri Mendeleev

Post-transition Metals

These metals are closer to semiconductors and are relatively inert. Aluminium (Al) and lead (Pb) have many uses while the rest are used as semiconductor dopes. Transition metals are on their left in the periodic table, while metalloids are represented on their right.

Metalloids

These are also known as semiconductors. They are used in modern electronics.

Non-metals

This is a diverse bunch of elements. Apart from selenium (Se), they are the elements most needed for life, such as carbon (C), nitrogen (N), oxygen (O), sulphur (S), and phosphorus (P). They are usually plastic (i.e. they will not regain their shape if bent) and cannot conduct electricity, as opposed to metals and metalloids that are elastic and can conduct electricity.

Halogens

These are the most reactive non-metallic elements. We use them for many purposes such as making lamp fillings, cleaning agents, and plastics; and they often partner with alkali metals in forming salts.

Noble Gases

These elements exist as gas in their natural state. Since they do not react with anything, they are called inert gases; and as they are not very abundant, they are also called rare gases.

Lanthanides

These elements are also called rare earths. They have many uses in modern electronic devices such as semiconductors and switches.

Actinides

Most of these are radioactive elements. Uranium (U) is the most important and is used in nuclear reactors to make electricity, while others like plutonium (Pu) are used in nuclear weapons.

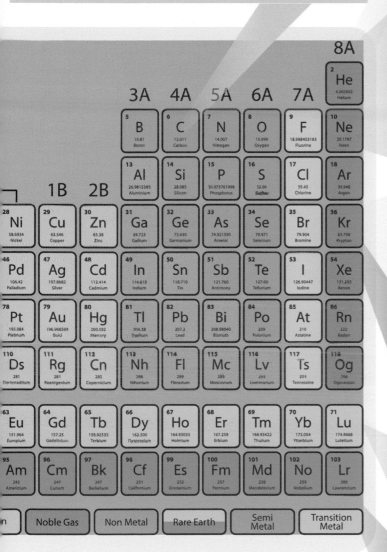

▲ *The periodic table showing all the 118 elements*

▼ *Atomic structure for Hydrogen, Oxygen, Carbon, and Nitrogen*

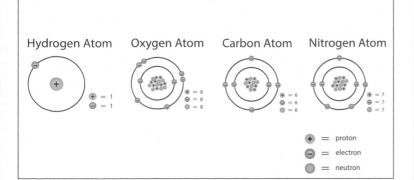

👤✓ In Real Life

An element that is yet to be discovered is named after its atomic number using Latin numbers and '-ium'. So, element no. 119 is called un-un-enn-ium. Once an element's discovery is verified by other scientists, the people who first discovered it are free to give it any name they like.

States of Matter

Chemists define matter as anything that can be touched or felt. At any given temperature and pressure, matter will exist in a phase (also called a state of matter), in which its atoms or molecules have a certain amount of freedom to move and can be separated from another phase by physical means. The natural phase of all materials is their physical condition at 20°–25°C ('room temperature'), and atmospheric pressure at sea level. For example, water is liquid in its natural state, but it turns to gas (steam) when heated above 100°C, and solid (ice) when cooled below 0°C.

If you heat or cool a material, at some temperature, it will change from one phase to another. Scientists call this a phase transition. Every material will change into another phase at a specific transition temperature. In daily life, there are two main transition temperatures. The melting point is when a solid becomes liquid, and when the opposite happens (liquid becomes solid), it is called the freezing point. Further, the boiling point is when a liquid becomes gas, and the condensation point is when gas becomes liquid.

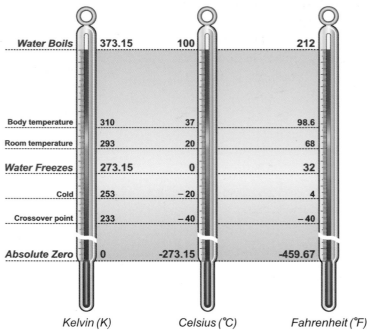

	Kelvin (K)	Celsius (°C)	Fahrenheit (°F)
Water Boils	373.15	100	212
Body temperature	310	37	98.6
Room temperature	293	20	68
Water Freezes	273.15	0	32
Cold	253	−20	4
Crossover point	233	−40	−40
Absolute Zero	0	-273.15	-459.67

▲ *Did you know that the Celsius scale is based on the melting and boiling points of water?*

▶ *Steam is the gas form of water. It is used to power engines and turbines*

🔍 Gas

This is a state of matter when all the atoms or molecules of a pure substance have complete freedom to move; imagine a classroom when the teacher is absent. This is called **fluidity**. Nitrogen (N), oxygen (O), hydrogen (H), the **halogens** (F, Cl, Br, I, At, Ts), and the **noble** gases (He, Ar, Xe, Kr, Rn, Og) are elemental gases, while carbon dioxide (CO_2), ammonia (NH_3), sulphur dioxide (SO_2), and methane (CH_4) are compound gases.

Plasma

A plasma is a special kind of gas that exists when there is very high electric current. Many kinds of atoms, especially those of metals, lose an electron or two and become positively charged (since now they have more protons). Other kinds of atoms gain an extra electron and become negatively charged. Both kinds of charged atoms are called ions. Plasmas are used in Plasma TVs and many other electrical applications.

◀ *Water dissolves so many things that it is called the universal solvent*

▲ *Lightning lights up the sky around 50–100 times per second around the planet*

Liquid

This is a state of matter when the atoms or molecules have lost some freedom to move; similar to a parade of soldiers moving under the officer's orders. Liquids move at a speed known as their **viscosity**—the more of it they have, the less fluid they are. Mercury (Hg) and iodine (I) are the only elemental liquids at room temperature. On the other hand, thousands of compounds are liquids at room temperature. Water (H_2O) is the best-known liquid. Many liquids are used as **solvents**, in which other solids or liquids (such as sugar or salt) can be dissolved for carrying out chemical reactions. You may often hear or read that glass is a very viscous liquid, but that is not true. Glass is an amorphous solid, that is, it has no internal structure.

Solid

When there's no freedom to move at all—like standing to attention for the national anthem—the atoms or molecules become a solid. Solids come in two forms: crystal, in which the atoms are arranged in rows and columns (called lattices) like soldiers in a parade; or amorphous, in which there is no organisation. One glass-like substance commonly called crystal is quartz, a mineral whose molecules are arranged in a regular lattice, which is transparent. Most elements and solid compounds are crystalline, such as sugar, salt, metals, and rocks. Many others, often made from living things, are amorphous, such as wood, chalk, cloth, and paper. Earth is a mixture of both kinds.

▲ *Ice is the crystalline form of solid water, while snow is its amorphous form*

Absolute Zero

The coldest temperature possible is –273.15°C, at which all the atoms and molecules of a substance completely freeze over. This is called absolute zero. In 1995, scientists found that near this temperature, atoms are no longer separate but merge to form a Bose-Einstein Condensate. Satyendra Nath Bose and Albert Einstein had predicted this in 1924. The Kelvin Scale of Temperature used by scientists is based on Absolute Zero. On this scale, –273.15°C is the same as 0°K (Kelvin), while 0°C is written as 273.15°K.

Purification Methods

When all the atoms or molecules in a material are of the same kind, it is called pure.
In real life, nothing is ever 100% pure. There are always other things called impurities that are mixed in. When there are lots of impurities, it is impossible to predict what will happen when the material is used for chemical reactions, or for making things. Therefore, chemists use purification methods to make a material as pure as humanly possible. Here are a few important ones, though there are many more.

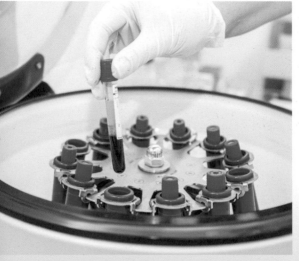

Sedimentation

This process uses gravity to separate solids from liquids. If you leave muddy water undisturbed in a glass, the mud will settle down and leave a clear layer of water above.

A machine called a **centrifuge** helps sedimentation happen faster by spinning mixtures in special tubes at very high speeds. The solid collected at the bottom is called sediment. Centrifugation is used in laboratories and chemical plants after a chemical reaction has produced a substance that is not soluble in water.

◄ *Centrifugation is used to separate plasma from blood cells before the plasma can be given to a patient who needs it*

Filtration

This is a method that makes use of the sizes of materials. A filter is a material that has holes of a certain size. Anything smaller than those holes will pass through, while bigger things will not. Filtration is used to separate floating particles from liquids and gases. When two solids are separated, it is called sieving.

Adsorption is a method by which impurities stick to a filter (usually finely powdered carbon) while water passes through.

▶ *Air conditioners have filters fitted in them to remove dust and other particles by adsorption*

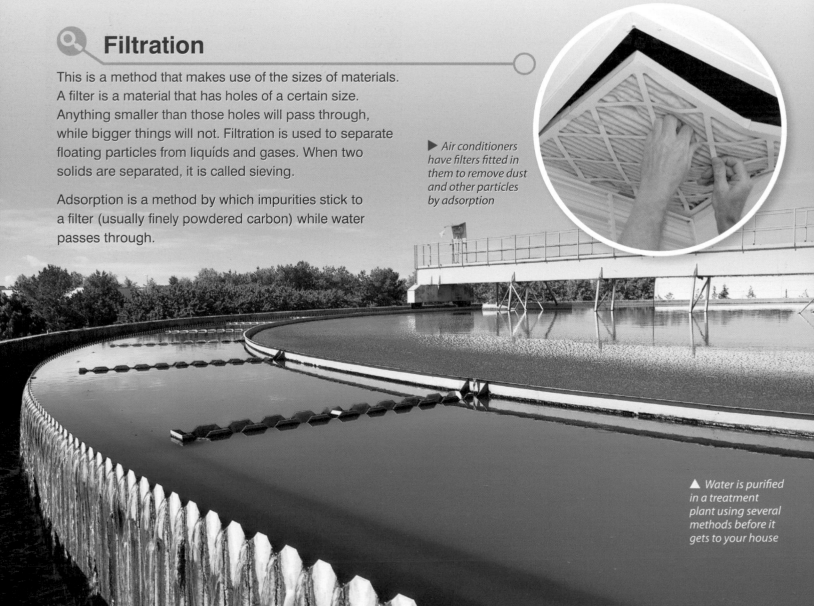

▲ *Water is purified in a treatment plant using several methods before it gets to your house*

Distillation

This is a method that makes use of the boiling point of a liquid. An impure liquid, like tap water, is boiled in a special distillation still. The water boils off, leaving solid impurities behind. At the other end of the still, the steam is condensed back to water.

One of the best-known methods for distillation is fractional distillation. Using this process, a mixture of two liquids, whose boiling points are far apart, is separated. For example, ethanol (C_2H_6O) boils at 78°C, while water boils at 100°C. By heating a mixture of ethanol and water at just above 78°C, ethanol can be distilled from water.

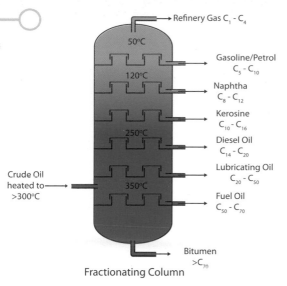

▲ *Fractional distillation is used to separate crude oil (petroleum) into useful chemicals. This is also called refining*

⊙ Incredible Individuals

Cleopatra the Alchemist (not to be confused with the queen of the same name) is believed to have lived in Egypt around the 2nd or 3rd century CE. She invented the alembic, a glass vessel used for distillation even today.

 ## Crystallisation

Try this: add salt to water in increasing amounts and watch it dissolve. After some time, the salt will stop dissolving with water. This is called saturation. If you heat this solution, the undissolved salt will dissolve, and you can keep adding more salt as the water heats further. Stop adding salt when you reach the boiling point. Now let the solution cool. It has now reached **supersaturation**. If you add a grain of salt to the solution now, you will see highly structured crystals of salt forming in the solution. This is called crystallisation and is used to purify soluble solids from supersaturated solutions.

▲ *Sea salt is made by evaporating seawater, and then purified by re-dissolving it in freshwater and crystallising it*

💡 Isn't It Amazing!

Crystallisation is used to study the molecular structure of chemical compounds by throwing X-rays on a purified crystal. The pattern made by the X-ray is then analysed through mathematics. In this way, Rosalind Franklin found the structure of DNA.

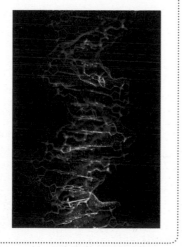

▶ *The structure of DNA was found by shining X-rays on it*

 ## Sublimation

Some solids directly turn to gas when heated without going through the liquid phase. This is called sublimation. Sublimation can be used to separate two solids, if one of them becomes gas on being heated. Sublimation in vacuum is used to purify the materials used in electronics.

Chemical Reactions and Bonds

Chemical reactions occur when one chemical meets another under specific conditions. The chemicals going into a reaction are called reactants, while those that are formed after the reaction are called products. To understand them, let's learn how electrons are arranged in an atom. They revolve around the nucleus, but different electrons move in different **orbitals**, just like the planets move around the Sun in different orbits. The farther an electron is from the nucleus, the less it is attracted to it. Reaction speeds then vary and depend on temperature.

Each orbital must have its electrons in pairs. If it doesn't, it is said to be unstable. Apart from noble gases, all elements have at least one unstable orbital, that is, they have only one electron. This unstable orbital is what causes chemical reactions.

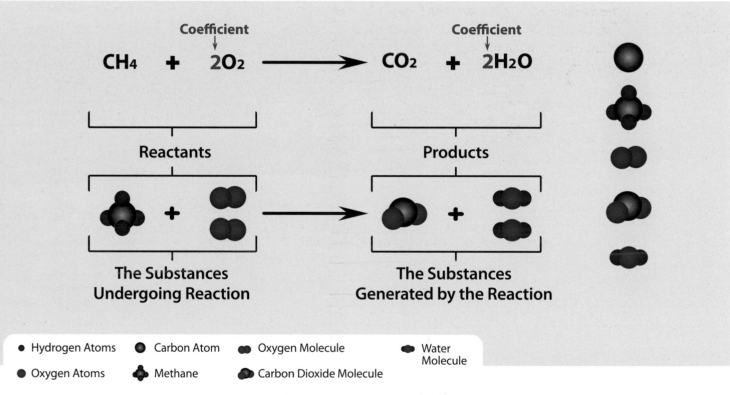

$$CH_4 \quad + \quad 2O_2 \quad \longrightarrow \quad CO_2 \quad + \quad 2H_2O$$

Coefficient · Coefficient

Reactants · Products

The Substances Undergoing Reaction · The Substances Generated by the Reaction

- Hydrogen Atoms
- Oxygen Atoms
- Carbon Atom
- Methane
- Oxygen Molecule
- Carbon Dioxide Molecule
- Water Molecule

▲ *How chemical reactions are written using symbols of elements*

🔍 Ionising Reactions

Unstable orbitals make an atom 'behave' in either of two ways. If the electron is far from the nucleus, the atom it belongs to may simply give it away to an atom that wants it. It now becomes an ion. As it has more protons than electrons, it has a positive electrical charge, so it is called a cation. Hydrogen and most metals form cations.

In the case where an atom takes electrons from other atoms, the receiving atom becomes an ion with a negative electrical charge called an anion. Most non-metals, halogens, and metalloids become anions.

A chemical reaction in which cations and anions are formed is called a redox reaction or an ionising reaction. The element or compound that gains electrons is said to have become reduced, while the element or compound that gave up electrons becomes oxidised. The resulting product is called a **salt**. The salt added to your food is just one kind of salt, sodium chloride (NaCl).

Ionic Bond

An ionising reaction creates one cation and one anion. They attract each other strongly because of opposite charges, forming an ionic compound. This attraction is strong enough to keep them bonded to each other, so it is called an electrovalent bond or an ionic bond. In the solid state, an ionic compound forms regular crystals.

Non-Ionic Reactions

The unstable orbitals of non-metallic elements can behave in another way. Instead of losing or gaining electrons, atoms of non-metals often 'share' electrons. This way, each atom's unstable orbital gets to have two electrons. A chemical reaction in which this happens is called a non-ionic reaction. The most common example of this is burning, when oxygen in the air reacts with heated fuels such as gasoline or diesel. The scientific name for this is combustion and it is used in the combustion engines that power cars.

IONIC BOND

Formation of an Ionic Bond

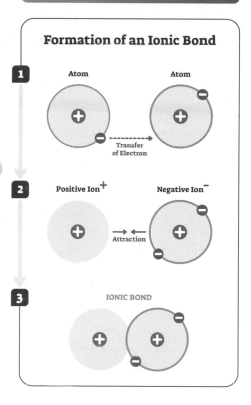

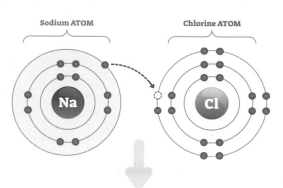

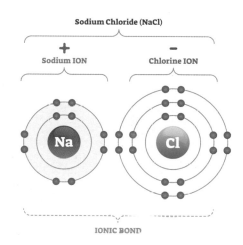

▲ A redox reaction leads to the formation of a compound with an electrovalent bond between its ions

Covalent Bond

A non-ionic reaction creates no ions but the atoms still stick around each other and share their electrons. The bond between them is called a covalent bond. Covalent compounds are often gases or liquids. In the solid state, they are often amorphous.

Hydrogen Bond

In water, hydrogen atoms share electrons with oxygen. The larger oxygen nucleus pulls the shared electrons closer to it, gaining a tiny negative charge. Hydrogen gains a matching positive charge. This makes hydrogen atoms weakly attract oxygen atoms from another water molecule. This is called a hydrogen bond, which is weaker than covalent bonds or ionic bonds.

⊙ Incredible Individuals

John Dalton (1766–1844) believed that the chemical properties of elements are because of the structure of their atoms. Until his time, it was believed that all elements were made of the same kinds of atoms, but he showed that each element has its own different atomic structure. Today, we know this as atomic theory.

▶ John Dalton laid the foundation of modern chemistry

Acids, Bases, and pH

In most books and films, an acid is shown as a coloured liquid fuming in a laboratory, or something that causes an upset stomach. However, scientists define acids and bases in a very different way. Acids and bases form much of the groundwork of modern chemistry and have hundreds of uses. They are often used to convert raw materials into the plastics, paints, medicines, preservatives, dyes, and many other chemicals we use in daily life. The balance of acids and bases in our body is an important part of staying healthy.

 Acid

Scientists define an acid as something that easily gives up a hydrogen ion (H^+) or ends up with extra electrons at the end of a reaction. Another definition of an acid is that it is any chemical in which one or more hydrogen atoms can be replaced by a positively charged ion (cation). The three most common acids used for chemical reactions are hydrochloric acid (HCl, which is also found in your stomach), sulphuric acid (H_2SO_4), and nitric acid (HNO_3).

Fatty acids, which are made of carbon molecules, do not dissolve in water. All others dissolve in water and break up into anions and hydrogen ions:

$$HCl + H_2O \rightarrow H^+ + Cl^- + H_2O$$

 Base

A base is the opposite of an acid. It is something that easily takes up a hydrogen ion (H^+) or ends up with fewer electrons at the end of a reaction. The three most common bases used for chemical reactions are sodium hydroxide (NaOH, also called caustic soda), potassium hydroxide (KOH, also called caustic potash), and ammonium hydroxide (NH_4OH). Bases that react really fast are called alkalis.

Bases dissolve in water and break up into cations and hydroxide ions:

$$NaOH + H_2O \rightarrow Na^+ + OH^- + H_2O$$

▼ *Many compound gases dissolve in water vapour to form acid droplets*

NO_2 SO_2

H_2O

◄ *Throughout the world, there are lakes that have become alkaline, like the Little Alkali Lake situated in California, USA*

💡 Isn't It Amazing!

Aqua regia is a mix of hydrochloric and nitric acid used to dissolve the metals gold and platinum. In 1940, when the Nazis invaded Denmark, they wanted to seize the Nobel Prize medals given to Jewish scientists Max von Laue and James Franck—but they could not find them. Another scientist, George Hevesy, had dissolved them in aqua regia. After the war, the gold was recovered and cast into new medals.

🔍 Salt

A salt is formed when an acid reacts with a base by the neutralisation reaction:

$$NaOH + HCl + H_2O \rightarrow Na^+ + Cl^- + 2H_2O$$

Many acids and bases react very strongly with each other, releasing a lot of heat. Such reactions are called exothermic reactions.

▶ Sea salt is mostly sodium chloride

🔍 pH

pH stands for potential of Hydrogen. It is a way of determining how acidic or basic a solution is, by measuring the number of hydrogen ions present in it. The pH scale is inverse logarithmic, that is, an increase of 1 on the scale means that there are 10 times fewer hydrogen ions. Closely related to it is the pOH scale, which measures the number of hydroxyl (OH-) ions. At a pH of 7, there are equal number of hydrogen ions and **hydroxyl ions**, so the solution is said to be neutral. Below 7, the solution is acidic and above 7, it is basic or alkaline.

$$H_2SO_4$$

$$HNO_3$$

Trees killed by acid rain

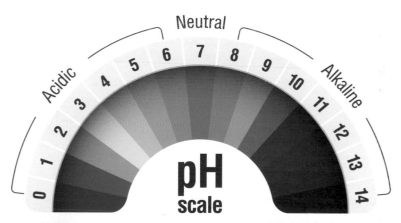

▲ The higher the pH, the fewer the hydrogen ions present

👤 In Real Life

Some chemicals change colours if the pH of their solution changes. They are therefore used as pH indicators. Your school lab may have pH papers, which are special paper strips soaked in chemical and dried. When dipped into an acidic or basic solution, the paper changes colour.

▲ A pH paper changing colour to show that there is alkali left over in a bar of soap, which may burn your skin

Catalysts

Some acids and bases react very easily and quickly with other things, so they are called strong acids and strong bases. Others react slowly, so they are called weak acids and weak bases. The ease with which a chemical reacts is called its **reactivity**. If you want to make a reaction go faster, you can heat the vessel containing the chemicals, or put a lot of pressure on it by placing a weight above it. Another way is by using a catalyst, a chemical that does not take part in the reaction or is re-formed at the end of the reaction. Among the most common catalysts in the world are enzymes—**proteins** created by our bodies while digesting food which help many other reactions inside our body.

Homogeneous catalysis happens when the catalyst and reactants are all in the same state of matter. For example, sodium bicarbonate ($NaHCO_3$) and citric acid ($C_6H_8O_7$) will not react with each other when they are in a dry form. When they are dissolved in water, the water acts as a catalyst and they react, forming carbon dioxide. This is used for making **antacids**.

$$NaHCO_3 + C_6H_8O_7 + H_2O \rightarrow NaC_6H_7O_7 + CO_2 + 2H_2O$$

Heterogeneous catalysis happens when the catalyst is in a different state of matter than the reactants. Graphite (a form of carbon), platinum (Pt), and palladium (Pd) are the most common catalysts. Iron (solid state) is used as a catalyst in the manufacture of ammonia from nitrogen and hydrogen (both gases).

▲ *Solid catalysts help increase the surface area and bring reactants together*

🔍 Enzymes

Enzymes work inside our bodies by a mechanism known as lock-and-key. There are thousands of enzymes in each of our cells and each enzyme catalyses only a single reaction. The enzyme's molecular structure has slots that allow different reactants to stick to it. Enzymes either join two reactants into one (called anabolism) or break a reactant into two (called catabolism). Anabolic enzymes are required for making proteins and other things that we need to grow, while catabolic enzymes are needed for digesting food and getting energy out of it. For example, pepsin, an enzyme made in our stomach, breaks down the proteins we eat.

▶ *Enzymes work by bringing reactants together and reducing activation energy*

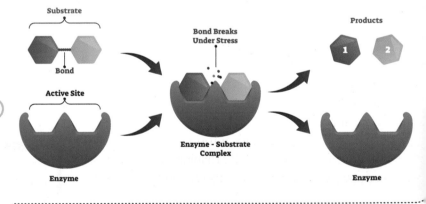

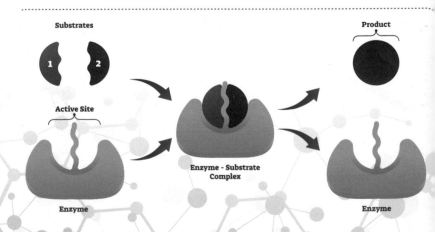

Metals

Chemically, a metal is an element that can form a cation by giving up an electron, and a non-metal is an element that forms an anion by accepting an electron. A common property of metals is that they should be malleable (easily hammered into sheets), or ductile (drawn into wires). They exist as crystalline solids in nature (except mercury, Hg), often do not react easily, and can readily conduct heat and electricity. They also have great tensile strength, that is, they can be stretched without breaking.

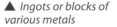

▲ *Ingots or blocks of various metals*

Silver, gold, copper, and iron are among the oldest metals known to humanity, along with bronze, an alloy of copper and tin. The history of humanity is divided into the Stone Age, the Bronze Age and the Iron Age. The Stone Age ended around 3300 BCE when humans discovered that they could make better tools out of metals instead of stone. As the hardest metallic substance available was bronze, the period is called the Bronze Age. Around 1200 BCE, humans discovered how to purify iron from its ore, thus starting the Iron Age. Iron is tougher and more flexible than bronze, and can be used for making many more things. We still live in the Iron Age.

Let's look at the periodic table on pages 6–7. Why do different kinds of metals take up so much space on it, and if they have common properties, why do they seem to be of different kinds?

Reactive Metals

Chemically, metals should be able to give up their electrons easily. Alkali metals, such as sodium and potassium, and alkaline earth metals, such as calcium and barium, do this the best. They almost never exist in pure form and will react with the oxygen in the air if purified.

▶ *Pieces of potassium. Potassium is so reactive with air that it has to be covered in unreactive mineral oil*

Transition Metals

These are what we commonly mean when we say metal. When they react with alkali metals, they can behave like non-metals. They are found in nature in a compound form called **ore** and can be converted to pure metal through a chemical process called refining. After refining, they stay in a pure state but react with the oxygen in the air very slowly by a process called corrosion. Some, such as gold and platinum, do not react at all and are known as noble metals.

Alloys

An alloy is a mixture of metals that is stronger than either of them separately and is used for many purposes. Brass (copper and zinc), bronze (copper and tin), and stainless steel (iron and carbon) are the most common alloys.

💡 Isn't It Amazing!

For long, the toughest swords were said to come from the city of Damascus (present day capital of Syria), with beautiful patterns on the surface. They were made of wootz steel found in southern India. While the technique was lost for a period, some individuals have recreated techniques that are of the calibre of original Damascus steel.

▲ *An antique knife made of Damascus steel*

Hydrogen and Helium

Did you know that 74% of the Universe is made of hydrogen (H), and another 8% is made of helium (He)? That just leaves 18% of the Universe's matter for the remaining 94 natural elements. But why is it so?

Hydrogen was the first element to be created when the Universe came into being during the Big Bang nearly 13.8 billion years ago. Therefore, it is called the mother of all elements. It is made of just one proton and one electron. It makes up the mass of all the stars, as well as a lot of **interstellar gas**. Deep inside stars, where the pressure is hundreds of millions of **pascals**, four hydrogens turn into one helium atom by a process called **nuclear fusion**. The electrons and protons of two atoms collapse into neutrons, which have no charge, while the other two protons join

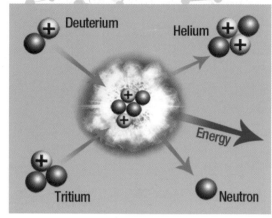

▲ *Hydrogen turns into helium deep inside stars, giving the energy that makes them glow*

them to make the helium nucleus. The remaining two electrons form a pair that orbits around the new nucleus. A lot of energy is released from this reaction, making stars glow.

🔍 Uses of Hydrogen

Elemental hydrogen is rarely found in nature as it is very reactive. It is produced industrially by making steam and methane (CH_4) react, with nickel (Ni) as a catalyst. This hydrogen is used for creating ammonia (NH_3), which is then used for making urea, which is used to make **fertilisers**. Hydrogen is also made to react with vegetable oils to turn them into margarine. These are just two of the numerous uses of hydrogen. It is also utilized in vehicles; in the production of electricity; in oil refineries; and so on.

◄ *Margarine is made by making hydrogen react with vegetable oils*

🔍 Isotopes of Hydrogen

Hydrogen has two isotopes. Deuterium is an isotope wherein the nucleus has a neutron in addition to a proton. As the electron has no weight, the deuterium nucleus is twice as heavy as the hydrogen nucleus. The isotope tritium has two neutrons, so it is thrice as heavy. Water that contains deuterium or tritium instead of plain hydrogen is called heavy water. It is used in nuclear reactors as a coolant.

💡 Isn't It Amazing!

The Large Hadron Collider, a giant detector built by physicists to detect subatomic particles, uses 90 tons of liquid helium to maintain a temperature of -271.3°C.

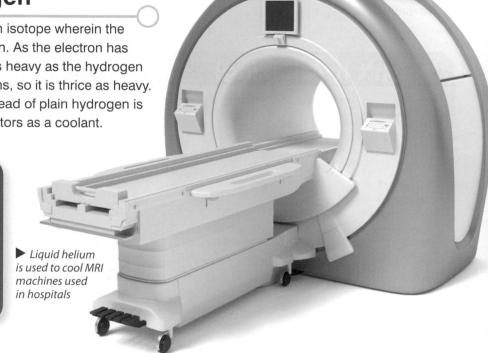

▶ *Liquid helium is used to cool MRI machines used in hospitals*

Noble Gases

Look at the last column of the periodic table on pages 6–7. This clubs together the elements helium (He), neon (Ne), argon (Ar), krypton (Kr), xenon (Xe), radon (Rn), and oganesson (Og) as noble gases. But why are they called that?

Each row (called a **period**) of the periodic table represents one shell of an atom. A shell is the space in which electrons move. Every element that has its outermost shell completely filled with electrons will neither give up electrons nor take any. Thus, it becomes chemically unreactive. Since they do not form ionic, covalent, or hydrogen bonds, they have low boiling points and are gases at normal temperatures.

In earlier times, elements were classified as base, which reacted with others, and noble, which did not react with anything. Gold is a noble metal because it does not react with anything. Iron is a base metal because it reacts with oxygen from the air and **rusts**. That is how the noble gases got their name. All these are arranged at the end of the period and make a vertical group, since they have similar chemical properties.

Row	Shells	Maximum Electrons in Outermost Shell	Elements
First	1	2	H, He
Second	2	8	Li to Ne
Third	3	8	Na to Ar
Fourth	4	18	K to Kr
Fifth	5	18	Rb to Xe
Sixth	6	32	Cs to Rn (including Lanthanides)
Seventh	7	32	Fr to Og (including Actinides)

86   **Radon**   Rn

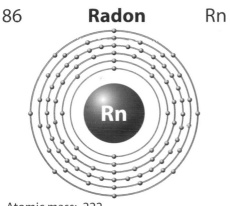

Atomic mass: 222
Electron configuration: 2, 8, 18, 32, 18, 8

▲ *An atom of radon showing all its 6 shells filled with electrons*

☀ Isn't It Amazing!

Noble gases can be turned into plasma under very strong electric current. This plasma then glows with a signature colour. This property is used to make glowing lights, which are often used as shop signs. The first to be used was neon (Ne), which gives a reddish-orange colour. These lights are called neon lights. Other noble gases project different colours.

▲ *Neon lights in Hong Kong. Different gases result in different colours when turned into plasma*

Nitrogen

Making 78% of the air around you, nitrogen is the most abundant gas in the atmosphere, which is good for us for it is a chemically unreactive gas in molecular form (N_2). Without it acting as a **damp**, almost everything would burn easily in oxygen. On the other hand, as an element, nitrogen is extremely reactive. It makes both a powerful acid (nitric acid, HNO_3) and a powerful base (ammonia, NH_3). It is named after **nitre** (KNO_3), which is used in making explosives such as firecrackers.

Nitrogen is one of the six elements critical to life, being an important part of proteins and nucleic acids. However, if most of the nitrogen on our planet is inert, how does it become such an important part of our lives?

👤✓ In Real Life

A number of bacteria can convert atmospheric nitrogen into ammonia, which is then used to make proteins and other biochemicals. Some of these bacteria live on their own, such as cyanobacteria. Others live together with plants such as legumes, inside a special structure in their roots, called root nodules. The plant gives them food in exchange for the ammonia that they make. Some of the ammonia is released into the soil. So farmers often grow a crop of legumes between other crops in order to enrich the soil with nitrogen again.

Root nodules

▲ *The root nodules of legumes contain bacteria that provide nitrogen for most living organisms through the food chain*

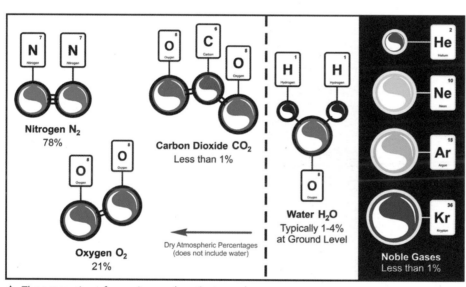

Nitrogen N_2
78%

Oxygen O_2
21%

Carbon Dioxide CO_2
Less than 1%

Water H_2O
Typically 1-4% at Ground Level

Dry Atmospheric Percentages (does not include water)

Noble Gases
Less than 1%

He, Ne, Ar, Kr

▲ *The proportion of gases in our planet's atmosphere*

🏅 Incredible Individuals

Carl Wilhelm Scheele (1742–1786) was a Swedish chemist who discovered many elements and compounds in his small laboratory. He discovered that air was made mostly of two gases—one that supported combustion (fire air), and another that did not (foul air), which we now know to be oxygen and nitrogen, respectively. Unfortunately, though he discovered chlorine, molybdenum, barium, tungsten, and hydrogen, he could never publish his discoveries in scientific journals, and the credit for his discoveries went to others. Today, however, he is recognised as one of the greatest chemists to have ever lived.

▶ *Sweden printed a postal stamp in 1942 to recognise Scheele's 200th birthday*

Oxygen

Though oxygen makes 21% of the atmosphere currently, did you know that there was no oxygen in the air three billion years ago? We owe the oxygen we breathe to certain blue-green bacteria that started making their own food through **photosynthesis** and released oxygen as a waste product. Although oxygen—like all other elements—is made in the stars by nuclear fusion, it is very reactive and becomes a part of various chemicals very quickly. Most of the oxygen on our planet is actually in the oceans, making 89% of seawater by weight.

▲ *Blue-green bacteria, now part of pond scum or ocean plankton, made all the oxygen in the atmosphere today*

🔍 Reactions of Life

Carbon is the main element that makes up all living organisms, but it is oxygen which takes part in the two great reactions that make up life. In photosynthesis, six molecules of water (H_2O) from the soil and six molecules of carbon dioxide (CO_2) from the air are combined in the presence of light to make one molecule of glucose ($C_6H_{12}O_6$). This reaction happens in blue-green bacteria, algae, and plants. Chlorophyll acts as the catalyst. Six molecules of oxygen (O_2) are released for each reaction and that's what we depend on for breathing.

$$6CO_2 + 6H_2O + light \rightarrow C_6H_{12}O_6 + 6O_2$$

The other great reaction is **respiration**, which happens in all living creatures. In photosynthetic creatures, it happens when there is no light. It is the exact reverse of photosynthesis, where glucose ($C_6H_{12}O_6$) reacts with oxygen (O_2) to form water (H_2O) and carbon dioxide (CO_2). Respiration turns the stored energy of light into the **chemical energy** that enables creatures to grow and move.

$$C_6H_{12}O_6 + 6O_2 \rightarrow 6CO_2 + 6H_2O + chemical\ energy$$

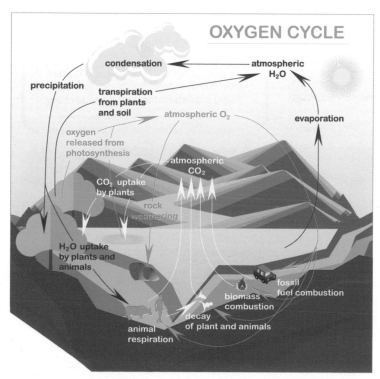

OXYGEN CYCLE

condensation — atmospheric H_2O

precipitation

transpiration from plants and soil

atmospheric O_2

evaporation

oxygen released from photosynthesis

atmospheric CO_2

CO_2 uptake by plants

rock weathering

H_2O uptake by plants and animals

fossil fuel combustion

biomass combustion

decay of plant and animals

animal respiration

▲ *The natural oxygen cycle between photosynthesis and respiration has now been disturbed by large-scale burning of fossil fuels*

⭐ Incredible Individuals

Oxygen was discovered by Joseph Priestley (1733–1804) and confirmed by his friend Antoine Lavoisier (1743–94). Lavoisier gave oxygen its name after he discovered that it is a part of many acids. In Greek, *oxys* means acid and *genes* means parent, so oxygen stands for that which gives rise to acids. Both Priestley and Lavoisier led difficult lives. Lavoisier was beheaded in the French Revolution, and Priestley had to flee England due to his political views.

▲ *We know much about oxygen due to the pioneering work of Joseph Priestley and Antoine Lavoisier*

Carbon

Carbon (C) is the element that makes us. Together with oxygen (O) and hydrogen (H), it makes the carbohydrates and fats that we eat. Twenty kinds of special compounds made of C, H, O, and nitrogen, called amino acids, make all the proteins in our body. Deoxyribose Nucleic Acid (DNA) is a complicated compound made of phosphorus (P) and all these elements. DNA is the chemical that stores our genetic code. Other compounds of carbon form the vitamins we need and a whole lot of other biochemicals in our body. To understand why carbon is so special, we must look at its atomic structure.

Atomic Structure

The carbon nucleus is made of six protons and six neutrons. It has two shells of electrons, one pair of electrons in the inner shell, and four unpaired electrons in the outer. The four unpaired electrons are always looking for a partner, which determines its **valency**. So, a carbon atom can make chemical bonds with four other atoms, which makes it a tetravalent element. Very often, the carbon atom will link to another carbon atom through a covalent bond. In this way, carbon atoms can make a long chain called a concatenation. Sometimes, the chain folds in on itself, forming a ring of carbon atoms.

▶ *Carbon has four unpaired electrons in its outer shell which give it a unique chemistry*

Isn't It Amazing!

Diamonds are a complex compound made entirely of carbon atoms in which each atom is bound to four others. This makes the compound very compact and so diamond is the hardest thing on Earth. On the other hand, another form of carbon is graphite, in which carbon atoms form rings of six each and these rings make flat sheets. The sheets are stacked one upon another, so they can slip and slide. This makes graphite one of the softest materials known to man.

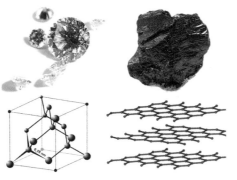

▲ *The chemical structures of graphite and diamond. Graphite is used in pencils, while diamond is used for cutting metal sheets*

▼ *Coal is burned in power plants to make steam, which drives the electric turbines*

Coal

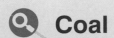

Coal is made from the remains of plants that died millions of years ago and were reduced to elemental carbon over time. Coal is used for various purposes; one such use is as fuel in electric power plants. Coal and petroleum are together known as **fossil fuels**.

formaldehyde   ethanol   quinine   benzene   cholesterol

acetylsalicylic acid   DDT   acetone   triclosan

▲ *Carbon atoms are shown as points in large organic compounds to save space. Unsaturated bonds are shown as double or triple lines*

🔍 Organic Compounds

There are several millions of compounds that can be made from carbon and thus it has its own field of chemistry called organic chemistry. Any chemical compound that has carbon and hydrogen atoms in it is an organic compound, though compounds containing only carbon and hydrogen are called hydrocarbons. Most hydrocarbons are obtained from petroleum, which is actually a mixture of hundreds of hydrocarbons found underground, or under the sea floor in many places around our planet.

Organic compounds containing other elements, such as oxygen, chlorine, or sulphur, can be made from hydrocarbons through chemical reactions. Hydrocarbons can be classified into two types:

1. Aliphatic compounds are made of carbon atoms lined up in long chains to which hydrogen atoms are attached. They are saturated and joined by a single bond. Chemicals such as acetone and ethanol are aliphatic compounds.

2. Aromatic compounds have their carbon atoms arranged in a ring. They are very stable and easily react with other substances. Chemicals such as benzene and quinine are aromatic compounds.

Organic compounds may be **saturated** or **unsaturated**. In saturated compounds, each carbon atom makes covalent bonds with four different atoms. In unsaturated compounds, there may be two or three covalent bonds between two carbon atoms. Most vegetable oils are unsaturated while the main compound in butter—butyric acid—is saturated.

Organic compounds are divided into two parts—a hydrocarbon backbone and functional groups. The backbone gives the compound its structure, while the functional groups such as acid (COOH), alcohol (-OH), amide (CONH$_2$) give it its chemical properties.

▲ *Coal is a finite resource, as new coal takes over a million years to form. Most of the coal we use today is over 300 million years old*

Sulphur and Phosphorus

Among non-metals, sulphur (S) and phosphorus (P) stand out for their usefulness, in both industry and biology. Sulphur is part of cysteine, an amino acid which is part of keratin, the protein which makes your hair and nails. Sulphur atoms in cystine form disulphide bridges, which tie two strands of keratin together, making the hair stronger.

On the other hand, phosphorus is an important part of DNA, where it forms the 'backbone' of the molecule. It is also part of adenosine triphosphate (ATP), a compound that stores the energy released from respiration. Our bodies 'couple' reactions, so that every time there is a need for energy in a reaction (say adding an amino acid to a protein chain), ATP is broken down to adenosine diphosphate (ADP) and a free phosphate (PO_4^{3-}) ion:

Protein chain + amino acid + ATP → longer protein chain + ADP + PO_4^{3-}

▲ *The progress of a country is at times measured by the amount of sulphuric acid it uses*

🔍 Sulphuric Acid

Scientists call sulphuric acid (H_2SO_4) the 'king of chemicals' because it is part of several reactions that are important to modern life. It is found in most cars as part of the lead-acid battery that gives electric power to the engine. The electric power is used to create a spark, which makes the fuel burn inside the engine, making it work. Sulphuric acid is also used for manufacturing hundreds of chemicals, including phosphate fertilisers. It is also used in the manufacture of other acids, the refining of petroleum, and the solubilising of ores.

🔍 Phosphate Fertilisers

Ammonium phosphate ((NH_4)$_3HPO_4$) is a common fertiliser that provides plants with both nitrogen (N) and phosphorus (P). It is made by treating two parts of ammonia (NH_3) with one part of phosphoric acid (H_3PO_4):

$$H_3PO_4 + 3NH_3 \rightarrow (NH_4)_3PO_4$$

▼ *Using phosphate fertilisers makes it possible to grow more crops in the same amount of land*

👤✓ In Real Life

Rubber is used widely to make tyres because it is elastic, strong, flexible, and light. However, natural rubber is prone to wearing off quickly unless it is vulcanised, which requires heating it with sulphur in large vats. The sulphur forms sulphide bridges between different rubber molecules, thus toughening it. This process was accidently discovered by Charles Goodyear in 1839.

Silicon, Semiconductors, and Ceramics

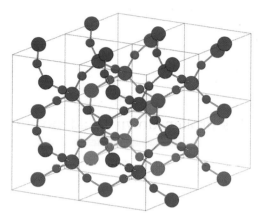

If you see the periodic table on pages 6–7, you will notice that silicon (Si) is placed in the same group (4A) as carbon. Elements in the same group (that is a vertical column of the periodic table) share similar chemical properties. Therefore, silicon, like carbon, is tetravalent, that is, it has four electrons to share. Like carbon, it also forms long chains. Silica (SiO_2), formed of silicon, and oxygen, is the most common compound in the crust of our planet, making up about 26% of it, and is found in sand, mud, and most rocks. Like diamond, it forms tetrahedral crystals called quartz.

◀ *The beautiful crystals of quartz are made from the tetrahedral arrangement of silicon dioxide molecules*

Semiconductors

If you look at the periodic table, you'll notice that silicon is part of a set of elements called metalloids, spread across periods and columns. All of them share a common property—they act as semiconductors of electricity. This means that they only allow a certain amount of current to pass through. Semiconductors are used today in a wide variety of electronics such as mobile phones, computers, and radiation sensors, among others.

▶ *An electronic board with a silicon chip in the centre will have millions of microscopic electronic circuits in it*

Ceramics

You see silicon all around your house—in the floor and wall tiles, in flowerpots and decorative vases, and even in the bricks that make your house. All of these are made of ceramics—things that are hardy, have low electric conductivity, and are chemically inert. They've been with us ever since the late Stone Age.

Clay from riverbeds is made of oxides of silicon and aluminium. These can be mixed with water to make a smooth dough that can be pressed into various shapes. When the moulded objects are dried and heated at a high temperature in a **kiln**, the silicon oxides form various interlinking structures that give the material its hardness but also make it brittle, that is, easily breakable.

▲ *A potter's wheel is used to shape wet clay before it is baked*

In Real Life

Supercooling happens when a liquid is cooled below freezing point but hasn't turned solid. Glass is supercooled silica, but it is so viscous that it behaves like an amorphous solid.

▶ *The art of stained-glass painting involves painting on glass pieces and heating them in a kiln so that the paint becomes transparent*

Currency Metals

Look at column 1B in the periodic table. It has the three metals: copper (Cu, from Latin *cuprum*), silver (Ag, from Latin *argentum*), and gold (Au, from Latin *aurum*). They are called currency metals, because they were used for making coins for a long time. They share similar properties of being very ductile (can be drawn into wires) and malleable (can be hammered into shapes).

Gold is often alloyed with silver or copper to make it more malleable, because pure gold can break on hammering. They also make it less dense and therefore, lighter. The purity of gold is measured in carats, with 24 carats being the purest form possible (99.9%). Most jewellery is 18 carats (75%), with 25% silver or copper.

▲ *Lumps of gold, copper, and silver. Due to certain scarcities, coupled with growing demand, the price for copper has shot up recently*

🔍 Corrosion

Corrosion is an occurrence wherein metals react with the air while water vapour acts as a catalyst. When silver corrodes, it is called **tarnish**. It reacts with hydrogen sulphide (H_2S) present in air to form silver sulphide (Ag_2S), which is black in colour. Copper reacts with the carbon dioxide present in damp air to form a greenish **patina**. When iron corrodes, it is called **rust**. But as long as metal objects are kept dry, they stay as they are. Gold does not react with anything except when it is pressurised under extreme conditions. That is why it was used as money since it does not lose its value.

▲ *Did you know that the Statue of Liberty is green because it is made of copper which has acquired a patina?*

👤✓ In Real Life

Numismatics is the art and science of studying coins. It can tell us a lot about life in the past, including the prices of things and how countries were governed.

▲ *Collecting coins is a very interesting hobby*

🔍 Other Metals and Alloys

Since 1866, the 5-cent coins of the USA have been made of nickel (Ni), and hence are called nickels. In our times, alloys of copper and nickel (cupro-nickel), stainless steel, zinc, and aluminium are used to make coins. Bronze (an alloy of copper and tin) and brass (an alloy of copper and zinc) are also used.

▲ *These coins are part of the European currency. Modern coins are made from a wide variety of metals and alloys*

Iron and Steel

The uses of iron and steel are so many that they would need a book of their own. Iron is a wonder metal. It is hard yet not brittle; it is ductile and malleable; and it is a great conductor of heat and electricity.

The science of metallurgy looks at how metals are purified (extracted) from their natural state. In nature, a metal is part of a compound, usually an oxide, sulphate, nitrate, or phosphate. These compounds are called minerals. Rocks are made of minerals of various kinds. The rocks that are rich in the mineral of a particular metal are called ores. The most common ores of iron are hematite (Fe_2O_3) and magnetite (Fe_3O_4).

Extraction of metal from an ore is called smelting. The ore is crushed to powder and mixed with flux, a chemical that reacts with the ore and reduces it to metal. For iron, a pure form of coal called coke is used. The ore and flux are melted in a smelter and the following reaction takes place:

$$Fe_3O_4 + 2C \rightarrow 3Fe + 2CO_2 \text{ and } Fe_2O_3 + 3CO \rightarrow 2Fe + 3CO_2$$

The pure iron is usually allowed to solidify as **ingots**.

💡 Isn't It Amazing!

In Delhi, the capital city of India, there is a pillar made of iron that has not rusted ever since it was built more than 1,600 years ago. This is because it is covered by a thin film of iron hydrogen phosphate ($FeHPO_4$) which stops air from reacting with the iron underneath.

▶ *The Iron Pillar in Delhi*

▶ *Molten refined iron being poured into rods which will be cut into rectangular ingots*

🔍 Steel

Most of the iron in the world is used as steel, an alloy that has up to 2% carbon and manganese. Carbon makes steel harder and less brittle than iron. Steel does not rust as easily as iron, and is more malleable and ductile. That is why it is used to make train tracks, bridges, vehicles of all kinds, and even cooking vessels. When steel rods are used as a frame over which cement is poured, it is called reinforced cement concrete (RCC).

Alloy Name	Carbon %	Manganese %	Used to make
Very Low Carbon Steel	0.1	0.4	Car body panels
Low Carbon Steel	0.1 – 0.3	1.5	Stamped and forged things
Medium Carbon Steel	0.3 – 0.6	0.6 – 1.65	Railway wheels and rails
High Carbon Steel	0.6 – 1.0	0.3 – 0.9	Springs and high-strength wires

Polymers, Plastics, and Rubber

So far we have seen how carbon atoms can link to themselves, forming long chains. They can also form long chains (polymers) of whole molecules called **monomers**. A **polymer** may be made of the same kind of molecule or one kind of monomeric unit called a homopolymer. For example, starch is made of glucose molecules linked together. If a polymer is made of different kinds of molecules, such as amino acids in a protein, it is called a heteropolymer. While nature makes many complex polymers, humans too have found ways to make them. Many of them have special industrial uses but some of them have become common in our lives—plastics, rubber, and synthetic fabrics.

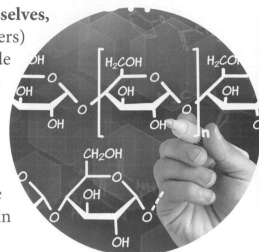

▲ *Starch is a homopolymer made of glucose molecules that are its monomers*

🔍 Petrochemicals

Petroleum is formed from the carbohydrates of dead plants and animals that were buried millions of years ago. In modern times, it is pumped out from the ground in **oil wells** (on land) or **oil rigs** (at sea). When it goes through fractional distillation (see page 11), it gives many different chemicals. Some of these are used as fuel in our cars, airplanes, and rockets, such as petrol (called gasoline in the USA), diesel, kerosene, and naphtha. A whole lot of others are used as raw materials to make petrochemicals. These include plastics of all kinds, paints, dyes, synthetic fabrics like nylon, vinyl, and synthetic rubber.

Plastics are made from monomers obtained from petroleum. The polymers may be in the form of long chains or branched networks of monomers. Long-chain polymers are favoured for making synthetic fabrics such as nylon. Branched polymers are preferred for making moulded items. Bakelite, a highly branched polymer (which makes it tough), is used for making brake pads, toys, and electric insulation.

Plastics are often named after the monomer used to make them. For example, PET, used to make bottles and food boxes, is Poly-Ethylene Terephthalate, and PVC, used for making pipes, is Poly Vinyl Chloride. Polyethylene is used for making disposable plastic bags and Polystyrene is used for disposable cups. They are now banned in many countries.

▼ *An oil rig pumps out petroleum from the sea floor and a giant ship called a tanker carries it to the shore where the petroleum is refined into fuels and petrochemicals*

Polyethylene	Polypropylene	Poly(vinyl chloride)	Polystyrene

polycaprolactone   polyhydroxybutyrate   polylactic acid

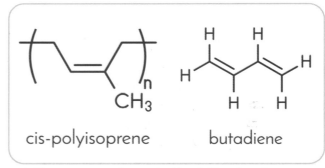

▲ Petrochemicals (left) are used as monomers to make a wide variety of plastics (right) and synthetic fabrics

🔍 Rubber

Rubber is a natural polymer made from the rubber tree. It has many uses in our lives, though most of it is used to make vehicle tyres. Rubber is also used to make gloves and waterproof clothing, insulation for electrical items, carpets, and also the erasers used to remove pencil marks. Indeed, that is how rubber gets its name in English.

The monomer of rubber is a compound called cis-polyisoprene. It is made from the rubber tree, *Hevea brasiliensis*. Synthetic rubber is made from a similarly shaped compound called butadiene.

cis-polyisoprene   butadiene

▲ The monomers of natural rubber (left) and synthetic rubber (right)

⭐ Incredible Individuals

Thousands of police officers and soldiers owe their lives to one woman—scientist Stephanie Kwolek (1923–2014). She invented a polymer called Poly-p-phenylene terephthalamide, which she found was resistant to tearing and breaking even by bullets. This polymer can be turned into a fabric called Kevlar, which is sewn into bulletproof vests.

▲ Bulletproof vests are made of a polymer called Kevlar, invented by Stephanie Kwolek

▲ Natural rubber is made from the sap of rubber trees

Nuclear Chemistry

On page 18, you read about nuclear fusion that happens deep within stars. There is another kind of **nuclear reaction** called **radioactive decay**, seen in the elements technetium (Tc), promethium (Pm), and all elements beyond bismuth. The atoms break down spontaneously into a smaller atom and an alpha particle, which is made of two protons and two neutrons (like a helium nucleus). For example, uranium (U, atomic weight 238, atomic number 92) decays into thorium (Th), releasing energy.

$$^{238}U_{92} \rightarrow {}^{234}Th_{90} + {}^{4}He_{2} + energy$$

There is another kind of radioactive decay, in which a neutron suddenly breaks up into a proton and a **beta particle** (similar to an electron). The atomic weight stays the same, but the atomic number goes up. For example, thorium beta decays into protactinium (Pa).

$$^{234}Th_{90} \rightarrow {}^{234}Pa_{91} + e^{-} + energy$$

Chain Reaction

The physicist Enrico Fermi discovered that if a neutron was shot at a nucleus, like a bullet at a target, it could make the nucleus break into two and release energy along with a few more neutrons. This is called nuclear fission. The released neutrons then hit other nuclei and break them up and so the process goes on and on. This is called a chain reaction. Nuclear fission chain reactions can be made to happen in a special building called a nuclear reactor. The energy thus released is then used to boil water to make steam, which turns a turbine, generating electricity. This is how a nuclear power plant works.

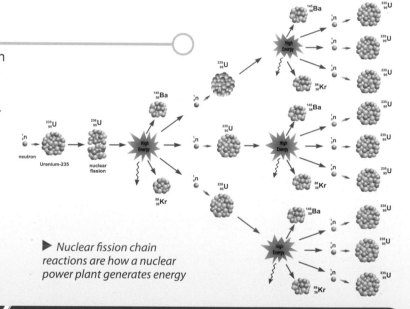

▶ Nuclear fission chain reactions are how a nuclear power plant generates energy

💡 Isn't It Amazing!

Did you know that out there in the Universe, there are stars that are made entirely of neutrons? They act like giant magnets and give out X-rays rather than light!

▲ Rotating neutron stars are also called pulsars

⊙ Incredible Individuals

Marie Sklodowska Curie (1867–1934) was a physicist and chemist who conducted pioneering research on radioactivity. She was the first woman to become a professor at the University of Paris. She discovered radioactive decay, as well as the elements polonium (Po; which she named after her birth country Poland) and radium (Ra). She received the Nobel Prize for Physics in 1903, and the Nobel Prize for Chemistry in 1911.

▶ Marie Curie discovered radioactivity

Green Chemistry

In the last two centuries, humankind has made a lot of progress. Developments in the field of Chemistry led to much of the progress, providing several new forms of materials and discovering new reactions. However, not all ideas have turned out so well. While plastics have been of great use in our daily lives, today they are polluting our forests and oceans, killing many innocent creatures. The CO_2 emitted by fossil fuels is causing global warming while many other chemicals that escape into the atmosphere cause acid rain and severe allergies. Today, chemists around the world are trying to find ways to reduce and even reverse these pollution-related problems.

▲ *Plastics kill thousands of sea creatures each year*

Fuel Cells

A fuel cell works much like an electric cell. But unlike an electric cell, a fuel cell uses hydrogen and oxygen gases instead of a solid anode and cathode. Inside the cell, the gases react with each other to form water and release chemical energy in the process. This energy is converted into electrical energy. In a fuel cell vehicle (FCV), the electricity is used to move the wheels. As these cars emit only water vapour, they cause no pollution.

Nevertheless, scientists are yet to find ways to generate fuel cells on a large scale.

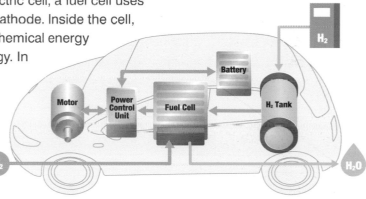

▲ *Fuel cells make hydrogen gas react with oxygen to make electric power, releasing water instead of smoke*

Biodegradables

Most natural chemicals decay. Metals corrode, termites eat wood, leather and cloth disintegrate in soil. However, nothing like this happens to plastics and they remain on our planet for millions of years. Many scientists have worked to replace regular plastic material with something which will disintegrate easily on its own in the presence of light or by the action of bacteria. Other scientists are experimenting with materials made from natural sources such as starch, cellulose, and wheat gluten. These are hardy and can withstand the pressures of daily life, but once discarded, these will degrade into simple chemicals such as carbon dioxide and water.

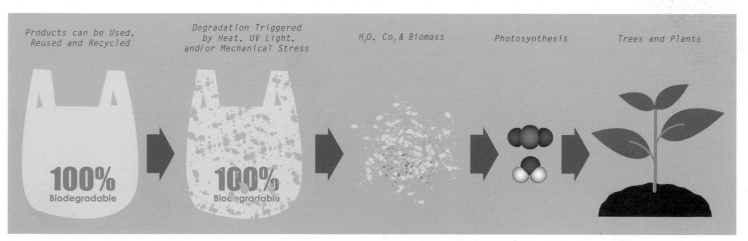

▲ *A biodegradable product can be broken down by bacteria and fungi into recyclable natural compounds*

ELECTRICITY
&
ELECTRONICS

OUR ELECTRIC WORLD

Think of what your house might have been like more than a hundred and fifty years ago. Mentally take out each electrical object and replace it with something that was done the old-fashioned way. Think of lanterns that burned whale oil in the living room, washing tubs with wooden bats, or kitchens with coal stoves. You would have travelled on foot, or in carts pulled by horses or bullocks. You would have to write a letter to someone living far away, and it would be weeks before the letter reached them and you received a reply.

Archaeologists have divided human history into three ages—the Stone Age, the Bronze Age, and the Iron Age. While each of these ages is based on changes that drove the evolution of society, nothing changed humanity more profoundly than the ability to harness electricity for its needs. It has helped us overcome our bodies' limitations, so we can talk to someone a continent away or travel safely at night.

Let's explore the world we have created in just a hundred years!

▼ *Electricity is part of our lives in ways that we often don't recognise*

Gadget Mania

The air-conditioning in our homes, cars and offices, the mobile phones we use to stay in touch with the world, the electric lights that help us stay awake far into the night and drive safely on roads, and, not to forget, the toaster that magically turns slices of bread into delicious toast! We've gotten so used to electricity that we can't even imagine what to do if there is a sudden blackout. So before we look into electricity, how it works, and how it helps us in our lives, let's have a look at some of the most interesting gadgets that were ever invented.

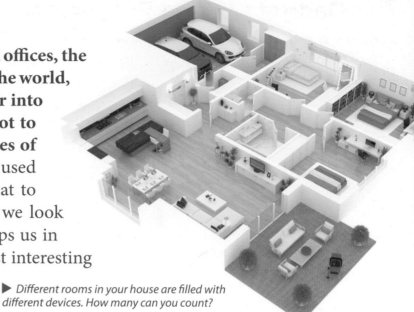

▶ Different rooms in your house are filled with different devices. How many can you count?

Electrical, Electronic and Electromechanical Devices

All the gadgets we use are of three types:

1. **Electrical devices:** These convert electrical energy into light or heat, like an incandescent light bulb or water heater; or they convert light into electricity, like a solar panel. Devices like transformers, capacitors, and high voltage electric lines are also electrical devices, because they store or transport electricity without converting it into any other kind of energy.

2. **Electromechanical devices:** These convert electricity into mechanical energy (kinetic or potential energy). Ceiling and table fans, vinyl record players, dial telephones, and electric bells are examples of such devices. Devices that convert mechanical energy into electricity, like the **turbines** in dams or the blades of windmills, are also electromechanical devices.

3. **Electronic devices:** These are devices that use complex electrical circuits, where 'gates' change the flow of electricity to create different outputs. Televisions, computers, and mobile phones are all electronic devices. They often involve tinier gadgets inside them that may be electrical or electromechanical devices. For example, televisions have tiny mechanical vibrators that convert electrical signals into sound signals, so that you can not only see what your favourite stars are doing in the movie you're watching, but hear them too.

▲ Electronic, electromechanical, and electrical devices

Isn't It Amazing!

There are some devices that we can wear, like earphones for listening to music or a smart watch that can tell us a lot more than just the time. Some people, like soldiers and firefighters, have electric jackets that adjust the temperature and glasses that take photos. In the future, we might see many electric devices become light enough to wear, rather than weigh down our pockets.

▲ Wearable electronics can even measure your pulse rate

Incredible Individuals

While Thomas Alva Edison is famous for inventing the electric light, did you know that the first electric light used for streets was invented by Humphry Davy? He is also known for inventing the Miners' Safety Lamp (or the Davy Lamp)

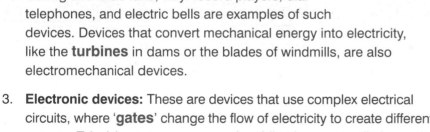

Gadgets We've Forgotten

In the 1890s, Nikola Tesla and Thomas Edison invented rival systems to distribute electricity to homes, using alternating current and direct current respectively. Ever since then, electricity became a cheaper way of providing energy for a home's needs, compared to oil or gas for lighting lamps and kitchen fires. Inventors began to make electric devices to do all kinds of jobs, from machines that wash clothes and keep food cool, to electric fans and lawnmowers. Electricity could also help us do things we could never do before, like speak to people in a different city, or listen to a famous singer over and over again.

Today, electronics have replaced many devices that were popular with earlier generations. Vinyl records came first and were popular from the 1920s-70s, then it was cassette tapes from the 1970s-2000s, and finally, it was compact discs from the 1990s-2010s. Devices that could play these media rose in parallel, especially portable versions such as the famous Walkman™. Here are other examples:

1. **Gramophones:** These were the first devices that could play music. They consisted of a turntable, on which the listener placed a vinyl record. A gramophone pin sensed the slight differences in the grooves on the record and converted that into sound.

2. **Jukeboxes:** These were machines that would let you select and play music by inserting coins into them. They were wildly popular from the 1930s to the 1950s.

3. **Cassettes and Compact Discs (CDs):** Cassettes worked like vinyl records, but used magnetic tape instead of grooves and plastic etchings. An electromagnetic head in the player would move up and down based on the magnetic charges and convert them into sound. CDs approached this using miniature bumps and lasers.

4. **Video Cassettes:** These were similar to cassette tapes, except that they could play video as well as audio. They made it possible for people to watch their favourite movies and TV shows at home. As these cassettes were comparatively expensive, video rental stores became common throughout the world from the 1970s to the 1990s. People would borrow movies just as we can borrow books from libraries. Rental stores died out with the increased accessibility of inexpensive Digital Video Discs (DVDs) in the 2000s.

▲ *The Grammy Awards, which are given every year to top musicians, are named after the gramophone, which was invented by Thomas Edison*

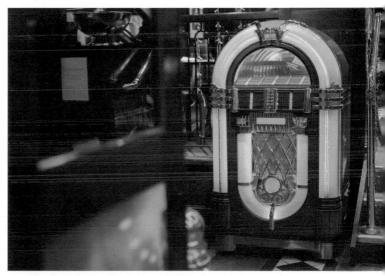

▲ *Jukeboxes were common in restaurants and haircutting salons, and many retro-themed restaurants have them specially made today*

◀ *To play a video cassette, one had to load it into a special device called a video cassette player (VCP), which in turn had to be connected to the TV*

▲ *Cassettes and portable cassette players made it possible for people to listen to their favourite music wherever they went. The Sony Walkman™ sold 385 million devices from 1979 to 2010*

Electricity: The Basics

Before we learn how our devices work, let's understand what electricity is. For that we need to understand a few terms of physics.

All electricity can be divided into two: static and current. **Static electricity** is what happens when your woollen clothes rub against rubber, or when lightning strikes the ground. This is because of opposite electric charges on them, as we will see ahead. **Current electricity** is what we commonly call electricity; it's 'current' because it is always on the move (dynamic). Both depend on a fundamental property of all things on Earth—an **electric charge**. Electric charges exist because of electrons, the tiny things that move around the nuclei of atoms.

Charge

Different materials have different charges on them. These charges arise because there are electrons on the surface of every atom, which move around the nucleus. Very often, these charges are balanced by an equal number of protons in the atoms, which stop the electrons from straying. This is because electrons have a negative charge and protons have a positive charge, and they attract each other. Such materials are called **dielectric**. Other materials, however, have an imbalance of electrons and protons. If there are fewer electrons, the material possesses a positive charge. If it has more electrons, the material has a negative charge.

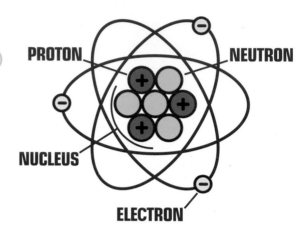

▲ *Materials become charged when they have too many or too few electrons*

Ions

The atoms of some elements can easily lose an electron or two to another atom. Such elements are called metals. When a metal atom loses an electron, it becomes a positively charged ion or cation. Other elements have atoms that are hungry for electrons. When they get an extra electron, they become negatively charged ions or anions. At very high temperatures, cations and anions can form a gas-like material called plasma. All stars are made of this material.

 In Real Life

Most clouds are made of plasma, in this case being comprised of charged water ions. When these ions come close to the Earth (or to a cloud with ions of opposite charge), they meet an opposite charge and are strongly attracted towards it. The clouds emit a spark, and the excess charge suddenly travels to the Earth, causing lightning.

◄ *Lightning is an example of a static electric discharge*

Electrons

When an electron moves, it produces a tiny **current**. In many metals, electrons can hop between atoms very easily. Some materials are rich in anions, while others are rich in cations. If you bring them together, there will be a chemical reaction. But if you keep them separate and connect them by a wire on one side and an electrode (a metal rod dipped in the substance) on the other side, the current will flow through the wire. This is because electrons will move from the anion-rich side (now called anode) to the cation-rich side (now called cathode). The difference in the charge between the anode and cathode is called the electric potential, which is also often called voltage.

▲ *Electric transmission happens when electrons move from an anode (from the power station) to a cathode (back to the power station), through the whole electric grid*

Isn't It Amazing!

AC/DC, the name of a famous rock band, does indeed stand for alternating current and direct current. As reported: "The band members Malcolm and Angus Young got the idea for the name from their sister, who saw the initials 'AC/DC' on a sewing machine."

Current

Current that flows only in one direction is called direct current or DC. But it can also be made to switch directions, which is called alternating current or AC. The latter happens because of **electromagnetism**. If you rotate a magnet, it creates a tiny electric field. If you put a metal coil around a rotating magnet, the electrons in it will start moving (this is called induction). However, for half a turn, current moves one way, and for the other half it changes direction. The more powerful the magnet, the stronger the current it generates.

▲ *Most devices (such as coffee makers) work either on AC or DC*

Current and Resistance

Why does electricity pass through metals, but not other materials? For this, we have to understand the idea of conduction and resistance. **Conduction** happens when there are enough loose electrons that will move when a potential is applied, that is, there is an anode and a cathode between which there is a difference of charge. What if there aren't any electrons to spare, or too many protons hungry for these electrons? Then there will be resistance to the flow of current. These two principles are how most electronic devices work.

▲ *Air is a bad conductor, but if two opposite charges are close enough, it allows a 'spark' to travel between them*

Good and Bad Conductors

Most materials will allow some electricity (i.e. some electrons) to pass through them, and resist the rest. A material that lets most of the electrons pass through it is called a good conductor. Most metals are good conductors, and that's why they are used as electric cables. A material that lets all the current pass through it with no resistance at all is called a superconductor. Most good conductors become superconductors only below -253°C, so none of them can be used to make cables that transmit electricity.

On the other hand, bad conductors let little electricity pass through them, which means they resist most electrons. Some materials, like wood and plastics, allow almost no electricity to pass at all. These are called insulators and are used to wrap electric cables so that electricity does not leak out of them.

Yet other materials are neither too bad nor too good and thus they are **semiconductors**. These are important in turning up or turning down the flow of current. Hence, they are the ones that make modern electronics possible.

▲ *Insulators protect conductors from leaking electricity and electrocuting people*

In Real Life

In theory, your body should be a bad conductor of electricity as 70% of it is made of water (since pure water is a bad conductor of electricity). But it will still let current pass through you, since the body has a lot of salt, which makes it a good conductor. This is why you can get an electric shock. You shouldn't touch an electric device when wet or sweaty as the salt in your skin can conduct electricity.

▶ *Electricians always work with safety equipment, including insulated gloves, hats, shoes, and glasses*

Resistors

So, what happens to electrons as they move along a conductor? Some of them get trapped by positive charges and are lost, reducing the current. This is called resistance (symbol R), and it was worked out by a person called Georg Ohm (1789–1854). The amount of resistance of a conductor can be calculated by measuring the current (symbol I) it lets through and the difference in voltage (symbol V) at either end of the conductor. This is called Ohm's Law, and the unit of resistance is called Ohm (symbol Ω) in his honour.

$$R = V/I$$

Yet other electrons are turned into different forms of electricity. The most common example you see is electric light. Some materials will emit light if current passes through them. This is because as electrons pass through them, they 'excite' the atom and transfer some energy to them. When the electron has passed, the atom becomes 'de-excited' and gives up that energy as a photon, the unit of light. Millions of electrons create millions of photons, and they light up a room. The reverse is also true, and that's how you get solar power. Other resistors turn electricity into heat or sound.

◀ *Electric devices work by converting electrical energy into other forms*

Optic Cables

These cables are used in connecting you to the internet, but they carry light inside them, not electricity. These work on a principle called total internal reflection. They are made of a material (called optical fibre) that reflects photons so that they bounce along the walls all the way from end to end with zero resistance. Hundreds of optical fibres are bundled together to form optical fibre cables (OFCs). These cables are laid all over the world, connecting computers across the globe.

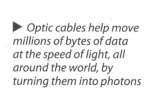

▶ *Optic cables help move millions of bytes of data at the speed of light, all around the world, by turning them into photons*

Making Electricity

We cannot actually make any electricity, because it is a form of energy. As you know, energy can neither be made nor destroyed, but only changed from one form to another. So when we 'generate' electricity, we are only turning some other form of energy into it. In great power plants, this could be thermal, nuclear or mechanical energy; in a battery (cell) or home generator, it is chemical energy which is released by a reaction. Batteries can be rechargeable, such as car batteries; or non-rechargeable, such as in TV remotes, which have to be discarded once exhausted.

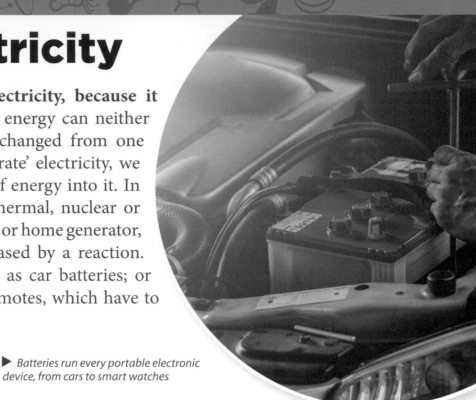

▶ *Batteries run every portable electronic device, from cars to smart watches*

How a Cell Works

Remember that you need an anode and cathode to create an electric potential for electricity to flow. A cell is a device where chemical reactions happen and create the necessary electric potential. Actually, there must be two reactions:

1. The **anode reaction**, which generates electrons that will travel through the electric cables.

2. The **cathode reaction**, which creates a lack of electrons, so that the electric potential is created.

But electricity will not pass unless there is something to connect the anode and cathode internally, so that the cycle is complete. This is called an electrolyte. The electrons come back into the cell, where they meet the cations and neutralise them, i.e. the charge disappears. These electric cycles are called circuits. Many reactions can turn chemical energy into electrical energy this way, but for them to work as a battery, they must be controllable by us.

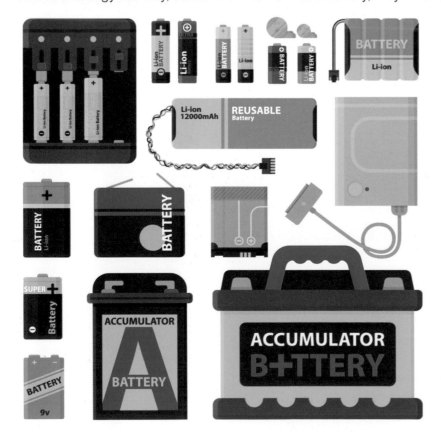

◀ *Batteries come in many sizes and shapes, but all are made of rows of electric cells*

In Real Life

A cell is a single unit that produces electricity. However, many cells can be coupled together in rows to increase the total amount of electricity generated. In the 19th century, when inventors worked on these, they were reminded of artillery guns lined up together in a battle. The word for that is 'battery', and that's why a group of cells working together is called a battery.

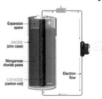

▶ *Four lead-acid cells are joined together to make one battery*

Non-Rechargeable Batteries

Most cells cannot be recharged. This is because once the chemical reaction has taken place, it cannot be reversed. Their main advantage is that they are cheap to make and can be made in large numbers, so they are used to power our flashlights, electric toys, music players, and hundreds of other devices. The most common ones use zinc (Zn) as the source of electrons (anode), and manganese dioxide (MnO_2) as the cathode, with a paste of ammonium chloride (NH_4Cl) as the electrolyte. A graphite (carbon) rod is used to take up the electrons, so the cell is also called a zinc-carbon cell.

Dry Cell Battery

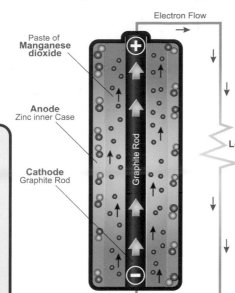

▲ Zinc-carbon cells are among the most commonly used and have a gel-like electrolyte in them

At the anode, zinc releases electrons into the circuit:

$$Zn \rightarrow Zn^{++} + 2e^-$$

At the cathode, the electrons arrive and make manganese dioxide react with ammonium chloride to make manganese trioxide, water and ammonia:

$$2MnO_2 + 2NH_4Cl + 2e^- \rightarrow Mn_2O_3 + 2NH_3 + H_2O + 2Cl^-$$

The chloride ions travel through the electrolyte to react with the zinc ions to make zinc chloride:

$$Zn^{++} + 2Cl^- \rightarrow ZnCl_2$$

Once all the MnO_2 is exhausted, the cell will stop working.

Rechargeable Batteries

Some chemical reactions can be made to run the other way if you apply an electric current to them. This is the principle used in car batteries and other rechargeable ones. The most common is the lead-acid battery, made of alternating plates of lead (symbol Pb) as anode and lead dioxide (symbol PbO_2) as cathode, both dipped in sulphuric acid (symbol H_2SO_4).

▲ Wireless charging of a smartphone battery

Anode reaction: $Pb + H_2SO_4 \rightarrow PbSO_4 + 2H^+ + 2e^-$

The hydrogen ions (H^+) travel to the cathode attracted by the electrons.

Cathode reaction: $PbO_2 + H_2SO_4 + 2H^+ + 2e^- \rightarrow PbSO_4 + 2H_2O$

When the car engine is running, it generates electricity that 'charges' the battery, and the lead and lead dioxide plates regenerate.

Inside a Power Plant

If you thought an electric power plant was just a giant battery, you could be no further from the truth. This is because electric power plants work on induction to generate huge amounts of electricity. But before that, we have to understand the principle of electromagnetism. It is a branch of physics that deals with how electricity and **magnetism** influence each other and is based on the findings of Michael Faraday and James Clerk Maxwell, who discovered that if you move a magnet in an electric field, it will make the electrons in the field move. The reverse is also true. A moving electron creates a tiny magnetic field of its own.

🔍 Induction Generator

When a giant magnet is made to rotate inside a metal coil, called an induction coil, it makes an alternating current run through it. This is called an **induction generator**. Lots of these are joined together to make a very large electric current which flows into the **electricity grid** that supplies power to your city. It isn't as simple as we make it out to be, but this is the general principle. Now we come to the question: how do we make the magnet rotate? Engineers attach the blades of a fan to the magnet, which can then be moved by water, wind, or steam.

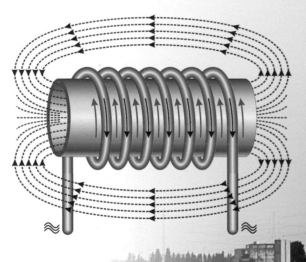

◀ *A rotating magnetic field (represented by the dotted arrows) triggers an alternating electric field (represented by the red and black arrows)*

▶ *Giant power plants are the bedrock of our modern industrial society*

⭐ Incredible Individuals

Nikola Tesla (1856–1943) made many important inventions that made it possible to produce electricity on a large scale and supply it to homes and factories. His most important invention was the rotating magnet for creating an alternating current. His magnets were installed at the Niagara Falls, where the force of the falling water rotated them.

▶ *Serbian-American engineer and physicist Nikola Tesla worked as an employee of Thomas Edison, and later went on to become his rival*

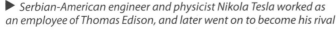

Steam Turbines

Wondering why we are talking about steam-driven machines, technology that disappeared nearly a hundred years ago? That's because we still live in the Age of Steam, at least in our power plants. Nuclear and thermal power plants use heat to boil water to make steam, which is then pressurised and passed into a chamber. The steam turns the wings of giant turbines that, in turn, rotate a magnet inside an induction coil, thereby generating electricity.

The heat for making steam comes in two ways: thermal power plants burn fuel such as coal or gas to generate heat, while nuclear power plants use a **nuclear reaction** to generate heat. A nuclear reaction is one in which a radioactive material, like uranium, breaks up to release energy (as heat), while turning into a new element.

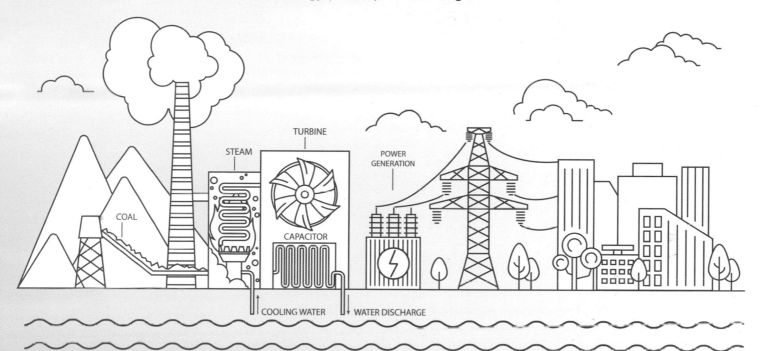

▲ The parts of a thermal power plant: Coal is burned to turn water into steam, which then flows through turbines to make electricity

Isn't It Amazing!

Dams use the power of falling water to turn the turbines which turn the rotor. China's Three Gorges Dam, with 34 generators, is the world's largest dam.

▲ Banks of capacitors are called electric substations

Capacitors

You know how a cell works. Now take the electrolyte of a cell, and replace it with a dielectric medium, one that conducts no current (see page 6). Run electricity into the cell. The anode and cathode will simply build up a charge, looking for somewhere to discharge it. Instead of a cell, you now have a capacitor. Capacitors are a big part of grids as they store the electricity generated in power plants. The amount of electricity a capacitor can store is called capacitance (symbol C, unit Farad [F]). When there is 'demand', that is when millions of people switch on a device at home, the capacitors are plugged into the network. Now that the circuit is complete, the electrons rush out of the anode to the cathode of the capacitor.

Electric Circuits

We've learned how power is generated from other sources of energy. But electricity only moves as a current if it can complete a circuit from the power source and back to it. On the way it will meet various kinds of resistors and other devices that will convert electrical energy to other forms of energy, which we use for our purposes—such as lighting and cooling a room, or powering TVs and computers. Some of the electricity will be used to power a motor (see pages 16–17). But not all devices use the same amount of electricity, nor do they need to be switched on all the time.

▼ Transformers at a power station

Transformers

In most countries, electricity travels through metal cables high in the air or underground at electric potentials of up to 765,000 volts, or 765 kilovolts (V and kV respectively). However, when it has to be connected to your home, it needs to be reduced to as little as 440V. For that, it needs a transformer.

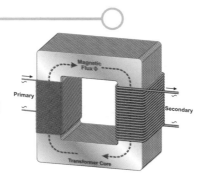

▲ The magnetic field generated by one coil affects the other, triggering a current in it

Transformers act on electricity like the volume controls on a TV remote, by a method you already know—electromagnetic induction. But now there's a twist. If an induction coil is placed next to another (without touching) and alternating current is passed through it, there will be a new current in the other coil! The current in that coil depends on the number of turns there are in that coil. So, if you have a coil with more turns than the first one, it will have more current. In this manner, you will have made a step-up transformer. If there are fewer turns in the coil than the first one, then you have a step-down transformer. Power companies pass the electricity they generate through several step-up transformers before it is loaded onto the electricity grid. The power from the grid passes through many of these before reaching your home.

Switches

A switch works in the simplest way—by breaking the circuit mechanically. Each light in your house is connected to the power grid by its own circuit. When you turn it off, the switch moves the cables away, and the device goes off. When you turn it on, the switch reconnects the circuit, and your device comes on. For gadgets like blenders or televisions, the switch is made by a power socket, into which you must plug in your device and then turn on the switch. The device's cable acts as a second switch.

▼ This is how electric switches work

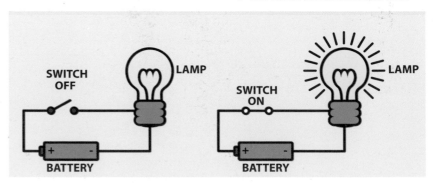

Series and Parallel

If you split a power cable, connect it to two electric devices, and then link up their cables back again, you create a **parallel circuit**. If you connect both electric devices to the same circuit, one after the other, you have made a **series circuit**. However, in a series circuit, if one device fails, it will turn the other one off too.

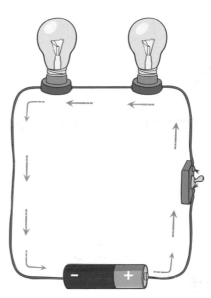

▲ *Parallel connections make sure that one device can keep running even if the other fails, as it doesn't break the circuit*

💡 Isn't It Amazing!

String lights, which have dozens of little lights in series, actually work in parallel circuits. That's why even if one light goes bad, the whole string does not go dark.

▶ *The strings are made of 22-gauge copper wire covered in coloured PVC plastic coating*

👥 In Real Life

Your home's bell is one of the simplest applications of electromagnetism. When you press the bell, electricity runs through a coil wrapped around a metal bar or horseshoe, magnetising it. It attracts another metal rod, which hits a gong. In doing so, it breaks the circuit, the magnetism stops and the rod goes back to its place.

▶ *The magnetic field generated by one coil affects the other, triggering a current in it*

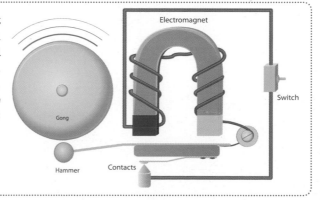

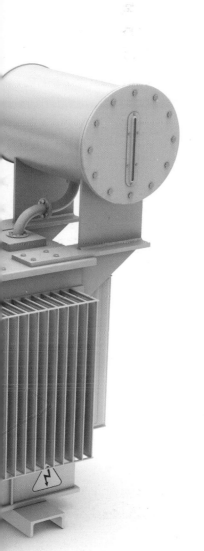

Motors and Magnetism

There are two ways by which electricity is put to work. One you know already—using resistors to turn electricity into heat, light, or sound. Another way is by induction, but this time the other way around. Passing electricity through a coil makes a magnet rotate. The rotating magnet can be fixed to other things to make them rotate too. This is the principle of the **electric motor**. You see them in familiar devices and day-to-day life, such as blenders, fans, and lawnmowers; but they also work in not-so-familiar devices such as mechanical toys, chainsaws, water pumps, electric trains, cars, and a whole lot of industrial machinery.

▲ An electric motor with its various parts

▼ An electric motor winding

⊛ Incredible Individuals

The Hungarian monk and school teacher Anyos Jedlik (1800-1895) invented one of the world's earliest working motors back in 1827.

🔍 Parts of a Motor

Every electric motor has two essential parts: one stationary and one that rotates. The stationary part of an electric motor, called the stator, has the electric coils. When electricity is run through it, it creates a magnetic field. The rotor is the metallic rod or shaft that rotates in response to the magnetic field created by the live stator. Ball bearings usually anchor the rotor to the motor's casing and help it rotate. A tiny device called commutator is present between the rotor and the stator, and is responsible for the conversion of direct current into alternating current.

👤✓ In Real Life

An electrical device, cable, or coil is said to be "live" when electricity is passing through it, and dormant otherwise. Electric transmission lines are live all the time, as are the electric boxes you see in substations and in your house's fuse box. This is why you should never touch them.

▲ Live power lines are usually kept away from populated areas

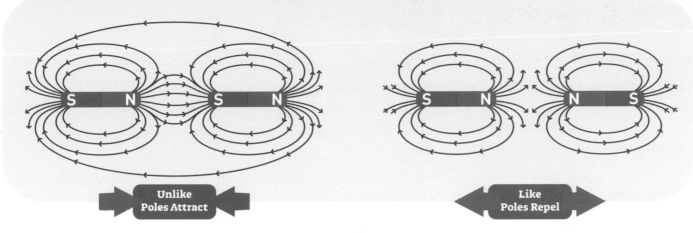

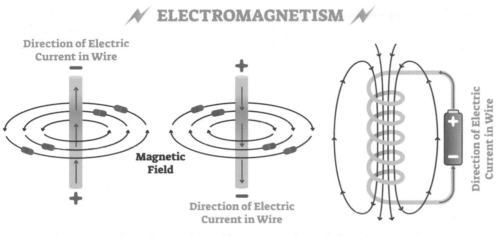

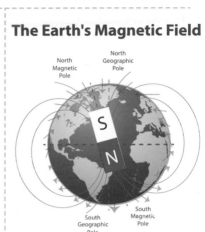

▲ Most metals can be transformed into magnets, but only for a short period

Magnetism

We've talked much about electricity causing a magnetic field, and the reverse. But what exactly is magnetism? Why do some materials, like iron, show it, and others, like copper, do not?

A magnetic field is a force produced at a right angle to the movement of a charge. Magnetic forces move within that field between its north and south poles (this field is called a dipole). The way opposite electric charges attract, opposite magnetic poles attract. And just as 'like' electric charges repel each other, like magnetic poles repel.

In most materials, electrons move in all directions, so their magnetic fields cancel each other out. These materials are called **diamagnetic**. However, in other materials such as good conductors, applying an electric charge can make all the electrons move in one direction, and so they get a magnetic field, though it does not last for long—These are **paramagnetic**. Lastly, in materials such as iron, the magnetic fields can be permanent if the current is run for a long time—These are **ferromagnetic**. Permanent magnets, like the ones seafarers use in a magnetic compass, are made of these.

Isn't It Amazing!

Our planet's core is made of a solid iron ball surrounded by molten iron. As the Earth rotates, this molten iron (which is charged) also moves, creating a gigantic magnetic field that covers the whole planet. It is roughly the same as the Earth's axis of rotation but is off by a few hundred miles. The North Magnetic Pole is is in the Canadian Arctic moving towards Russia, while the South Magnetic Pole is located off the coast of Antarctica.

▲ Powerful horseshoe magnets are used in recycling yards to separate metals from non-metals

Semiconductors

Look at the electronic devices around you today—smartphones, laptops, automatic washing machines, programmable microwaves, remote-controlled fans, and LEDs. If you ask your grandparents, fifty years ago the 'smartest' device out there would have been a pocket calculator, which is now reduced to an app on your phone. What made all this possible?

The answer is that these are all semiconductor devices. Once, these were large and expensive devices, which could do only the simplest of programming tasks. But as we learned more about them, we learned to fit more and more electronic circuits into a smaller space on a semiconductor **chip**. These devices became smaller and cheaper, and several of us own devices with semiconductors today.

What are semiconductors?

Silicon, selenium, and germanium are all examples of semiconductor materials. They have too few 'loose' electrons to be good conductors, but enough of them to not be insulators. In the last two centuries, physicists discovered that their partial conduction of electricity could be useful to regulate how it flowed, and to use them as 'gates' in a circuit. This means they can make electrons flow in one direction and stop them from another. Further, they can combine two streams of electrons into one; they can 'decide' to let one current pass instead of another, and so on. Using this, they can be programmed to do tasks like doing sums or control other electronic devices.

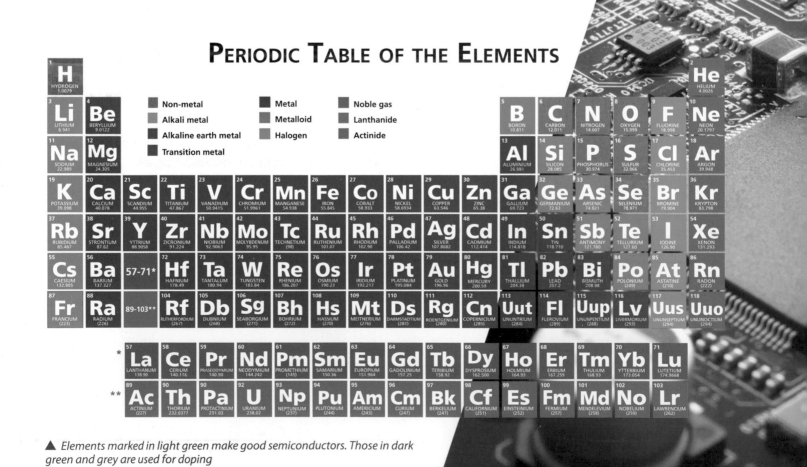

PERIODIC TABLE OF THE ELEMENTS

Non-metal | Metal | Noble gas
Alkali metal | Metalloid | Lanthanide
Alkaline earth metal | Halogen | Actinide
Transition metal

▲ Elements marked in light green make good semiconductors. Those in dark green and grey are used for doping

Doping

In the 20th century, many scientists who worked together discovered that semiconductors can be 'doped'. By doping, they mean that a pure semiconductor crystal could be deliberately adulterated with another material that increases or decreases the amount of electricity that it can conduct. If you add small amounts of phosphorus (5 electrons to spare) to silicon (4 electrons to spare), you get an **n-doped** semiconductor, which has a slight negative charge. Similarly, by adding boron (3 electrons to spare) to silicon, you get a **p-doped** semiconductor with a slight positive charge. Now, by putting the two together, you get a **p-n junction**. If you run a small current with n first and p later, the current will flow easily, but if you reverse the current, it does not go past p, as it takes up the electrons to make up for the ones it is missing. Thus, a p-n junction acts like a one-way gate.

P–N JUNCTION

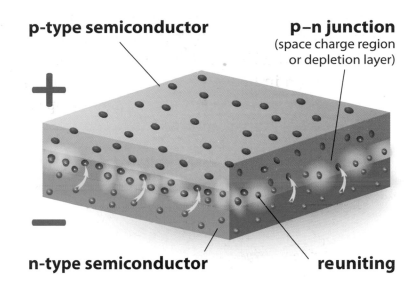

p-type semiconductor

p–n junction
(space charge region or depletion layer)

n-type semiconductor

reuniting

▲ *p-n junctions are used as gates in electronic circuits*

Transistors

What if we make complicated junctions such as n-p-n or p-n-p? We can make another device called a transistor. This device controls how much electricity can flow through it, by using a second current to modify the conductivity of one of the semiconductors. The incoming power is called the source, and the outgoing power is called the drain. The part of the transmitter that receives the source is called the collector, while the part from which the drain leaves is called the emitter. Between them is a third connection, called the base (which receives the 'gate' current) that adjusts the conductivity. You can thus use transistors as tiny transformers to increase or decrease signal.

▲ *A transistor with the source, gate and drain*

💡 Isn't It Amazing!

John Bardeen, Walter H. Brattain, and William B. Shockley invented semiconductor transistors. Their first use was in making 'pocket' radios, which people could carry with them.

▶ *To most people in the 1960s and 1970s, a transistor meant a pocket radio*

Diodes and Displays

In electronics, a diode is a device which offers high resistance when current is passed one way, and low resistance the other way. You've already seen how p-n junctions work; they make the best diodes. Before that, diodes were made of a glass tube, in which a rod-shaped cathode and a plate-shaped anode were fitted with a vacuum in between. Electricity can only pass from cathode to anode; if you plug in the diode the other way, it will stop the circuit.

These big diodes (and related devices called triodes, which acted as transistors) were used in building the first electronic circuits in which electricity could be put to use in making calculations, keeping track of time and other things. Diodes can deduct electrons or add them. Multiple diodes can conduct more complex jobs. In the 1950s, the vacuum tubes (which would break down easily) were replaced by semiconductor diodes. Over time, these diodes were reduced in size, becoming smaller and smaller to such an extent that today thousands of diodes (and transistors) can be fitted onto a silicon chip smaller than a fingernail! This is called a microprocessor.

▲ *The first diodes were vacuum tubes, which would easily go bust. Today's diodes are tiny and much more reliable*

LED Lighting

White light is made by mixing several colours. Another method of making white light is by using phosphor, a substance that absorbs light of one colour and emits another. Tube lights and compact fluorescent lamps work on the same principle. In an LED lamp, a blue LED emits light, which falls on the phosphor that has been coated inside the light. It absorbs some of the light and emits yellow light. The yellow light mixes with the remaining blue light to make white light.

▼ *Streets lit with LED lights save your municipality a lot of money*

Light-emitting Diode

Some p-n semiconductor junction diodes emit light when electricity passes through them. This is the principle used in LED lamps, that are fast replacing the earlier incandescent and fluorescent lamps. They are brighter and need a lot less electric power, although they may also be more expensive. The LED technology is also used in making screens of TVs, computers, touch phones and other devices.

Different combinations (dopes) of semiconductors emit lights of different colours (see the table below). A multicolour LED display is made of several such tiny diodes.

Light Colour	Combination
Red	Aluminium gallium arsenide (AlGaAs)
Orange	Gallium arsenide phosphide (GaAsP)
Yellow	Aluminium gallium indium phosphide (AlGaInP)
Green	Gallium (III) nitride (GaN)
Blue	Zinc selenide (ZnSe)

Other colours can be obtained by placing different colour LEDs in the same diode, as per the colour chart.

▲ LED lights in many colours at an airport

Isn't It Amazing!

The world's largest LED 3D screen was installed in Gothenburg in 2011 to show fans the Union of European Football Associations (UEFA) Cup final (which happened in London), where Barcelona beat Manchester United 3–1. The screen measured 6,192 mm by 3,483 mm.

LED Display

Most screens, whether in TVs, phones, or computers, are switching to LED displays. This works by putting three microscopic LEDs into a **pixel**, which is the unit of space in all digital screens. These LEDs give off red, blue, and green light when live. When a digital signal comes into the screen, it has information for each pixel—which LEDs need to be switched on and with how much intensity. This leads to the various colours and pictures that we see on the screen.

▶ The more pixels on an LED screen, the sharper the image displayed

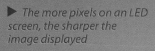

Interesting Electrical Phenomena

Alongside magnetism, there are other phenomena which can generate electric currents. Some are useful to us and can power gadgets, while others can create problems that we have to be careful about.

Piezoelectricity is a phenomenon when electricity is generated in some types of crystals when they are pressed.

Triboelectricity occurs when two materials are rubbed together, causing charged particles to appear on their surface.

Pyroelectricity is the property of some materials to generate a voltage difference when heated or cooled.

Thermoelectricity is a phenomenon that happens when two different materials, with different electric and thermal conductivity, are joined together. A difference in temperature between them also leads to a difference in voltage.

Let's look at some of these in detail, and how scientists and engineers use them to generate electricity and make many kinds of devices work.

▼ As electricity is a form of energy, any other kind of energy can be converted into it, using the right materials

Piezoelectricity

Piezoelectricity (*piezo* is 'to press' in Greek) was discovered by the brothers Jacques Curie and Pierre Curie (husband of Marie Curie) in 1880. They demonstrated that if you put pressure on crystals of tourmaline, quartz, and even sugar, they will generate a tiny electric current. It also works the other way round—a current passed through these crystals can cause them to deform. The piezoelectric effect is used in many devices, such as electric balances for weighing diamonds, guitar pick-ups, electronic drums, and kitchen lighters. Scientists are trying to figure out a way to use the piezoelectric effect to make electricity from car tyres.

▶ When you push the lighter button, it strikes a piezoelectric crystal which generates a tiny current, which in turn creates a spark that ignites the gas

Triboelectricity

Triboelectricity (*tribo* is 'to rub' in Greek) happens when two charged surfaces rub against each other, such as running a comb through hair or rubbing a glass with fur. Triboelectricity is the main source of static electricity. The rubbing causes electrons to come loose on the surface of the material. When an electrically conductive surface (like your skin) comes in touch with the charged material, the electrons travel onto it. This causes a mild electric shock.

Triboelectricity is the reason rockets are not launched during storms. In a storm, the air is full of charged particles, and if the rocket rubbed past them, the static electricity generated would interfere with the radio signals between the rocket and the control centre.

▲ *The triboelectric effect can also affect electronic chips as the static voltage caused by accidental rubbing of the chip can overwhelm the tiny currents of the chips*

Pyroelectricity

Pyroelectricity (*pyro* is 'fire' in Greek) is a phenomenon seen in certain kinds of crystals, like gallium nitride. When the crystal is heated even by a tiny amount, it generates an electric current, because the increased vibration caused by heating the molecules causes them to shed electrons. The pyroelectric effect is used in infrared sensors, in which the heat given off in the form of infrared electromagnetic waves can be captured by the sensor. These are used in automatic switches, which can turn the lights on or off in a room by sensing your presence through your body heat. They are also used in camera traps for photographing wild animals.

▶ *An infrared camera trap can sense the heat of an animal when it comes close to it and trigger the camera to take a photograph*

Thermoelectric Effect

The thermoelectric effect (*thermo* is 'heat' in Greek) was discovered by Thomas Seebeck in 1821. He noticed that two metals that are joined at the ends will have different electric conductivity because of the difference in their heat conductivity. This is also known as the Seebeck effect.

Scientists use this principle to build electronic thermometers using a device called a thermocouple made of wires of different metals or alloys. Thermocouples are very sensitive to even slight differences in temperature, and can also be used for measuring very high temperatures, such as in gas stoves or in the furnaces of factories where metals are refined from their ores.

▶ *The long wire you see is the thermocouple which senses the temperature, which the device then converts into a digital display*

Analogue and Digital

Engineers divide measurements into two kinds—analogue and digital. Analogue things are those that come in continuous measures, such as time, space, temperature, or speed. When you measure them, you can express the measurements in decimals. For instance, your body's normal temperature is 37.5°C, acceleration due to the Earth's gravity is 9.80665 m/s² and so on. Analogue devices, such as the mercury thermometer or a clock with gears, measure these things on a continuous basis.

On the other hand, digital things are those that come in whole numbers. The most common digital things are light waves and sound waves, because there cannot be such a thing as half a wave. After the introduction of **quantum theory**, we know that many natural forces are actually discrete, that is, they come in quanta, because they are made up of particles. Electricity is made of moving electrons; light (including X-rays and Gamma rays) is made of photons; and nuclear radiation is made of alpha or beta particles.

Electronic engineers therefore face a puzzle. Most of their measurements are in analogue, but the tools they make to measure them are digital. Converting analogue signals to digital ones that can be displayed takes up much of their time.

In Real Life

We often use analogue as a shorthand for things that are not electronic, and digital for those that are. But many non-electronic things, such as cameras that use film, are also digital. The camera film is made of molecules, and each molecule carries colour information, which makes it digital at a fundamental level.

▲ *An analogue watch shows time as it passes, whereas a digital watch can show you the time only once every second*

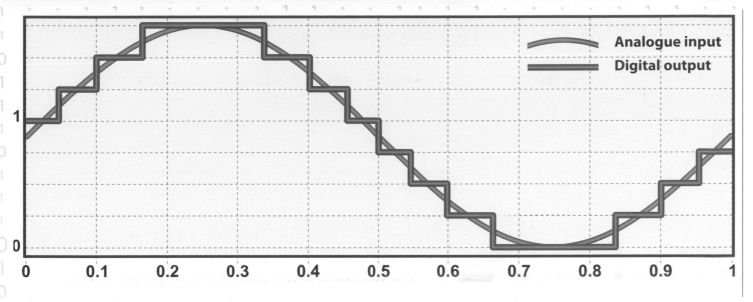

▲ *Analogue-to-digital conversion turns a continuous measure into a discrete one*

Analogue to Digital Conversion

Digital (derived from the Latin word 'digit', which means 'finger', that we all use to count) means that any measure, that engineers call a signal, has to be represented as an integer (i.e. a number that can be counted on the fingers). Therefore, a digital device can only 'sample' a continuous signal and produce snippets of that signal (see above image). This is called analogue-to-digital conversion. For electronic engineers, this means that to get a digital signal which represents the original as accurately as possible, they need to become more and more precise, so that the smallest changes in the analogue signal can be picked up. This is important where many decisions have to be made at very high speeds, such as in a radar detecting a flying plane.

They do this by trying to build sensors that are extremely small through a process called **miniaturisation**. With our improved understanding of semiconductors, we have been able to build devices on very small scales. Today, with nanotechnology, we can go down to the molecular level and get as accurate a signal as is physically possible.

Digital to Analogue Conversion

Digital displays face a different problem—turning a digital signal into an analogue one, so that we can make sense of them. Otherwise we wouldn't be able to hear our friends on the phone or see an image on the TV. Engineers solve this, again, through miniaturisation, and that's why you see TVs and cameras sold based on megapixels. A pixel is a unit of space which counts as one digital unit; a megapixel is one million pixels. The smaller the pixel, the better the resolution of a digital image.

▼ *The more pixels (digital units of space) an image packs, the sharper it is*

Making Computers

Did you know that computers in the 1950s were so big that they would take up an entire room? It is only with the invention of semiconductor-based diodes and transistors that electronic circuits could become smaller, allowing more computing power to be built up in the same space. Over time, computers became as small as a cupboard (mainframe), to a device that could sit on your table (desktop), and then on your lap (laptop). Now the device fits in your palm and is called a smartphone. But there's more to them getting smaller than just the microprocessor.

▲ *Early computers took up entire rooms and had lesser computing power than your mobile phone*

Integrated Circuit

An integrated circuit (IC) puts transistors, resistors, diodes, and capacitors—all microscopic in size—onto a semiconductor chip. After an engineer designs the circuit, it is printed onto a chip by a method called photolithography. Conducting metal strips are laid onto the chip, while other areas are modified chemically to make n-p junctions.

Data Storage

For a computer to work, it must be able to store data in a device called a **memory chip**. All data is stored as bits—a simple binary signal in a computer circuit that is either on (1) or off (0). Eight bits make a byte. Read Only Memory (ROM) stores data permanently, while Random Access Memory (RAM) stores the data temporarily while doing calculations. This is the same as how you hold 1,245 in your head while you try to mentally add 6,567 to it: you need to remember the places (tens, hundreds, thousands) of the digits. The processing power of a computer is usually expressed in terms of the total number of bytes its RAM has.

▲ *An electronic circuit board has dozens of IC-chips pasted onto it along with other microelectronics*

◀ *Data storage devices have evolved over time, from paper tapes, cellulose film, magnetic (floppy) discs, and compact discs to modern micro SD cards*

🛈 In Real Life

In 1965, Gordon Moore, a computer scientist, predicted that the number of transistors on a microprocessor would double each year. He turned out to be nearly right, since they do double roughly once every 18 months. This is now called Moore's Law. Today, over 23 billion transistors can fit onto one chip!

Programming

An algorithm or programme is a set of steps that the computer follows to know what it has to do. Thousands of algorithms are needed to run your computer smoothly (the **operating system**), while others come bundled in packages that help you do calculations, process natural languages (word processors), connect to the internet, listen to music or watch movies—these are called **applications**. Together, they are called **software**, while the physical parts of the computer (or smartphone) are known as **hardware**. The science of creating algorithms is called programming. In most modern computers, programming is done through various codes called **computer languages**. They come in two main categories: Low Level Languages and High Level Languages. The first type mainly interact with the hardware of computers, helping in operations and handling instructions by converting input into machine language—1 and 0. The second comprise of programming languages for different utilities and purposes such as Java, C++, FORTRAN, PASCAL, and Python.

⊙ Incredible Individuals

Ada Lovelace (1815–1852) left behind a step-by-step manual of how to calculate a complex kind of number called a 'Bernoulli number' for which a new kind of device—the Analytical Engine—was to be built by her friend, Charles Babbage, in 1843. For this, she is celebrated as the first programmer ever. The second Tuesday of every October is celebrated as Ada Lovelace Day.

▲ Ada Lovelace

▼ *The world's first-ever computer programme, created by Ada Lovelace in 1843*

Diagram for the computation by the Engine of the Numbers of Bernoulli. See Note G. (page 722 et seq.)

[Table: complex mathematical diagram for the computation of Bernoulli numbers, with columns for Number of Operation, Nature of Operation, Variables acted upon, Variables receiving results, Indication of change in the value on any Variable, Statement of Results, Data, Working Variables, and Result Variables. The table contents are too detailed to transcribe accurately.]

Here follows a repetition of Operations thirteen to twenty-three.

Mobile Phones

When we say 'phone' today, a little rectangular object that can connect to the internet and search for information, and contains messaging apps and social networks, comes to mind. But if you ever saw a telephone from the 1970s or '80s, you would wonder how it should be used.

▶ *The telephones of older times, invented by Alexander Graham Bell and patented in 1876, look nothing like the modern telephones we use today*

🔍 Speaking and Listening

So how does a smartphone work? Inside most mobile phones, you'll find the following six things: a central processing unit, an LED display, a microphone, a speaker, a camera, and a battery to power them all. The microphone is made of a tiny magnetic membrane called a **diaphragm**. When you speak, sound waves from your mouth reach the diaphragm and make it vibrate. As it vibrates, it triggers electric current in an **electrode** just next to it, which passes through an analogue-to-digital convertor and becomes a digital signal. This signal is then sent to the mobile network, which sends it to your friend's phone.

In your friend's phone, the digital signal passes through a digital-to-analogue convertor and then a tiny electromagnet. The magnet attracts or repels another diaphragm. The movement of this diaphragm makes sound waves in the air, which reach your friend's ear as an analogue signal. Most telephones are quite precise, but not perfect, so sometimes people sound different in real life and over the phone.

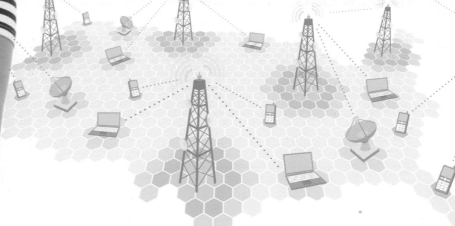

▲ *A modern mobile phone network*

◀ A modern mobile phone with multitasking applications

▶ A modern mobile phone tower

Sending and Receiving

Your phone has an in-built antenna, which converts the digital signal into a radio wave. Before that, the **Subscriber Identity Module (SIM)** card in your phone tacks on a code that helps the network identify you and where you are. The signal reaches the telephone tower or base station nearest to you, where it is again converted into an electric signal that can travel by cable, or into a more powerful radio signal that is transmitted to a communication satellite. It then passes through many telephone exchanges, which identify the receiver's number and switch them onto the right path (which is why telephone numbers have a country and an area code before your actual number). Finally, the signal reaches the cell your friend is in, and a radio signal passes to their phone, which rings. The geographic area served by each base station is called a cell, and that's why the whole process is referred to as cellular telephony.

⭐ Incredible Individuals

Before the telephone, there was the telegraph, a device that sent signals over long cables. Your message (in writing) had to be encoded into a series of short and long beeps called Morse code, and the code then had to be decoded at the other end. People who did this were called telegraph operators. In 1866, Mathilde Fibiger became one of the first women to be hired for the job, which was earlier thought to be suitable only for men.

▶ Mathilde Fibiger (bottom) and the telegraph equipment she would have used (top).

Renewable Energy

In the last few decades, people around the world have become concerned with what is happening to the wonderful nature and environment around us. Human activities are stuffing the air with millions of tonnes of carbon dioxide and causing climate change, plastics are polluting the ocean, and pesticides and other chemicals are killing insects and other wildlife. The generation of electricity is one of the biggest causes of climate change—from thermal power plants that emit CO_2, to the big dams that cause a lot of harm to the ecology around them. On the other hand, nuclear power is not leading to pollution, but it poses a threat if there is a leakage of radioactive material. Another problem is the fuel used for nuclear and thermal plants, which is expected to exhaust one day. That is why scientists and engineers across the world have been trying to find ways to generate electricity from a fuel source that will not run out or pollute the Earth.

⭐ Incredible Individuals

In 1962, the marine biologist Rachel Carson published the book *Silent Spring*, which warned of the dangers caused to the environment by modern industry. The book inspired many people to think of ways to reduce our impact on Earth, and was a great inspiration for people researching renewable energy.

▲ *Rachel Carson's book inspired many people to work on renewable energy*

🔍 Solar Power

This power depends on a source of energy that will eventually run out, but only after a few billion years. Light from the Sun is renewed every day and we can easily turn it into electricity. The device that does this is called a photovoltaic cell. It is made of silicon crystals. When photons from sunlight fall on the silicon crystals, the electrons in them become 'excited'. If these crystals are connected to an electrical circuit, these excited electrons start moving, forming an electric current. Solar is increasingly becoming popular as an alternative to conventional energy production.

▲ *Solar panels, made of solar cells, make the wings of satellites and give them the electricity they need*

Wind Power

People, in order to create energy, especially for running flourmills, have long been using windmills. In the 20th century, as turbine technology improved, windmills were used for generating electricity. In a place that's extremely windy, the blades of the fan would automatically move, and a turbine would then convert this motion into electricity.

 # Geothermal Power

▲ *Traditional windmills*

The earth releases heat from its interiors to its surface through **volcanism**. In many places (such as Iceland) this heat makes ground water escape as steam (making a geyser) or turns it **super hot** if trapped inside.

A geothermal power plant captures the released steam and makes it run through a turbine to produce electricity. In other places where steam does not escape naturally, a pipe is drilled to reach the water. As the water rises, it turns into steam because the pressure falls, and is directed to turn a turbine. The steam is condensed and pumped back into the earth, where it can be heated again.

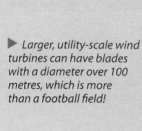

▲ *A geyser in Strokkur, Iceland*

Tidal Power

Tidal power uses the energy stored in tides as they rise and fall. Tidal power engineers build a dam that captures water when the tide rises. When the tide recedes, the gates of the dam open and the water flows out into the sea. As it flows, it turns a turbine. In other places, the natural ocean current is directly used to move a turbine.

▶ *Larger, utility-scale wind turbines can have blades with a diameter over 100 metres, which is more than a football field!*

▶ *A tidal barrage with turbines*

FORCE &
MOVEMENT

THE BASIS OF THE UNIVERSE

Our Universe is made of two things—matter and energy. Matter is all that you can touch, feel, and see. Energy is what makes things move and work. Both matter and energy are made of tiny particles. Matter is made of atoms, which are themselves made of electrons, protons, and neutrons. Protons and neutrons are made of tinier particles called quarks, which are made of tinier particles themselves.

Energy is made of tiny weightless photons. When energy meets matter, like when you kick a ball or shine a flashlight onto something, it makes matter move. When you kick a ball, the potential energy in your foot creates a mechanical force on the ball and drives it towards the goal. When light falls on the atoms of an object, the photons in it make the electrons in the atoms move and therefore produce a tiny electromagnetic force. You cannot feel this force, but you can see this as the 'shine' on the object.

This book will help you understand what force and movement are, and why the Universe is the way it is. On the way you will understand how machines work, how rockets take off, why planes don't fall from the sky, and even how the planets move in their orbits around the Sun.

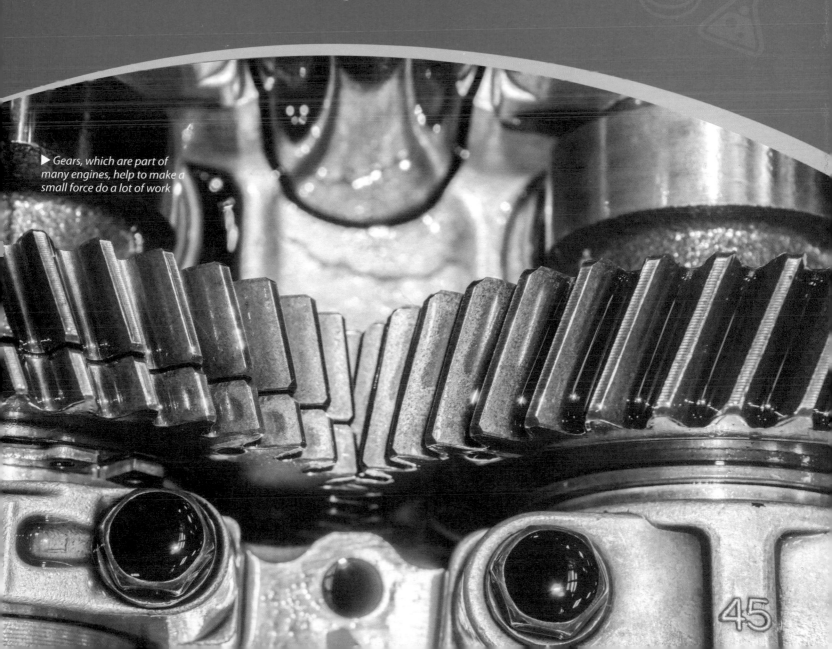

▶ *Gears, which are part of many engines, help to make a small force do a lot of work*

Force: Making Things Move

Force is what makes things move. It may be a giant planet revolving around giant stars, your mother dragging you out of bed to go to school, or it might be electrons jumping from one atom to another, causing a chemical reaction. It may even go right down to the fundamental particles of the Universe, pulling and pushing each other to make the vast fabric of space and time.

But science is more specific. Force, according to science, is an entity that creates motion *in a specific direction*. It is, therefore, a **vector** quantity. Your body **experiences** weight due to the force of the Earth always pulling you downwards. On the other hand, your body **possesses** mass—the total number of atoms and molecules that make you up. This is a **scalar** quantity, because you have the same mass whichever way you are headed. All measurements in physics are determined based on whether they are vectors or scalars.

Types of Force

The Universe has four fundamental forces. With these forces, you can explain almost anything that is going on.

The first of these is gravity, the force that makes two bodies attract each other.

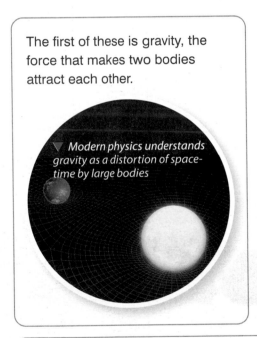

▼ *Modern physics understands gravity as a distortion of space-time by large bodies*

▼ *Electromagnetism is a force that explains electricity, magnetism, heat, and light*

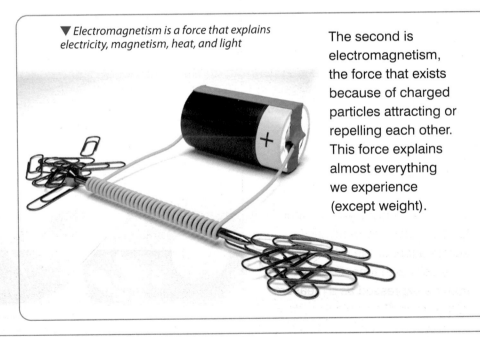

The second is electromagnetism, the force that exists because of charged particles attracting or repelling each other. This force explains almost everything we experience (except weight).

The third force is a strong force, also called the strong nuclear interaction. This force holds protons and neutrons together in a nucleus.

▼ *The strong and weak forces work at the level of the nucleus, electromagnetic force works on atomic scales, and gravity works at the galactic level*

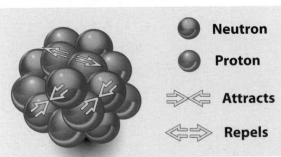

Neutron

Proton

Attracts

Repels

The fourth is the weak force, or the weak nuclear interaction. This also works only inside an atom's nucleus. Without this force, nuclear fusion would be difficult and stars, such as the Sun, would not exist. The continued study of these two forces will only lead to a greater understanding of natural mechanics and the universe.

Momentum

Momentum (symbol p) is what a body with some mass (symbol m) has when it has no force acting on it. When an object is standing still, that is, when it has no **velocity** (v), its momentum is zero. When it has some velocity, its momentum has a value. A small object at high speed (a ball hit by a bat) and a large object at low speed (a roadroller) may share the same momentum.

$$p = mv$$

▶ *It takes a lot of force to change a roadroller's momentum*

Mechanical Force

In mechanical terms, force (symbol f) is the change in momentum with respect to time (symbol t). A catcher stops a ball with a small mass, whereas it takes something huge to stop a roadroller. The force may be electrical (like charges repel, opposite charges attract), magnetic (like poles repel, opposite poles attract), or it may be a property of the density and hardness of the material (friction, elasticity, etc.).

$$f = \frac{mv}{t}$$

The value v/t gives you another fundamental idea of physics: acceleration, or the rate of change of velocity with time. Force can then be expressed as a measure of the mass of an object, and the change it undergoes in its acceleration when the object meets the force.

$$f = ma$$

▼ *The dog's mass and forward acceleration stop the balls' momentum*

What Makes Us Move

Force changes the momentum of an object and therefore changes it from one state of inertia to another (inertia means a body remaining in the same state, whether moving or staying still). This change of inertia can be used to make the device do work that is useful to us, such as using the force of your feet to pedal a bicycle. But what produces that force in the first place?

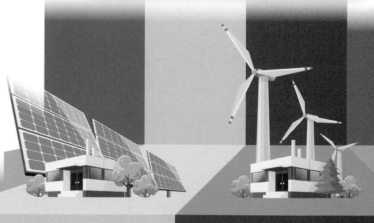

It is **energy**. It is the same thing that you get by eating food, or a car gets from its fuel. All the energy on our planet ultimately comes from the Sun, which gets its energy through nuclear fission. It takes a lot to explain energy, but we can share two interesting things:

- Energy is related to mass by Albert Einstein's famous Theory of Special Relativity.

- Energy can neither be created nor destroyed, but only converted from one form to another. This is the Law of Conservation of Energy.

▲ All the energy we use ultimately comes from nuclear reactions in the Sun

🔍 Work

The conversion of energy, from one form to another, results in some work being done. When you ride a bicycle, your body uses some of the chemical energy it got from food. Your muscles turn the chemical energy to kinetic energy, and this creates the force that pushes the pedal. In physics, the total work done (W) can be explained as the distance the bicycle travelled multiplied by the total force (f) that you applied. But remember that force is a vector. Therefore, the distance that matters is the **displacement** (symbol s), which is the linear distance between the starting point and the ending point, and not the path you have travelled.

$$W = fs$$

Work is of two types—**internal** and **external**. Your heartbeat is an example of internal work; you do external work when bicycling. In internal work, all the energy is spent in keeping the system going (like your body), while in external work, the energy spent makes the body do something, such as pushing the bike's pedals.

💡 Isn't It Amazing!

Scientists have a short way of writing extremely large numbers. So, instead of writing our planet's mass as 598,000,000,000,000,000,000,000,000 kg, we can write it as 5.98×10^{24} kg. The number written as superscript on 10 tells you the **order of magnitude**.

▶ The Sun delivers 3.6×10^{26} kgm²/s³ of power every second. This unit can be further simplified as Joules per second or Watts

WATER   **SOLAR**   **WIND**

Potential and Kinetic Energy

Kinetic energy is the energy a system has when it is moving or doing work (the energy your leg has while pedalling a bicycle). If an object is at rest then it doesn't have kinetic energy. **Potential energy** is the energy available to a system due to inertia (e.g. the unspent energy from your food), or the energy it is transferring as it does work (the energy that is now part of your bicycle's inertia of movement). Sadly, your bicycle won't have much of this kinetic energy left by the end of the journey, since most will be lost due to **friction** with the ground.

▶ The relation between work and energy. The units of both are written as Newton-metres or Joules

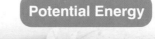

Potential Energy

Kinetic Energy

Power

Displacement

Work done

Power

If you look at electric batteries or lights, they are denoted by the power (symbol P) that they deliver. Something is powerful when it gives a lot of energy (which you experience as force) in a small amount of time, like a wrestler bending a bar of iron. Physicists write power as the rate at which a machine can do work (W) in each unit of time which is usually in seconds.

$$P = \frac{W}{t}$$

◀ Types of energy. We often talk of energy in terms of anything that can be converted into electricity

FOSSIL   NUCLEAR

In Real Life

When James Watt (1736–1819) tried to sell his improved steam engine to mills, they could not understand how it would do more work than the horses they used to pull loads. Being a clever physicist, Watt denoted the energy his engine could deliver every minute (power) in terms of the amount of work a horse could do per minute. The mill owners were impressed, and that's how we got the unit we still use: horsepower.

▲ One horsepower is how much a healthy, untired horse can draw: 33,000 pounds by a foot every

What We are Made Of

Matter is the part that makes up the Universe. If something has **mass**, then it can be touched or felt, or at least measured. Matter is made of protons, electrons, and neutrons, which are themselves made of tinier (subatomic) particles called quarks. Albert Einstein's Special Theory of Relativity redefines matter as a form of energy (e). His equation for it has probably become the most famous equation in the world:

$$e = mc^2$$

Where c is the velocity of light in vacuum and m is its mass. Matter is of two types:

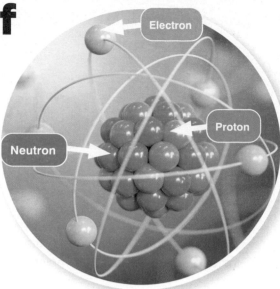

▲ *Matter is made of subatomic particles, which make up electrons, protons and neutrons, which in turn make atoms*

- **Light matter**, which interacts with photons and can be perceived by us either directly (like a football), or by using scientific instruments (for particles such as quarks).

- **Dark matter**, which does not interact with photons. We cannot perceive it at all, but we know it exists because it exerts gravity. Dark matter makes up 27% of the Universe.

Mass and Weight

The definition of mass (symbol m), useful to us in daily life, is that it is the amount of **inertia** that an object has. This is in turn proportional to the number of atoms and molecules in it (i.e. **density**), and the atomic or molecular mass of the elements and compounds it is made of. If you see two boxes of the same size on a table, how would you know which has more mass? You'd have to apply a force, by either pushing or lifting them.

Weight is how our bodies experience mass. In physical terms, the Earth exerts the force upon us. So, by the definition of force, your weight is your mass multiplied by the acceleration due to gravity (g). This lead to the SI unit for weight being Newtons. If your mass is 34 kg, your weight will be 34×9.8 kgm/s², which is 333.2 Newtons.

▼ *Weight (the gravitational pull of the Earth) is how we measure mass on a weighing balance*

💡 Isn't It Amazing!

Your weight (but not mass) will be different on different planets, because they have different accelerations due to gravity (g). If you weigh 333.2 Newtons on Earth, you'll only weigh 55.3 Newtons on the Moon, but 842.3 Newtons on Jupiter.

▲ *If you ever managed to land on Pluto, you would weigh only 22.3 Newtons (you would still be 34 kg though)*

Cohesion

Cohesion refers to the forces that stop things from breaking apart. There are two main forces that hold things together:

1. Ionic attraction: Salts, acids, and alkalis are materials made of ions which have opposite electric charges. Ions of opposite charge attract each other strongly and those of the same charge repel each other. In a solid state, these ions form themselves in a repeating **lattice** of alternating positive and negative charges. The attraction is strong and it takes a lot of energy (heat or mechanical) to break them. That's why things made of metal are so strong.

2. Electric dipole: Substances that are not ionic still have weak dipoles—tiny electrical charges (called $\delta+$ and $\delta-$) at each end of the molecule. The dipoles create weak attraction between different molecules, which keeps them together. It takes less energy to break these forces, which are also called **van der Waals forces**. Cake is held together by such forces, which is why it crumbles so easily.

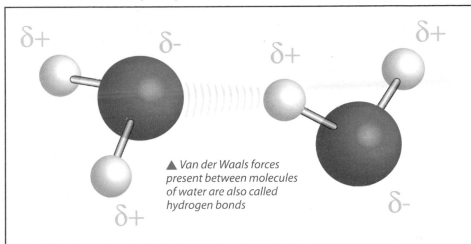

▲ Van der Waals forces present between molecules of water are also called hydrogen bonds

Normal Force

When standing or moving on a bridge, you experience three forces:

• the **frictional force**, that is, the force required to move you;

• your weight (force due to gravity); and

• the **normal force** that acts at right angles to friction.

The normal force is the force exerted by the cohesion of the bridge on you, without which you would crash through it.

A bridge's normal force depends on the density of the materials it is made of

When Things Move in a Straight Line

Have you observed dust particles in a sunbeam? They seem to move in a completely jumbled fashion, darting about and suddenly changing direction. This motion, which seems to be random, is called Brownian motion, named after Robert Brown (1773–1858). However, it is not random. It is governed by the Laws of Motion, which were first written down by Isaac Newton after many years of observation and experimentation.

These laws form the basis of **mechanics**—the science of making things move. As we saw on page 5, every movement must have velocity and direction.

▲ *Brownian motion can be explained by Newton's Laws of Motion*

Lift

Weight

Thrust

Newton's First Law of Motion

In simple language, this law says that an object will not change its state of motion on its own, unless some force acts upon it. An object has only two states of motion: at rest or moving in one direction. This is known as the Law of Inertia.

Imagine that you've gone to the edge of the solar system with your friends (no atmosphere, no gravity) to play cricket. Your friend bowls and you hit the ball hard. It will fly out of the solar system and to the end of the Universe. That's because the force of your hit gave it motion, and unless it crashes into something, there's no force to stop it. This won't happen on Earth because air **drag** will slow the ball down and gravity will pull it back to Earth.

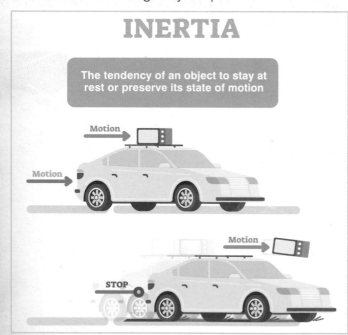

INERTIA

The tendency of an object to stay at rest or preserve its state of motion

Motion

Motion

Motion

STOP

▲ *Things fall frontwards when you brake a moving car because of inertia*

Newton's Second Law of Motion

This law says that the amount (magnitude) and direction of the net force (F_{net}) that acts on an object can be measured by:

1. the mass (m) of the object

2. the direction it moves in

3. the acceleration (a) it undergoes

Think of a football. When it's on the ground, it experiences several forces on it. When you kick it, your foot has to give it enough force to overcome gravity, normal force, friction force, and the drag due to air. The final acceleration of the ball is proportional to whatever is left of the force of your kick. Therefore,

$$F_{net} = ma$$

▶ *Understanding Newton's Second Law of Motion could help you win many football matches*

Newton's Third Law of Motion

According to this law, for every force, there will be another force equal to it, which acts in the opposite direction. You have seen one such force—the normal force, which stops an object from crashing through the solid it is placed on. This force makes a ball bounce off the ground or the wall. When you drag something on the ground, the friction provides resistance. Another such force is **buoyancy**, which makes things float on liquids. When you dive into a pool, you can feel the water pushing you up. Yet another is drag, the friction caused by moving through a fluid—this also acts in air, which is considered to be fluid in nature.

◀ *When you hit a ball, you will experience recoil, the equal and opposite force to the ball hitting your bat*

When Things Don't Move in a Straight Line

Though we think of motion as something that goes in a straight line, there are other kinds too. One of them is like the swaying of a clothesline, known as vibration. The movement of a swing is another kind of motion, called oscillation. The linear movement of an oscillating body is called **propagation**. When it moves forward while oscillating, we get a **wave**. The **rotation** of the Earth on its axis is circular motion; and the **revolution** of our planet around the Sun is combination of both linear and circular motions.

▲ *The pendulum of a grandfather clock oscillates, while the hands of the clock face rotate*

Vibration

Vibration is the movement of an object around a mean position. When you pull the string of a violin and let it go, the string goes back to its resting state with some force. But its momentum is so much that the string goes right past the resting point to the other end, along the same distance as you pulled on the other side. As the string swings back, its momentum makes it go past the resting point again. This to-and-fro movement is called vibration. If there were no drag due to air, this would go on endlessly.

To vibrate, there has to be a motive force pulling the object away and a resisting force pulling it back to the original state. It is often the same force, which changes direction once the vibrating entity has reached one end. In a metal string, it is the **strain** (the extent to which the atoms can be pulled apart).

 The energy of a vibrating string is transmitted to us as sound waves

Oscillation

When something moves and comes back to its place again and again, physicists say that it undergoes periodic motion. An object that vibrates with a defined time period is said to oscillate. That's how a playground swing works. At the subatomic level, everything oscillates—atoms, nuclei, electrons, quarks, and photons. The energy to oscillate comes from their electromagnetic field. Frequency is the measure of the number of oscillations a particle does in one second. It is measured in Hertz (Hz). Every particle has its own natural frequency of oscillation, which depends on the amount of energy it possesses.

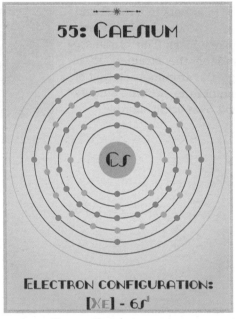

55: CAESIUM

ELECTRON CONFIGURATION: [XE] - 6s¹

▲ *The oscillation of a Caesium-133 atom is used to define a 'second', the unit of measuring time*

Wave Motion

A wave propagates when oscillating objects also move linearly. Waves are longitudinal, when the direction of propagation and oscillation are the same. Our ears catch longitudinal waves in the air as sound. In a transverse wave, the particles oscillate perpendicular to the direction of propagation. Light and radio waves travel this way.

▶ *Types of waves*

LONGITUDINAL WAVES

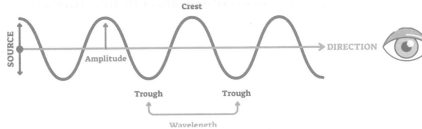

EXAMPLE

Music System
Sound Waves

Amplitude
Expansion
SOURCE
DIRECTION
Compression
Wavelength

TRANSVERSE WAVES

EXAMPLE

Television
Visible Light

SOURCE
Crest
Amplitude
DIRECTION
Trough   Trough
Wavelength

Circular Motion

Circular motion is how a wheel or a disc moves. To calculate how fast a rotating or revolving object is moving, you must measure the angle it moves at, not the distance. This measure is called **angular velocity** and it is measured in degrees per second. As the Earth rotates, all places on the same longitude have the same angular velocity. Nevertheless, they all have different linear velocities. If you stand at the Equator, you have 24 hours to cover 40,075 km, the circumference of the Earth. At the North or South Pole though, you don't have to move at all!

▼ *The angular velocity of a point on the edge of a wheel is the same as its centre. However, its linear velocity is much faster, as it has to travel the full circumference*

In Real Life

All the members in a rock band use the power of oscillation to make music. The guitarists depend on the strain of their strings, the drummers on that of the membrane, and the singers on their own vocal chords!

▲ *Music depends on making a harmonious mix of the natural frequencies of all oscillating things*

How the Planets Move

Why do the planets all seem to go around the Sun in neat paths? Nothing holds them in place after all, no rails or cables. They are actually held together by gravity and move according to special laws. Many of these laws were discovered by Johannes Kepler (1571–1630) after several years of observation of the night sky. Kepler's Laws are based on the **heliocentric theory**—the idea that the Earth goes around the Sun, and not, as it seems every day, that the Sun goes around the Earth.

 ## Kepler's First Law

The orbit of every planet is elliptical with the Sun at one of its foci.

Think of an ellipse as a stretched circle, so it would have two centres (called foci). Planets go around the Sun in a slightly elliptical orbit, not a round one. How much the orbit is off from being a full circle is called its orbital eccentricity (symbol e). For example, our Earth has an eccentricity of 0.017, while the dwarf planet Pluto, the most elliptical, has an eccentricity of 0.248 (it would be zero for a fully circular orbit). Because of this elliptical orbit, the Earth comes closest to the Sun on January 3 (called Perihelion) and moves the fastest, and goes farthest from the Sun on July 4 (called Aphelion) and moves the slowest. Planets (and moons) have elliptical orbits because they pull each other as well as the Sun. Planets change their eccentricity as they come closer or go farther from each other.

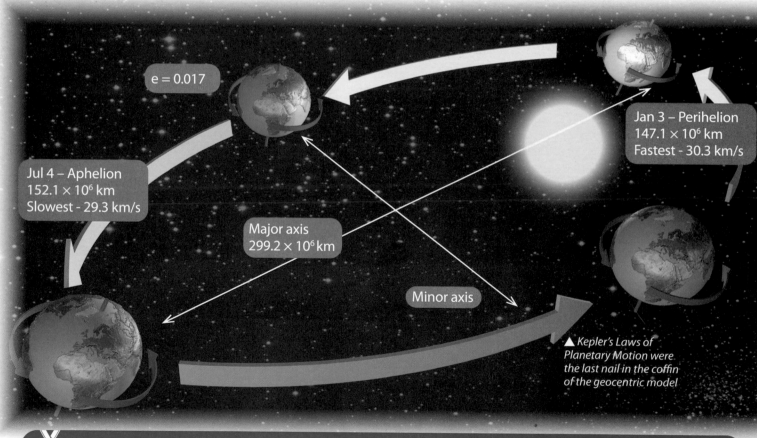

e = 0.017

Jul 4 – Aphelion
152.1 × 10⁶ km
Slowest - 29.3 km/s

Jan 3 – Perihelion
147.1 × 10⁶ km
Fastest - 30.3 km/s

Major axis
299.2 × 10⁶ km

Minor axis

▲ Kepler's Laws of Planetary Motion were the last nail in the coffin of the geocentric model

Incredible Individuals

For most of history, people thought that the Earth was flat and that it was the stars and other planets that went around it (**geocentric theory**). In Europe, astronomers Nicolaus Copernicus (in 1543) and Galileo Galilei (in 1615) published their observations that suggested it was the Earth that went around the Sun instead, but they got in trouble with the Catholic Church for doing so. Only when Johannes Kepler provided a convincing mathematical explanation in 1609, did heliocentrism slowly get accepted.

▲ Galileo Galilei   ▲ Nicolaus Copernicus

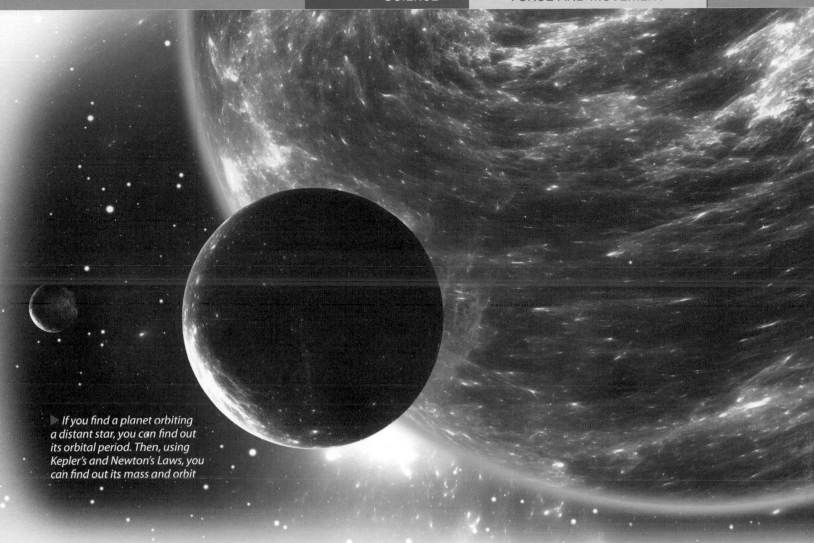

► If you find a planet orbiting a distant star, you can find out its orbital period. Then, using Kepler's and Newton's Laws, you can find out its mass and orbit

Kepler's Second Law

A planet travels faster when near the Sun, and slower when farther.

This is because gravity accelerates the planet as it comes closer to the Sun. The Earth takes 365 days to complete a trip around the Sun, so it clearly travels some distance each day. As it comes closer to the Sun, it covers a longer distance along its orbit, and as it goes farther away, it travels for a smaller distance.

Kepler's Third Law

The square of a planet's orbital period is proportional to the cube of half its major axis.

A planet's **orbital period** is the time it takes to go around the Sun. The major axis is the longest line from the ends of the ellipse that runs through both foci. Astronomers use this law to calculate how long a planet will take to go around the Sun, if they know the major axis of its orbit. They then use this to know when the distance between our planet and another will be the smallest, which is useful for launching spacecrafts in order to minimize the distance to be travelled.

Isn't It Amazing!

After Uranus was discovered in 1781, astronomical calculations of its orbit did not match observations, suggesting that another planet was interfering. In 1846, the French astronomer Urbain Jean Joseph Le Verrier (1811–77) calculated where this new planet could be. No French observatory agreed to look for it, so he wrote to Johann Gottfried Galle (1812–1910) at the Berlin observatory in Germany. His letter reached Galle on 23 September 1846, and Galle found Neptune that very night!

► Neptune was discovered at a location just 1° off from where Verrier had said it would be

Why Things Fall Down

When learning about gravity, you may come across a story that says that Isaac Newton discovered gravity when he was sitting under a tree and an apple fell on him. But the story of Newton's discovery is more complex than that. Let's talk about this discovery and how it changed the world.

☀ Isn't It Amazing!

Did you know that the apple tree that inspired Newton still stands? It grows in Woolsthorpe Manor in Lincolnshire, England, which was Newton's childhood home, and is now over 350 years old.

Newton's Law of Universal Gravitation

Although we know that the Earth attracts all things to itself, Newton suggested that the reverse was also true: all things attract the Earth to themselves too. He figured out that the force of the attraction (symbol F_g) was proportional to the mass of the two bodies attracting each other (symbols m_1 and m_2), and inversely proportional to the square of the distance between them (r). Another factor is the gravitational constant (G), whose value is $6.673 \times 10\text{-}11$ N m²/kg².

$$F_g = \frac{Gm_1m_2}{r^2}$$

So, you could say that not only does an apple fall towards the Earth, but the Earth moves towards the apple too. But since the mass of the apple (a few grams) is nothing compared to the Earth's mass (5.97×10^{24} kg), and the distance between the Earth and the apple is only a tiny fraction as compared to the Earth's radius (6.37×10^6 m or 6370 km), the force of attraction (F_g) between the apple and the Earth depends only on the Earth. Therefore, when you do the math, $F_g = 9.8$ Newtons.

$$F_g = \frac{6.673 \times 10^{-11} \times 5.97 \times 10^{24}}{(6.37 \times 10^6)^2} = 9.8 \text{ N}$$

Now, from Newton's Laws of Motion, we know that F = mass (m) times acceleration (a). But since the mass is negligible, the acceleration due to gravity (g) is effectively a constant everywhere on Earth, that is, 9.8 m/s².

General Relativity

Over time, Newton's law has failed to explain many aspects of gravity. Albert Einstein proposed a radical new solution: space-time. Space-time is the fabric of the Universe, made of the three dimensions of space and one of time. Everything in space is embedded in space-time but huge objects such as planets and stars can bend it around them. To imagine how this happens, get your friends to stretch a cloth flat. Place a football on it. Doesn't it bend the sheet around itself?

▲ *The bending of space-time causes smaller objects to be drawn to the larger ones*

▼ Gravity holds the solar system together

Gravitational Waves

Einstein's theory of space-time acting as a fabric means that it will have ripples going through it when something big happens (such as two stars crashing). These "ripples" are called **gravitational waves** and have the same speed as light. Unlike electromagnetic waves though, they are not known to be made of any particle till now.

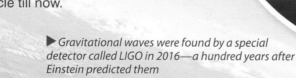

▶ Gravitational waves were found by a special detector called LIGO in 2016—a hundred years after Einstein predicted them

Incredible Individuals

The Binomial theorem, laws of motion, force and mass, acceleration, inertia, universal gravitation, differential calculus, momentum, weight, vector addition, projectile motion, centripetal acceleration, circular motion, satellite motion, tidal forces, the precession of the equinoxes, and optics—one scientist discovered them all. His name is Isaac Newton, the Father of the Scientific Revolution.

▶ Newton humbly said of his discoveries, "If I have seen further, it is by standing on the shoulders of giants."

Forces of Resistance

When you pull a heavy box across the floor, why does it seem so hard to pull? This is because of friction, which is a perpendicular force resisting your forward motion. Much of friction is caused by forces of **adhesion** between the atoms and molecules of the two solids in contact. As you saw on page 9, these are ionic attraction and van der Waals forces.

In reality, friction between two things should be small because their surfaces are not entirely smooth, even if they appear so. That's because they have microscopic hills and valleys called asperities. But when an object has been resting, the force of gravity (mg) works with the adhesive forces to pull it down and crush the asperities. In turn, this increases the surface of contact and the adhesion becomes stronger. That's why it's harder to make an object move than to keep it moving.

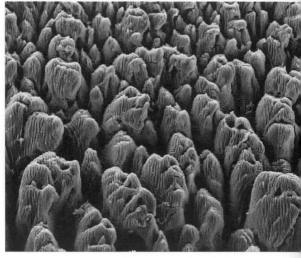

▲ *The surface of silicon, seen under an electron microscope. What looks smooth and shiny to the naked eye is in fact a microscopically rough surface*

Friction

As friction depends on adhesive forces, it depends on the materials in contact. Physicists use a measure called the coefficient of friction (symbol μ) to measure how two solids will interact. It is the ratio of the force required to pull (F), to the weight of the material (called load, L). Therefore, $\mu = F/L$. If the ratio is 1, it means as much force is needed to pull the load as its weight.

However, there are two coefficients of friction—one for calculating how much effort is needed to make a standing thing move (**coefficient of static friction**, symbol μ_s) and one for keeping a moving thing moving (**coefficient of kinetic friction**, symbol μ_k). To make a car that weighs 1,000 Newtons move, you will need 840 Newtons of force, but only 720 Newtons once it is moving. That's because the μ_s for friction between rubber (your car's tire) and concrete (the road's surface) is 0.84, while the μ_k is only 0.72.

▶ *When skating on ice, the steel blades need just 3 Newtons of force to move 100 Newtons of weight ($\mu_k = 0.03$)*

In Real Life

Why can lizards stick to walls, ceilings, and even glass windows without falling? That's because their feet have hundreds of tiny hair. This increases the total surface in contact and the total van der Waals forces, and therefore increases friction.

▶ *Gecko legs maximise friction to the extent that their legs "stick" to walls*

Drag

Drag is the resistance that a fluid offers to a solid object moving through it. You feel drag when walking into the wind or while swimming. It depends on the density and viscosity of the fluid, the speed at which the object is moving, the area that's exposed to the fluid, and the shape of the moving object.

▼ A bullet train's "nose" is designed to minimise the drag it faces while moving at high speed. This is called streamlining

Viscosity of Fluids

Fluids (gases and liquids) have fewer atoms or molecules and therefore less cohesion. Nevertheless, they have some friction within them, called viscosity. Viscosity depends on how close the atoms or molecules are to each other. A thin liquid (like water) has low viscosity, while a thick liquid (like oil) has high viscosity. Viscosity decides how fast a fluid will "flow". The viscosity of a liquid decreases if you heat it, since its atoms or molecules go further apart.

▲ If you cool honey in the fridge, it will become a lot more viscous

Lubrication

Lubrication is a way to reduce friction between two solids, by introducing a liquid between them. The lubricant must have high viscosity to ensure that the friction between it and the solid surfaces does not tear it apart; otherwise, the solids will come in contact. Lubricants must also resist changing viscosity too much when they get heated in the process.

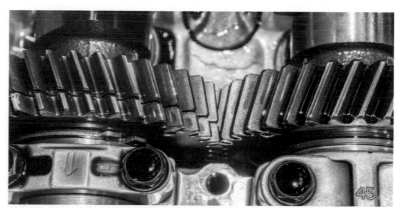

▲ Lubricant in a machine makes sure that its gear wheels don't jam each other through friction

Machines

The word 'machine' makes you think of things with a number of gears and screws and complicated moving parts. But that's not what a machine means to physicists. To them, a machine is any device that transfers work done at one end (called the input work, W_{in}) to another end (the output work, W_{out}). Thus, in a robotic arm that's making a car, there will be a large number of tiny machines that make the whole arm, each transferring work till the end.

In an ideal machine, all the work would be transferred without loss of energy, but in the real world, there's always friction (because of solid parts touching each other) and drag (because of air). Therefore, the usefulness of a machine is measured in terms of Efficiency (η), the fraction of the input that is delivered as final work.

$$\eta = \frac{W_{out}}{W_{in}} = \frac{Energy_{out}}{Energy_{in}} = \frac{F_{out} * s_{out}}{F_{in} * s_{in}}$$

You read that work is the product of the force (F) and the length moved by the mass (displacement, s). So, if the displacement of the input can be doubled, the force can be halved. The ratio of the output force to the input force is called a mechanical advantage (MA).

$$MA = \frac{F_{out}}{F_{in}}$$

Inclined Plane

This is the simplest machine in which one end is higher than the other. It is used to raise a load (P) for a distance (s), by actually dragging it at an angle, rather than pulling or pushing it upwards directly. The work done is the work required to overcome the pull of gravity. The smaller the angle of the incline (its **gradient**), the smaller the force required to counter the pull of gravity and raise the load. This is why we feel less tired going up a gentle slope than a steep staircase.

Lever

A lever is a machine made of three parts: a load arm, an effort arm, and a fulcrum. The length of the two arms makes the most difference, as does the location of the fulcrum, which divides levers into three classes.

Classes of Lever

1st Class Lever	2nd Class Lever	3rd Class Lever
Effort — Load	Load	Load
Fulcrum	Effort / Fulcrum	Fulcrum / Effort

◄ *Your body's joints act as fulcra, muscles as effort and bones as the load*

Isn't It Amazing!

Trains have difficulty going up mountains. As they have very little friction, they can slip on the tracks if the slope is too steep. They need to ascend as gradually as possible, so the track has to be laid so that it goes round and round the mountain, with many tunnels and bridges. This also reduces the force required to counteract gravity, making them go faster.

▲ *The low gradient makes the train spend very little energy climbing*

Wheel and Axle

A wheel and axle convert linear motion into rotational motion, greatly minimising friction and increasing **efficiency**. The longer the radius of the wheel, the less effort you need to put in to move. You see this type of machine everywhere: in motor vehicles, in machines, in toys, and even the wheels of your suitcase!

▶ *Cranes use a wheel and axle called a windlass to convert rotational motion into linear motion*

Pulley

A pulley is a wheel over which a cable runs carrying a load. The most common use of it is in an elevator, where a counterbalancing weight going down pulls the elevator car up.

◀ *By using a combination of pulleys, the length of the rope can be increased, so that the counterweight can be made lighter*

Wedge

A wedge turns the force applied in one direction by an angle. A knife is a good example of a wedge: by pressing your knife down on a carrot, you drive the two pieces away till they split. Humans have been making wedges since the Early Stone Age, in the form of stone axes and cutters.

▲ *Pizza knives combine wedges and wheels*

Screw

A screw is an inclined plane (the ribs of the screw) arranged in a spiral around an axis, to convert rotational motion to linear motion. Screws are used in presses to crush things with little force.

▶ *Screw-presses are used traditionally in Asia to press milk from coconuts*

⊛ Incredible Individuals

James Starley (1830–1881) and his nephew John Starley (1854–1901) perfected the modern bicycle. Through a simple combination of pulleys, wheels, and levers, it efficiently converts your input (pedalling) into motion.

◀ *All modern bicycles are based on Starleys' safety bicycle*

Density and Buoyancy

Density (symbol d) is simply a measure of how much matter there is in a unit of space. We use mass (m) as a measure of the amount of matter and volume (V) as the measure of space. Therefore, the formula for calculating density is simply:

$$d = \frac{m}{V}$$

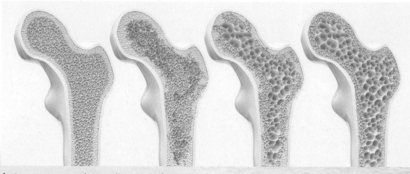

▲ *As we age, our bone density reduces, making them prone to breaking*

Density is expressed as kilogrammes per cubic metre (kg/m³) or grams per cubic centimetre (g/cm³). (These units are now the standard units throughout the world.) When the metric system was defined, the density of pure water at 4°C was fixed as 1 g/cm³, and the densities of all other materials are compared to it (**relative density**). Density is an important character of a substance and has a strong role in determining what that substance may be used for.

🔍 Floating and Sinking

Why do some things—such as iron nails—sink in water, while others—such as wooden nails—float? It is because of their density (d). Density increases the force on the object due to the Earth's gravity (g). The heavier mass will be pulled faster towards the Earth.

If you put an object in water, it will experience normal force that counteracts gravity, called buoyancy. Buoyancy is the resistance of the fluid to being displaced. The van der Waals forces between a liquid's atoms or molecules have to be broken by an object sinking through it (or in the case of a ship, moving horizontally). An object denser than water will have a force (m*g) strong enough to break through it, so it sinks. An object less dense (rarer) than water will not have enough force to break through, so it floats.

As gases have weaker van der Waals forces than liquid, they have lesser buoyancy and viscosity.

▶ *Iron-bodied ships float because their hold is full of air (or crude oil), so that the total density is less than that of water*

Isn't It Amazing!

As air is heated, its molecules move away from each other, reducing its density. The buoyancy of the cooler air below will push it upwards. This is the principle used in flying hot air balloons. Helium and hydrogen are lighter than air, so balloons filled with them also float.

▶ Zeppelins are hydrogen balloons coupled with propellers. They were used for air transport in the early 20th century

Specific Gravity and Purity

▼ The purity of gold objects is measured in carats. 1 carat is equal to a gold content of 4.166% in the object

Relative density is the density of a substance expressed as a fraction of the density of a reference substance. When water is used, this is called **specific gravity**. This measure is used to determine whether an object is pure or contaminated, by the Archimedes Principle. If an object is put in water, it will displace water equal to its own volume. Two dense objects of the same weight will displace different volumes of water, which you can measure.

Gold is an expensive and very dense metal. It is often mixed with silver or copper for making jewellery and other things. If an object made of gold displaces more water (by volume) than a nugget of gold of the same weight, you know that it is impure.

Freshwater and Seawater

W – Winter Temperate Seawater

S – Summer Temperate Seawater

T – Tropical Seawater

TF – Tropical Freshwater

F – Fresh Water

Salt dissolved in water adds to its mass without changing its volume. That makes seawater, which is rich in salts, denser and therefore more buoyant than water in river deltas. Ships moving from freshwater ports to the open sea experience more buoyancy, while those moving in the reverse direction sink a bit.

◀ Plimsoll Lines indicate how much a ship's hull may sink safely in freshwater and seawater in summer and winter. The numbers show the depth to which the ship's bottom (keel) has sunk below the surface

Engines

Humans have always dreamed of mechanical motion. One inventor attempted to use windmills as propellers to drive carts in 1714. Another one tried to run a car powered by wound-up clockwork in 1748. But neither were reliable.

During the Industrial Revolution, the science of converting heat energy into work (thermodynamics) was developed. Engineers wondered whether they could build practical engines that could actually do work, especially hauling loads of coal out of coal mines and carrying the loads into factories. Nicolas Cugnot built a steam-powered car in 1769 that could run for 20 minutes, but then had to rest for the next 20. Thomas Savery, Thomas Newcomen, James Watt, and Richard Trevithick, each one improved

on the other's design of the steam engine, making them much lighter and faster. Other inventors, such as Karl Benz and Gottfried Daimler, both from Germany, worked on internal combustion engines, which were much lighter than steam engines.

▲ *This exhibit in the Metiers Art Museum, Paris, is the world's oldest surviving motor vehicle, though some parts of it are new*

Steam Power

Steam is full of energy, and if confined in a chamber, will try to push its way out. A piston is a lid, like a disc of metal, which can be used to make the chamber bigger or smaller. If the piston is attached to a rod, the force of the steam pushing against it can be converted into work. This is the idea behind a steam engine.

In the picture on the right, you see four stages of the engine at work. First, the steam is boiled and enters the piston chamber. As it enters, it pushes against the piston. As the energy is converted to mechanical energy that moves the wheel, the steam cools and is drained off. A second rod attached to the wheel controls a moving sluice. Once the piston is pushed to the end, the wheel has rotated half a circle. The rod now closes one inlet of steam and opens the inlet on the other end. Steam rushes into that side and pushes the piston back, completing one turn of the wheel. This is called a double-acting engine.

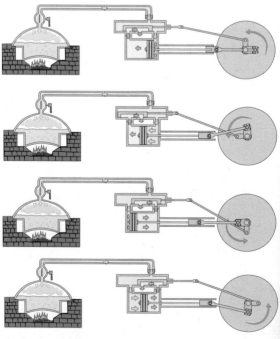

▲ *A double acting steam engine conserves power and does nearly double the work*

In Real Life

As steam-powered engines were heavy, they were run on railroads, so that the iron wheels running on iron tracks would have minimum friction.

◄ *Steel wheels on steel tracks allow really high speeds as rolling friction is near zero*

Internal Combustion Engine

The weight of the water and the coal used to power the steam engine made it very heavy. What if the gas released as the fuel burns could be used to push the piston, instead of using steam? This is the idea behind the internal combustion engine.

Modern internal combustion engines have a piston chamber (cylinder) like steam engines. On the intake stroke (see 1 in the picture), the engine takes in air from the atmosphere and a small amount of fuel from the fuel tank. It compresses it in the compression stroke (2). In the power (or combustion) stroke (3), an electric spark ignites the fuel. The heat of the combustion causes the air to expand rapidly, pushing the piston forcefully. In the final exhaust stroke (4), the burnt fuel and air are removed from the cylinder.

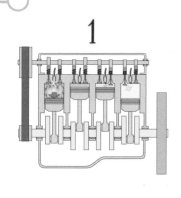
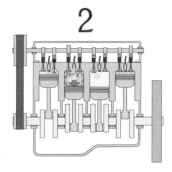
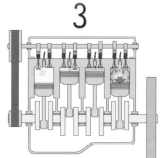
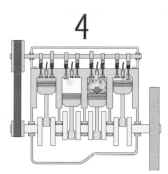

▲ Linking four cylinders in different stages produces a more efficient conversion of heat to work

◀ Belts connect the engine's crankshaft to the axles, so that the energy from the engine can be transmitted to the wheels as mechanical force

▼ The black cylinder is the steam boiler, while the black box below it, in front of the wheels, is the piston box

⭐ Incredible Individuals

Bertha Benz made the first long distance car journey with her sons Eugene and Richard in 1888 from Mannheim to Pforzheim in Germany. Her trip attracted large crowds and people began to see the advantages of a lightweight self-powered carriage.

▲ Bertha Benz (left) and the BenzPatent Motorwagen (right). She was the main investor in her husband Karl Benz's factory, and also invented brake pads

Flight

Humans have always wanted to fly. Greek mythology tells the story of Daedalus, a talented artisan who, along with his son Icarus, was imprisoned by Minos, the king of the island of Crete. Daedalus made wings out of feathers and wax for himself and Icarus. As they flew out of prison, Icarus flew too close to the Sun, whose heat melted the wax. Icarus fell into the sea and drowned.

The only problem with this invention is that humans don't have the bones or the muscles needed to fly, even if we make better wings. But we can use the power of physics to make flying devices, and we'll learn about them here.

◀ *The Fall of Icarus, painted by Jacob Peter Gowy, in the Museo del Prado, Madrid, Spain*

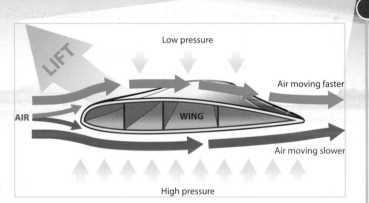

◀ *An aerofoil is a special design that makes planes fly if they move very fast*

🔍 Lift

You've read how balloons fly using buoyancy. But there's another way, which scientists have known for centuries, called the **lift**. An object experiences drag caused by viscosity when moving through a fluid. As the object moves forward, it displaces the fluid, causing it to turn. This turn causes lift, a force that acts perpendicular to drag.

A special design of plane wings, called an aerofoil, ensures that lift acts upwards while the plane is moving forward. It makes use of the tiny differences in air pressure created by the aerofoil design, so that air is of lower pressure and higher speed above, and higher pressure and lower speed below. The difference in pressures pushes the wings upward. The faster the plane, the higher the lift. Planes at take-off need to have high velocity, so they have to speed up on a runway.

⭐ Incredible Individuals

The first woman to get a pilot's license and fly on her own was Raymonde de la Roche of France. She got her license on 8 March 1910; just six years after the Wright brothers made the first aeroplane flight on 17 December 1903.

▲ *In 1919, Raymonde de la Roche flew a plane 16,000 feet above sea level, setting a world record*

Isn't It Amazing!

If a propeller can fan air downwards, the thrust becomes the same as lift, so the plane rises. This is the basis of a helicopter.

▲ *The horizontal propeller provides lift, while the vertical propeller in the tail prevents the helicopter from spinning*

Propellers

If you jump off a cliff using a glider, the buoyancy of the air will keep you up while the lift is being generated But for airplanes, a more reliable way is required. After many attempts by many people, the Wright brothers got it right. They perfected a screw propeller, which has twisted aerofoil blades. When it rotates, it fans air behind it, so the pressure in front reduces and that behind increases. This pressure difference pushes the plane forward very fast (thrust).

▶ *Propellers can be used to create thrust (forward) or lift (upward)*

Jet Propulsion

If you force water out of a garden hose at top pressure, you can feel the pushback (Newton's Third Law of Motion). This is the principle of the **jet**. A jet engine is an internal combustion engine paired with an air compressor. Compressed air meets the burning fuel and is pushed out through a turbine. As it rapidly expands in the atmosphere, it generates a huge amount of thrust.

▶ *Jet engines team up with aerofoils to create thrust and lift that power modern long-distance flight*

To Space

Getting to space has been a human dream for millennia.
It finally came true between 9:07 am and 10:55 am
(Moscow time) on 12 April 1961, when Yuri Gagarin
orbited the Earth. But how did he get there? What was the
science that made it possible?

Getting to space involves a lot of really simple physics.
You have to achieve escape velocity (v_e) to beat the
Earth's gravity to get out there. You have to learn to build
spacecrafts that are powerful enough to go a long, long
way. You have to understand how to use gravity to give
the spacecraft a boost.

 ## Thrust

You saw how planes rise by generating lift on pages 26–27. However, the lift is not
enough to get a rocket to achieve escape velocity. So, it uses another principle
called **thrust**. Thrust is the force with which the rocket pushes against the Earth
first, and as it lifts off against the air. A rocket must have enough thrust to beat
drag, weight, and the potential energy it will keep gaining as it rises. Most rockets
generate thrust by jet propulsion.

 ## Escape Velocity

Newton's Laws of Motion tell you that things accelerate as they fall to the Earth because of the
Earth's gravitational pull (symbol g). As you go higher into the atmosphere (h), your potential
energy rises too. For a rocket to beat this, it must have kinetic energy ($\frac{1}{2}mv^2$) equal to or more
than the potential energy due to gravity (mgh) that it will acquire as it rises. It must therefore go
fast enough to overcome this pull. To escape from Earth, you need to shoot out at 11 kilometres
per second. And that's before taking into account the friction of the atmosphere.

$$\text{If} \quad \tfrac{1}{2}mv^2 \geq mgh \quad \text{then} \quad v_e = \sqrt{2gh}$$

 ## ⊛ Incredible Individuals

French satirical writer Savinien Cyrano de Bergerac
(1619–1655) imagined curious ways of flying to the
moon in his novel *Comical History of the States and
Empires of the Moon.* He imagined an engine consisting
of concave mirrors, which focus sunlight onto the air in
it, making it rush out of the engine like a jet.

▶ *Savinien Cyrano de Bergerac also suggested that one could travel
towards the Moon by tying bottles of dew to oneself*

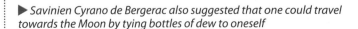

In Real Life

At orbital velocity, you can neither escape a planet (or a star) nor crash into it. Therefore, you end up going in circles, like the Moon goes around the Earth, or the Earth goes around the Sun.

▲ *The moon's orbital velocity is 1.022 km/s*

Gravity Assist

As a spacecraft approaches a planet, it will accelerate due to that planet's gravity. If it is moving fast enough already, it can reach the escape velocity of that planet, with which it can shoot out further into space. Most crafts going to outer space use the Moon to do this.

▲ *The Moon has no atmosphere because its escape velocity is less than that of gas molecules heated by sunlight*

Materials Science

The lighter the weight of the rocket and more powerful the fuel, the faster the thrust can take the rocket up. Therefore, most of 'rocket science' is really about fuel efficiency and learning how to build lighter rockets. Rockets are often made of high strength, low weight alloys. They are coated with ceramics so that the drag due to the atmosphere does not burn them up (this is especially important for returning spacecrafts).

Fuels (called propellants) are usually solids stored at very cold temperatures, so they take up less space and more can be filled in.

The Metric System

All the measurements you have seen in this book are expressed in units of the metric system. But did you know that there are many other systems in the world for measuring length, area, mass, volume, force, etc.? Though almost all countries use the metric system now, the USA still largely uses the Imperial System.

The metric system originated in France after the 1789 French Revolution. The new Republican government was concerned that the hundreds of systems of weights and measures used in different parts of France would cause a lot of confusion. To address this, the government created a new system whose units of length, volume, mass, and time would be based on properties of nature itself. Everything would be based on the metre, which is how the system got its name.

The metre was to be one-ten-millionth (1/10,000,000) of the longitudinal distance from the North Pole to the South Pole. The gram would be the mass of one cubic centimetre of water at its maximum density, and the litre would be one-thousandth of a cubic metre. In 1799, a platinum block measured to be one kilogram and a platinum-iridium rod measured to be 1 metre became the standards by which all measuring and weighing devices were to be calibrated.

◀ *This block of platinum was the international prototype of the kilogram till 20 May 2019, after which the weight was defined by the Planck's constant*

Metric Scale

The great advantage of the metric system is that it follows the decimal system, so that the calculation of units becomes easy. Greek prefixes are used for multiples of the metre, gram, and litre, and Latin ones for fractions. This way, 100 metres is a hectometre, a million litres is a megalitre, and one-tenth of a gram is a decigram.

Prefix	Size in meters	Examples	Prefix	Size in meters	Examples
Exa (E)	1 quintillion	105 light years	deci (d)	1/10th	compact disk
Peta (P)	1 quadrillion	ten light years	centi (c)	1/100th	children's fingers (width)
Tera (T)	1 trillion	one light-hour	milli (m)	1/1000th	flea
Giga (G)	1 billion	the Sun	micro (µ)	1-millionth	red blood cell
Mega (M)	1 million	dwarf planet Ceres	nano (n)	1-billionth	DNA (width)
kilo (k)	1000	Sydney Harbour bridge (length)	pico (p)	1-trillionth	X-ray wavelength
hecto (h)	100	football field	femto (f)	1-quadrillionth	atomic nucleus
deca (da)	10	school bus	atto (a)	1-quadrillionth	quarks
	1	walking stick			

SI Units

In 1875, the International Bureau of Weights and Measures was established in Sèvres near Paris, and other countries began to adopt the metric system. In 1960, a few changes were made to clear the confusion amongst scientists, and the new system was named the *Système Internationale* (French for 'International System'). It replaced the old definitions with those based on absolute, unchanging properties of nature, because many of the original standards changed over time.

The metre is now defined as the distance light travels in a vacuum in 1/299,792,458th of a second, since the speed of light in vacuum (symbol c) is exactly 299,792,458 m/s.

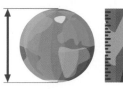

Metre

The kilogram is defined using the values of metre and second, and the Planck's constant (symbol h), whose value has been determined to be precisely $6.626,070,15 \times 10^{-34}$ kgm²/s. Therefore,

Kilogram

$$1 \text{ kg} = \frac{(299,792,458)2}{6.626,070,15 \times 10^{-34} \times 9,192,631,770} \text{ hs/m}^2$$

The second is equal to the duration of 9,192,631,770 periods of the radiation corresponding to the transition between the two hyperfine levels of the unperturbed ground state of one atom of Caesium-133 undisturbed by any other radiation.

Second

The Kelvin, the SI unit of temperature, is defined using the other three (metre, kilogram, and second), and the Boltzmann constant (symbol k), whose value has been determined to be $1.380,649 \times 10^{-23}$ kgm²/s²K. Therefore,

Kelvin

$$1 \text{ K} = \frac{1.380,649 \times 10^{-23}}{6.626,070,15 \times 10^{-34} \times 9,192,631,770} \text{ kgm}^2/\text{s}^2$$

▲ *The Système Internationale defines seven basic units, from which all others are derived*

The ampere is the unit of electric current, and is expressed as the amount of electrical charge (written in Coulombs) that passes through a conductor in 1 second. Its definition is based on the charge of the electron, which has been fixed as $-1.602\ 176\ 634 \times 10^{-19}$ Coulombs. 1 Ampere is 1 Coulomb per second.

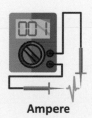

Ampere

The mole is the unit for the amount of a substance (n), which is a measure of the number of elementary entities such as atoms, molecules, ions, electrons, or subatomic particles. One mole is defined as exactly $6.02214076 \times 10^{23}$ elementary entities. This number is called the Avogadro number.

Mole

The candela is the SI unit for luminous efficacy (the scientific way to refer to 'brightness') of light sources in a given direction, such as an electric bulb or the Sun. One candela is defined as 1/683rd of the luminous efficacy of electromagnetic radiation of frequency 540×10^{12} Hz in one direction.

Candela

Isn't It Amazing!

The French also divided the circle into 400 degrees, instead of 360 degrees. Though it made calculations easier, people never adopted this system.

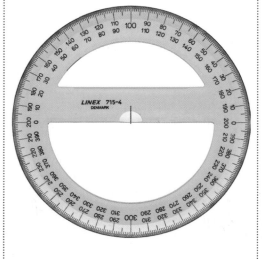

▲ *A protractor showing metric and common degrees.*

FUTURE SCIENCE
&
TECHNOLOGY

THE MARCH OF SCIENCE

You have probably never seen a typewriter. Its invention at the end of the 19th century revolutionised human life. The invention of the typewriter led to the creation of hundreds of thousands of jobs for young people as typists and secretaries, even as several old jobs disappeared. But the advent of the modern computer in the 1980s began to turn the typewriter obsolete, as writing and recording information became easier. Yet, the typewriter lives on in our digital QWERTY keyboards.

New devices help us understand the natural world better—through the sciences of physics, chemistry, and biology. Engineers take the new ideas of science and use them to build better things—better forms of transport, **genetic engineering**, and **cloning** to fight disease, robots and artificial intelligence to manufacture better products, and aid in various sectors of industry and service. These, in turn, help us push the frontiers of science, which then helps us build new technologies.

Thousands of jobs are lost as new technologies reduce the need to employ humans (this is called automation). But many new kinds of jobs are created too, and we need to learn them anew. Who would have imagined jobs such as a web designer or a drone pilot a few decades ago? Economists have called this **creative destruction**. Let's have a look at a few advances in science and technology that will change our lives.

▼ *The evolution of science and technology cannot be predicted and, at times, is beyond our imagination*

Nanotechnology

As humans, our bodies are limited by nature. Without technology, we cannot stand temperatures that are too cold or too hot, nor can we fly in the sky or dive into the seas. But technology is often cumbersome and uncomfortable, such as the oxygen cylinders used by divers and mountaineers. Scientists who work with different kinds of materials are always looking to make things lighter, more flexible, and, of course, cheaper. That's where nanotechnology comes in.

The term 'nano' in nanotechnology comes from the word nanometre (nm), a unit of length one-billionth (1/1,000,000,000) of a metre; the size at which atoms and molecules exist. Nanotechnology is the science of creating materials by building them one atom or molecule at a time, while strictly controlling how they are arranged, using what we know of their chemical properties. Nanotechnology creates novel atomic structures that are not common in nature.

◀ *Graphene is a form of carbon made by nanotechnology. Here you see it acting as a molecule-sized filter (black) that only allows water molecules (red and blue) through*

🔍 Nanoelectronics

With every passing year, electronic devices such as computers and mobile phones are becoming more complicated than ever. There are already millions of transistors on microprocessor chips. In 2016, scientists found a way to make transistors as small as 1 nm wide. If there was a way to manufacture them on a large scale, then computers would get much tinier, much faster, and a lot more flexible than they currently are.

Another use is in creating nanometre-sized sensors. These would be tiny electrical devices that can detect pollution, heat, and movement, among other things, and transmit the information to a mobile computer. Such sensors could be sewn into clothes or even implanted under your skin, to monitor blood sugar, for example.

▶ *Nanosensors sewed onto clothes could be used to detect low blood sugar levels and warn patients to eat something*

👤✓ In Real Life

A lot of nanotechnology is inspired by nature. For example, lotus leaves have microscopic structures that repel water and keep the plant waterproof. Scientists have designed a vanadium dioxide nano-coating for windows that mimics the lotus leaves.

Nanomedicine

Doctors are very excited about what nanotechnology can do for medicine. One line of research uses graphene, a form of carbon which exists as thin sheets. Atoms of carbon can be laid down as nanometre-sized ribbons of graphene, to create a frame in which nerve cells (neurons) can be grown, and their axons can be made to follow a pre-decided path to meet other neurons. This way, people with brain damage who have lost the ability to do math or recognise faces could regain some ability.

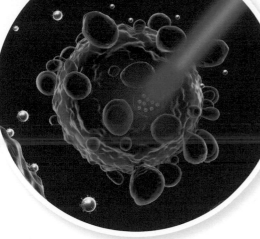

Another line of research looks at using balls of gold just a few nanometres wide (nanoparticles) to kill cancer cells in combination with radiation therapy. When a patient's body is injected with these particles, cancer cells absorb them at a greater rate than normal ones. In turn, the particles make them take in more radiation than they normally would, causing them to die.

◀ *One day, nanoribbons could help Alzheimer's patients regrow neurons in their brains*

Nano energy

Many nanotechnologists work with graphene —a form of carbon that can be made into sheets that can then be rolled into carbon nanotubes. Nanotubes are very conductive to electricity and offer little resistance. Scientists are looking to see if they can be used to replace metal wires to make transmission of electricity cheaper, while also making electric cables lighter.

Another use of carbon nanotubes is in building sturdier yet lighter materials, such as the blades of windmills. Lighter windmill blades convert more wind energy into electricity. Using the same thought, turbine blades in other power plants can be made lighter, so that energy is not wasted in overcoming the resistance of the material due to its weight.

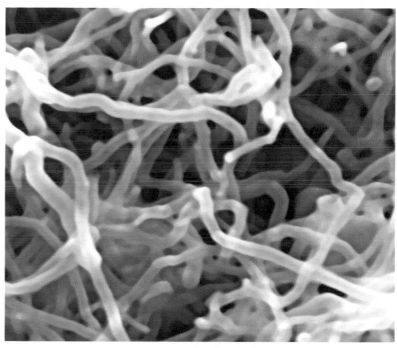

▲ *An electron microscope picture of what carbon nanotubes look like*

Other Uses

Yet another use of nanotechnology is in making paints and clothes that can resist the growth of bacteria and fungi. Nano-materials are also being used in garments to make them self-cleaning so that the use of chemical detergents can be reduced. Scientists are experimenting with nano-structures made of graphene for many things, such as building artificial organs and tools for removing pollutants from the atmosphere. Graphene structures are being made to purify sea water and polluted water, so that it can be made fit for drinking. As the human population grows, so does the demand for clean water.

▲ *Nano clothes could one day keep you safe from germs while you play outside*

Wearable Electronics

When visiting a foreign country, not knowing the local language can make things very difficult. But, what if you could wear an ear device and suddenly every language sounds like English, or one that you are familiar with?!

This is not science fiction but the exciting new field of wearable electronics. Glasses that double up as cameras, earphones that translate on the go, and even smart socks that tell you how much you have walked! Upcoming technologies such as nanotechnology and artificial intelligence play a big role in this.

☢ Wearable Eyegear

What if your glasses could automatically adjust themselves to the brightness of the light? So they would be darker outdoors and brighter inside. These are called smart glasses, which have tiny light sensors in the lens. Another kind of wearable eye gear, such as Google Glass, features a tiny camera that communicates with a mobile device, and a detector that monitors eye movement. So you can capture photographs by just blinking your eyes!

☢ E-book

Using nanotechnology, scientists are looking to make flexible screens that can help you read or watch videos on the go. When you're done, you just fold up the screen and put it in your pocket.

☢ Fitness Bands

These wristbands have sensors that can track your movements, and measure your pulse, blood sugar, and skin conductance. In the future, they could communicate with microscopic robots injected into your body to monitor other aspects of health, such as how cancer cells are being found and destroyed.

☢ Wearable Charger

Nanotechnology is also helping us convert the heat of our body (thermoelectricity) into electrical power using a glass-based fabric. So while you do your morning exercise, the heat you generate can be used to charge your phone using a thin wearable device.

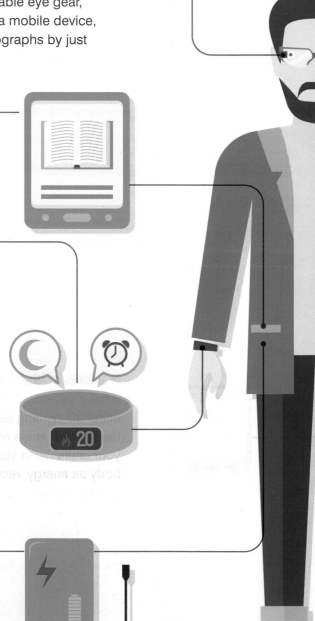

▶ *With wearable technology, we would not need to lug around big gadgets*

⊛ Incredible Individuals

Kay McNulty, Betty Jennings, Betty Snyder, Marlyn Wescoff, Frances Bilas, and Ruth Lichterman Teitelbaum were the six women who helped programme ENIAC (Electronic Numerical Integrator and Computer), one of America's first computers. Although few remember them today, their work set off the advances in computer science, which have now made them small enough to wear on your wrist.

▶ *Marlyn Wescoff and Ruth Lichterman Teitelbaum demonstrate the ENIAC*

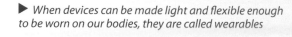
▶ *When devices can be made light and flexible enough to be worn on our bodies, they are called wearables*

⊛ Wearable Ear-gear

Today we have earphones that communicate with our phones without wires. The next step: an earphone that can hear information in one language and translate it, in real time, to another that you are comfortable with.

⊛ Smartwatch

Your parents probably have one which helps them respond to emails or messages or alarms, without having to pull out their phones each time. What if we said that with the help of nanotechnology, they might replace phones altogether, and come equipped with incredible computing power?

⊛ Smart Clothing

What if you could make your clothes using 3D-printing technology? You could then add all kinds of smart materials, so your clothes can store the heat of your body as energy, recognise your gestures, or even control your other devices.

⊛ In Real Life

What if instead of wearing electronics, they were implanted into your body? You would be a cyborg—a cybernetic organism. Some scientists think that in this way, some defective organs of a human can be replaced with tiny electronic devices.

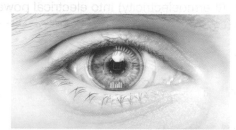

▲ *People with defects in their retina could see using cyborg eyes, which work using implanted electronic light sensors*

⊛ Smart Socks

Smart socks can help many patients who have trouble walking. They can be programmed to tell you to stop walking before it becomes painful.

Artificial Intelligence

What is intelligence? Scientists have suggested that there are four aspects to it, which are as follows:

1. **Perception:** The nervous system interprets the environment around us through sight, hearing, smell, taste, and touch. How these senses can be integrated by the brain is a measure of intelligence.

2. **Learning:** Perception is stored in the brain as memory—a library of everything you have perceived in the past. Learning is the making of memory. You learn facts by **rote** (such as the letters of the alphabet), and relationships by association (such as what happens to you if your mom catches you sneaking cookies).

3. **Reasoning:** This is the part that most people think is real intelligence.

   - **Inductive reasoning** relies on past actions. If you got into trouble for sneaking cookies yesterday, you could get into trouble today.

   - **Deductive reasoning** relies on current information. If there were four oranges on the table this morning, and now there are three, someone's eaten an orange.

4. **Problem Solving:** This takes the above three and sees if they work in a new situation that you have no memory of. For example, if $2 \times 3 = 6$ and $2 \times 6 = 12$, will $3 \times 2 \times 2$ also make 12?

▲ *Language and deception were thought to be unique parts of human intelligence*

Artificial Intelligence (AI)

If we enable a computer to master all the four powers above (Perception, Learning, Reasoning, and Problem Solving), we could call it an intelligent machine. Computers already do quite a lot—storing memory (they never forget), solving mathematical problems (way better than us), and sensing the environment (e.g. face recognition software). However, their inductive reasoning powers and the ability to solve non-mathematical problems are still limited.

However, humans have other superpowers. They understand and speak **language**, making up new sentences on the fly. AI scientists focus on getting computers to 'get' language as well as possible. That's how we have Siri and Cortana, the voice assistants in Apple and Microsoft phones and computers respectively. Humans have another power: deception, making a person believe the opposite of the truth. This is applied to computers through the Turing Test: if you cannot tell a computer apart from a human, it is intelligent.

◀ *In a Turing Test, you face two screens, one that gives answers typed by a human, and one that gives answers from an AI programme. You have to guess which is which, by asking smart questions*

Symbolic Learning

This is how most computers learn their tasks. They store a huge number of 'programmes', which are instructions on what to do. They use these instructions to build up a memory of things, for example, spellings of words. When a word does not match those in the stored dictionary, they either point out the right spelling or ask you to record the new word.

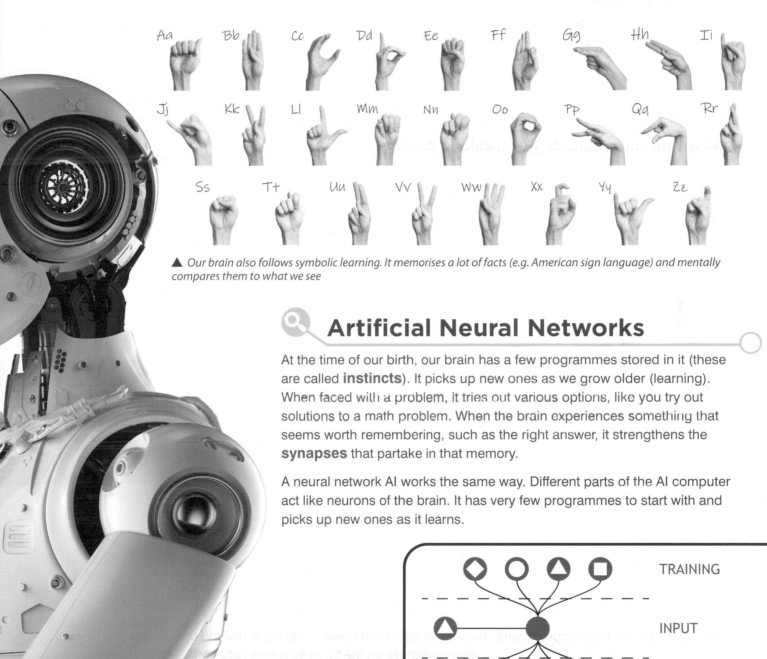

Aa Bb Cc Dd Ee Ff Gg Hh Ii

Jj Kk Ll Mm Nn Oo Pp Qq Rr

Ss Tt Uu Vv Ww Xx Yy Zz

▲ Our brain also follows symbolic learning. It memorises a lot of facts (e.g. American sign language) and mentally compares them to what we see

Artificial Neural Networks

At the time of our birth, our brain has a few programmes stored in it (these are called **instincts**). It picks up new ones as we grow older (learning). When faced with a problem, it tries out various options, like you try out solutions to a math problem. When the brain experiences something that seems worth remembering, such as the right answer, it strengthens the **synapses** that partake in that memory.

A neural network AI works the same way. Different parts of the AI computer act like neurons of the brain. It has very few programmes to start with and picks up new ones as it learns.

▶ A neural network works by being trained on a data set (say, recognising shapes), and then being tested on what it learned

◀ Cybernetics is a field of science that combines robotics, artificial intelligence, and biotechnology to artificially enhance our body

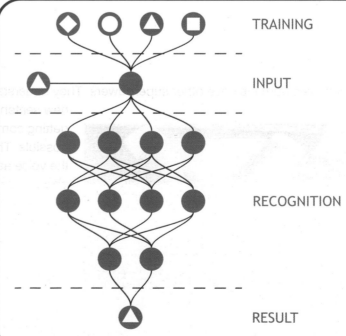

TRAINING

INPUT

RECOGNITION

RESULT

Robotics

If you have read science fiction, you must have come across several stories on robots. Robots are a kind of automaton—machines that operate by themselves. The Chinese built some of the earliest automata, including a completely mechanical orchestra. But today, if you want to be a robotics engineer, you'll have to learn several things: computing, artificial intelligence, electronics, and mechanics.

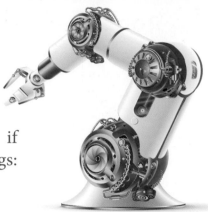

Unlike the ones in stories, most modern robots do not look like humans, except some toys. They are used for manufacturing electronic appliances, automobiles, and other goods. They are also being tried out for performing surgeries where very tiny cuts and stitches need to be made, which doctors cannot perform.

Automation

Would you consider your washing machine a robot? Once you've loaded it and switched it on, it does all the work by itself. The idea behind robots is automation—getting work done without human involvement. The Industrial Revolution of the 19th century was driven by automation. Inventors created elevators and escalators, machines that could weave cloth out of threads, and wagons that could move without being pulled by horses. Yet, we still don't consider them as robots.

◀ *It may look like a box, but a washing machine is a robot too!*

Industrial Robots

We think of robots as machines that can move around and use their arms and legs as we do. Modern robotics uses electricity and computer science to make large metallic 'arms' move about and do precise tasks. These robots come in two types:

1. Fixed robots: These are bolted down into one place. Such robots are used in factories to make the movements required to weld parts of a car together, or to make tiny parts for electronics such as mobile phones.

2. Mobile robots: These can move on wheels. They can go to places where it is dangerous for humans (such as deep inside a nuclear plant, outer space, or a chemical spill), and carry out either pre-programmed instructions or instructions given from a remote location by radio.

⊛ Incredible Individuals

The word 'robot' comes from the Czech word for slave labour, *robota*. It was coined by the playwright Karel Čapek in *R. U. R.*, a play about artificial human beings who are slaves at first, but ultimately destroy real humans and take over the world.

▶ *Poster for the play R.U.R., in which the word robot was used for the first time*

Robo-Surgery

Robotic 'fingers' can be really tiny and can move precise distances, measured in millimetres, in a way our hands cannot. This comes in use when you need to make tiny cuts and stitches when doing surgery—so surgeons love them. Instead of being nervous about making a mistake, a surgeon can sit outside the operation theatre, watching the operation on a giant screen while guiding the robot through a computer.

▶ *Surgeons can direct robots from afar in the future, avoiding human error and achieving higher precision*

▼ *Industrial robots can be programmed to do repetitive yet dangerous jobs, such as high-temperature welding*

Injectable Robots

You read about nanotechnology on pages 4–5. Now imagine that applied to robots. Machines can be made tinier than a pinhead, which can then be injected into the blood. They can travel through the blood, find cancer cells and kill them. Or they can go right inside the cell's nucleus, locate bad DNA and 'edit' it so that you can be cured of **genetic diseases**.

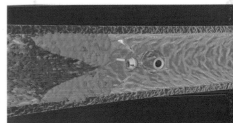

▲ *Nanometre-sized robots can be used to remove arterial plaques in the future*

Isn't It Amazing!

Rube Goldberg (1883–1970) was an American cartoonist who drew cartoons of complicated, convoluted machines performing simple tasks. In the field of robotics, a Rube Goldberg machine is an over-engineered machine, that is, a machine which would have done equally well with fewer parts.

▲ *Example of a Rube Goldberg Machine*

Autonomous Vehicles

Autonomous vehicles, also called driverless cars, aren't even the future. They are here today. In some cities, they are being tried out to map streets or to deliver pizza. Driverless trains already transport people in many cities and pilotless planes (drones) are used for warfare in many countries. But autonomous cars go a lot further. They integrate artificial intelligence, **visual recognition**, motion sensing, robotics, and the 'internet of things' so that the cars can be reliable and accident-free. Many corporations are investing in research to manufacture them, so that they can be used as cabs that come to you at the press of a button!

▼ *Autonomous vehicles are a combination of many technologies*

Learning on the Go

To get your driving license, you must learn all the road signs, drive for hours under the guidance of an instructor, and pass a driving test. While a driverless car may not need a license, it must still go through all these steps. The first is easy, your car will learn all the street-signs by symbolic learning. But it needs to be able to recognise them from a distance while travelling at top speed. So, designers of autonomous vehicles use neural networks and other 'deep learning' methods to make it work.

The autonomous vehicle will need to learn many things, for example:

- How to avoid crashing into people and dashing across the road
- How to drive in heavy rain, ice or snow, or in windy conditions
- How to recognise roads in poor shape, or drive on dirt tracks
- How to drive uphill or downhill or navigate sharp turns
- How to recognise street signs that may be faded or broken

▼ *London's Docklands Light Railway has trains without drivers. They are run by a central computer system instead*

Motion Sensing

Did a cop ever pull over your parents or anyone you know because they broke the speed limit? The cop might have used a laser to detect the speed at which the car was being driven. Similar technology is being used in cars to detect vehicles in front of them and behind them, and what speeds they are travelling at. These motion sensors communicate with the on-board computer, which decides whether to brake, speed up, overtake, or get to one side. More importantly, they need to be able to detect any humans or animals on the road. This ensures that the car will not cause an accident.

▲ *The internet of things connects devices to work independently of human control*

Internet of Things

The Internet of Things (IoT) connects all electronic devices in homes, on roads and in workplaces to the internet. This allows information to be shared between devices. For example, IoT helps your autonomous car communicate with all the other autonomous cars around it, thus making sure all cars keep a safe distance between themselves. It can also use GPS to find the best route, and to know when to turn right or left. This kind of artificial thinking, without any humans involved, is called ambient intelligence. What's more, it could also connect with fuelling stations and drive you to one when it is running low on fuel. Once there, a robot will probably refuel your car. All you will need to do is pay!

⊙ Incredible Individuals

Bill Joy, the co-founder of Sun Microsystems, predicted the Internet of Things in 1999, in a presentation made at the World Economic Forum in Davos, Switzerland, as a web of devices communicating with each other.

Blockchain

Today we carry out millions of transactions over the internet. We send and receive messages, we buy and sell things. Many big companies transfer millions of dollars of money around the world. Almost all of this data is recorded in a central server or a data centre located in a single place (say, the basement of the bank's headquarters or your network service provider). Although the data is kept safe in many ways, if a terrorist or a hacker got access to this data, they could cause a lot of damage.

Japanese scientist Satoshi Nakamoto came up with a way to overcome this fear. His thought was to make the storage of data decentralised. Instead of one central database, all the data is stored on thousands of databases. Each time there is a new transaction (called a block), say, for example, you buy a new video game on the internet, this information will be updated in all the databases. As each database is like a chain of transactions, the whole process is called a blockchain. So even if one database is hacked, the rest are still intact.

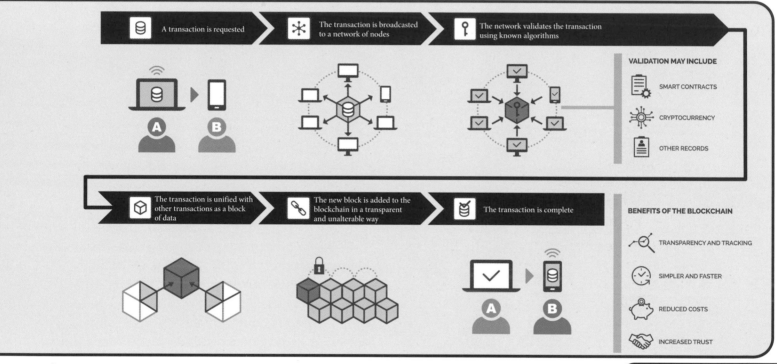

▲ *Blockchain is used to make each online transaction safe*

🔍 E-verification

Verification is used by governments and banks to confirm that it is indeed you who is making transactions (such as withdrawing money or paying taxes), and not a fraudster. Blockchain makes verification simple by giving you an **encryption key**. Each time you make a transaction, you use the key. The key tells the system that it is you, and makes you invisible to any hacker. All the databases in the system 'verify' that the key matches the information they have about you. Once you are verified, your transaction is added to each and every database.

💡 Isn't It Amazing!

Blockchain is used to create digital payments without bank accounts, coins, or notes. These are called cryptocurrencies because they are not issued by any country. Instead, the e-verification makes sure that the transaction is a safe and honest one.

▶ *Many governments are looking at adopting blockchain to make the internet safer*

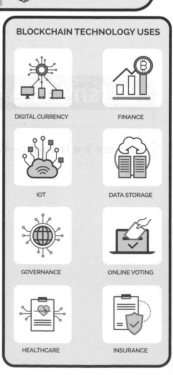

BLOCKCHAIN TECHNOLOGY USES

DIGITAL CURRENCY

FINANCE

IOT

DATA STORAGE

GOVERNANCE

ONLINE VOTING

HEALTHCARE

INSURANCE

3D Printing

If a machine breaks down, often you have to go around hunting for a spare part or order it online and wait for days. What if you could make it yourself? That is the idea behind three-dimensional (3D) printing. Just as a printer deposits ink on paper, a 3D printer is designed to 'print' an object layer by layer.

▲ *3D printing is also used to make prototype models and spare parts for machines*

You create a design on your computer and order a print. The printer deposits some powder onto a smooth, non-stick surface. A roller then flattens it into a thin layer. Then a printer head applies glue in the exact pattern that you designed, so that only those particles stick. The printer head rises slightly and a layer of powder is applied again and rolled over. In this manner, the machine 'prints' each layer till the whole object is complete. It sounds like a lengthy process, but it is very fast. 3D printing is now being used to make replacement teeth and bones, so patients can get them in the exact shape of the ones they have broken.

🔍 Laser Sintering

Sintering is the process of joining two metal surfaces together by partly melting the surfaces that need to be joined. Laser sintering uses a laser whose energy heats the metal atoms to a melting point. As a laser can be focused very precisely, it can be used in place of a glue gun in a 3D printer head, to make the metal powder particles melt and merge.

◀ *Laser sintering helps make a 3D-printed metal object into a whole solid without using adhesive*

💡 Isn't It Amazing!

Here's a thought—what if spare organs for our body could be made using 3D printing, just like machine spares? Biologists are working towards making any organ we may need by directing a tiny pipette to deposit stem cells onto a scaffold, and then inducing them to differentiate into various kinds of tissues, such as muscles, blood vessels, connective tissue, and epithelium.

▶ *3D bioprinting could one day grow you a new organ from your own stem cells*

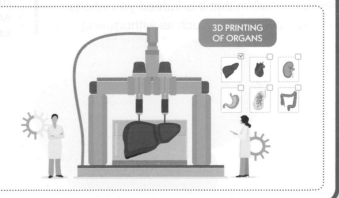

3D PRINTING OF ORGANS

Superfast Trains

If you bring two magnets together, with the same poles facing each other, you'll notice that they repel each other. Now imagine if a whole train was built like that. The 'engine' of the train is made of electromagnets, and the track is made of permanent magnets, with alternating north and south poles. When the engine is switched on, the north poles in the track pull the south poles in the engine, pulling the train forward (magnetic suction). But as it moves forward, the engine meets the south poles in the track, which pushes the train by magnetic repulsion.

A small motor in the train makes sure the train moves forward, and not backward. The total repulsion keeps the train from touching the track, so when it moves, there is no friction with the track. This is called magnetic levitation (maglev for short). Maglev trains can, therefore, move at speeds of up to 430 km an hour.

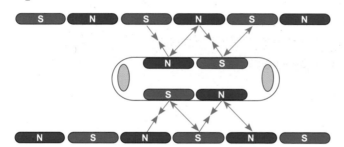

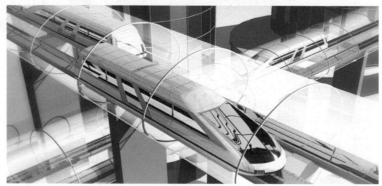

▲ *A maglev train in Shanghai, China. Only Germany, China, Japan, and South Korea have maglev trains right now*

◄ *How magnetic levitation works*

⊙ Incredible Individuals

Robert Goddard (1882–1945) was an American inventor who pioneered many of the ideas that are used in modern rocket science. He was fascinated with space travel and high-speed travel ever since he was a child. As a college student, he wrote an essay called *Travelling in 1950*. He imagined a system of transport in which cars would travel by alternate magnetic attraction and repulsion through vacuum tubes to avoid air friction which reduces speed.

▲ *NASA named its space flight centre in Maryland, USA, after Robert Goddard*

🔍 Hyperloop

Scientists are now taking Goddard's ideas forward with the Hyperloop concept, which runs maglev trains through vacuum tubes at very high speeds and no friction. While maglev trains are now possible, the science of building and maintaining high-strength vacuum tubes over many hundreds of kilometres is still a work in progress. The first passengers travelled safely on 20 November 2020 at 160 km per hour. To achieve extremely high speeds (say 1,200 km per hour), the tubes have to run straight for hundreds of miles, and the vacuum pumps must be able to pump out hundreds of tonnes of air without a pause.

▲ *The Hyperloop has been proposed as a transportation network for future colonies on Mars. As Mars' atmosphere is only 1% as dense as that of Earth, vacuum tubes won't be needed*

Smart Cities

While you can zip through the countryside in a maglev in the future, you might still face the dreaded traffic jams between your home and the station. The concept of a smart city suggests that internet devices communicating between cars and a traffic control centre can predict traffic patterns and stop jams from building up.

The smart city is a concept that emerged among scientists and urban planners towards the end of the 20th century. Advances in electronics and computer science have made it possible for all kinds of information to be collected and processed in giant **data centres**. A smart city will have thousands of sensors placed on streets, transit stations, sewers, and buildings. Offices and schools will share data on how many people are coming and going, drugstores will report medicines in short supply, and hospitals can report an increase in the incidences of diseases.

A smart city's government could then act accordingly, sending crews to unblock sewers or rush medicines to a hospital, before it is too late.

▲ A smart city would use data science, artificial intelligence, and advanced electronic sensors to deliver daily services

Surveillance Cities

Some people have criticised the idea of a smart city. They believe that surveillance, i.e. collecting data on citizens' movements, almost minute by minute, is not right. It would destroy their privacy and reduce their freedom to do the many things that make a city lively, just so the city can run smoothly. This is one of the many ethical problems facing future science.

▲ Surveillance could help keep people safe, but it would also deny them their freedom and privacy

In Real Life

In 2015, Amsterdam converted one of its popular shopping streets, *Utrechtsestraat*, into a smart street. Here, the city government installed:
- Smart plugs, which switch off a device automatically when not in use, to stop energy leakage.
- Smart street lights that dim when there's nobody on the street.
- Smart meters, which allow homes and shops to reduce unwanted electricity usage.

The project has helped the people on the street save on electricity bills and reduce carbon emissions.

▲ Lights on Utrechtsestraat become dimmer when there's no one around, and brighten if you walk past them

Space Travel

Dennis Tito (born 1940) was a NASA engineer who worked on the Mars missions. He later entered the world of finance, where he made millions of dollars. But what he is really famous for is being the world's first 'space tourist'. Unlike an astronaut, who goes to space for work, a space tourist has to pay to go there on holiday, but it can be expensive. Tito paid 20 million USD to stay at the International Space Station for just six days!

▲ Did you know that Anousheh Ansari of USA is the only woman to have been a space tourist?

Space Elevator

▲ Space flight would become affordable for all if space elevators could be built. Here you see little space stations with elevators extending down to Earth in a futuristic world

Why is space tourism so expensive? It's because of all the fuel that rockets need to beat the Earth's gravity. Konstantin Tsiolkovsky, a Russian scientist, thought of an alternative—an elevator that goes hundreds of kilometers above the Earth, where the planet's gravity is weak. He imagined a space station in low-Earth orbit that holds a gigantic pulley with cables that go all the way to the Earth. Fresh supplies could be pulled up by balancing them against the used-up waste (or things mined from other planets) that goes down. Once up, a tourist could be launched to the Moon or to Mars very easily. Though he imagined it back in 1895, scientists today still haven't been able to make an elevator cable tough enough.

Planetary Slingshot

A spacecraft approaching a planet will speed up, because gravity makes it gain momentum. However, if you put it in the right place, this momentum will instead make it shoot right past the planet (instead of crashing into it), go around it and away in the opposite direction. If you want to travel past Jupiter, your spacecraft will have to do this to get the speed to escape the pull of the planet. This is also called **gravity assist**.

In Real Life

Scientists working on Einstein's Theory of General Relativity (which says gravity is a geometric property of spacetime, and that gigantic objects can bend spacetime) discovered that it predicted a strange phenomenon: a sort of tunnel (called a wormhole) between two black holes, such that you go into one and come out of the other, billions of miles away. But can it ever work for space travel?

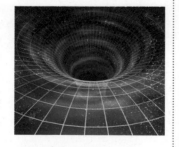

▲ An imaginary wormhole. We still don't understand the physics behind them completely

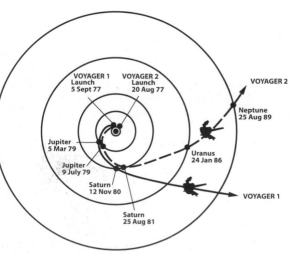

▲ The spacecrafts Voyager I and Voyager II sent by the USA used Jupiter, Saturn, Uranus, and Neptune as slingshots to get enough speed to leave the solar system

Living in Space

If travelling to the Moon and back became really cheap, would you consider moving there permanently? Scientists, as well as legislators, have considered the idea, as a way of reducing overcrowding on Earth, to harness minerals from the moon and to launch spacecrafts to other planets. Some thinkers have even visualised a second base on Mars, from which astronauts can set out on intergalactic journeys. But with no atmosphere or gravity, living on the Moon is impossible, unless there's a way to recreate the conditions of our planet there.

▲ *The Moon could be a valuable source of Helium-3, a fuel required for nuclear fusion*

🔍 Living on the Moon

As the Moon has one-sixth of the Earth's gravity, scientists would have to create artificial gravity for a Moon colony, or train people to live in low gravity. We don't quite know how our bodies would react to low or zero gravity. Astronauts live on the International Space Station for months together just so they can study this.

Humans who plan to live on the Moon or Mars will also need to figure out how to make electricity for their colony, grow food, get water, and produce oxygen to breathe. Electricity could come from solar or nuclear power, and food could be grown from seeds and soil brought from Earth. Getting water (H_2O) is more complex. Hydrogen (H_2) has to be captured from the **solar wind** and made to react with oxides of silicon and iron in the new planet's soil. That would also be a way to get valuable silicon (Si) or iron (Fe) that could be sold back to Earth, getting the colony some money.

$$2H_2 + SiO_2 \rightarrow 2H_2O + Si$$

H_2 = Hydrogen SiO_2= Silicon dioxide H_2O =Water   Si = Silica

▲ *A permanent Moon colony could be possible if the cost of transport between the Earth and the Moon reduced considerably*

👥 In Real Life

Biosphere 2 was an experiment carried out by a group of eight scientists from 1991 to 1993 in the Arizona desert in USA. They created a giant greenhouse, which had all the animals and plants necessary to sustain human life, while being completely cut off from the rest of the planet's ecosystems. This is how a space colony would be set up on the Moon or any other planet.

▼ *Biosphere 2 in 1992. A Moon or Mars Colony might look like this*

Genetic Engineering

Genetic engineering (GE) has been around ever since humans learned to domesticate plants and animals in the Neolithic Period (the New Stone Age). By selective breeding, ancient farmers removed **traits** that they didn't want in their domestic animals and plants. That's how wolves who were aggressive became dogs that listen to humans.

But when people talk of genetic engineering today, they mean the artificial modification of DNA in a laboratory (DNA is a molecule that carries our genes). When this DNA is injected into plants and animals, they begin to show the required traits. For example, you might have heard of BtCrops in the news. These are crops that have been modified in the lab to carry a gene that originally belongs to the bacterium *Bacillus thuringiensis* (Bt). This gene makes the plants create a protein that is toxic to insects if they eat them, but not to humans.

◀ *The idea behind genetically modified (GM) cotton is to reduce the destruction caused by the cotton weevil, and thus reduce pesticide use*

 ## Plasmids

Bacteria have small, circular molecules of DNA called plasmids. Most of the research in genetic engineering has been carried out in plasmids. Geneticists cut plasmids with a special kind of enzyme called restriction endonuclease, add new DNA to it, and stitch up the DNA using another enzyme called a DNA ligase. The plasmid is put back into bacteria and it multiplies inside them to make many copies. This way, plasmids can be modified to carry genes for human proteins.

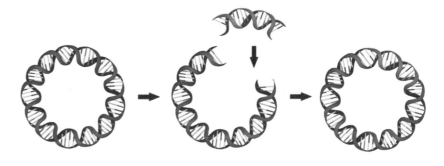

▲ *Plasmids are used to make bacteria produce biological chemicals needed by humans, like insulin*

 ## Human Genetic Engineering

You may have heard of the phrase '**designer baby**'. This is the idea that humans can genetically engineer their own cells to eliminate defective genes, or modify the genome to create 'superhumans'. Thus, babies born from such cells will have been 'designed'. However, some people fear that this could be misused to create a race of slaves or 'robotised' humans.

💡 Isn't It Amazing!

Some diabetes patients have to take regular **insulin** injections to live normally, as their body cannot make enough insulin. Getting enough insulin from human donors would be impossible. So most injectable insulin made today comes from GM bacteria that carry the gene for human insulin in a plasmid.

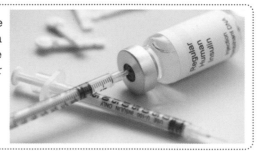

▶ *Artificial insulin made by genetically engineered bacteria*

Gene Editing

This exciting new technology may help us fight cancer and other genetic diseases. Instead of using stem cells, the DNA of the defective cells can be 'edited' using an enzyme called Cas9. This enzyme recognises a kind of DNA sequence called CRISPR (Clustered Regularly Interspaced Short Palindromic Repeats). It is guided into the defective gene by a molecule called a guide RNA, whose sequence is complementary to the defective gene. The Cas9 then cuts out the CRISPR on either side of the 'bad' DNA. It carries with it a spare piece of 'good' DNA that is then stuck in place of the bad DNA. These systems have reduced the price, time, and complexity of genetic engineering.

Scientists are trying to develop injectable solutions so that every defective cell of an organ can have its DNA repaired.

▼ *The double helix structure of DNA is common to all living organisms. It makes it possible to make new DNA from old*

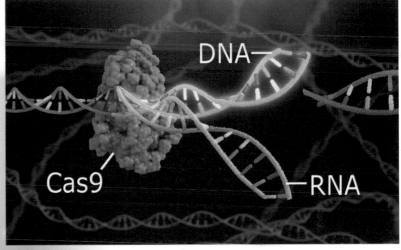

▲ *How gene editing works*

 ## Incredible Individuals

In the early days of genetics, scientists did not understand that DNA could recombine at specific places. In the 1940s, Barbara McClintock (1902–92), while studying the genetics of maize, discovered that genes 'jumping' from one place to another could only explain certain changes in maize from one generation to another. This would be one of the first steps towards genetic engineering. Sadly, her work was ignored for many decades.

▲ *In 1983, Barbara McClintock became the first woman to win the Nobel Prize for Medicine or Physiology solo*

Stem Cells

Like leaves in a plant come out from the stem, the cells in your body come from stem cells. These are cells that have not **differentiated** or turned themselves into other kinds of cells. There are two types: embryonic stem cells and adult stem cells. The first type of cells are present in babies as they grow inside their mother's womb. These embryonic cells change into different kinds of cells—liver cells, bone cells, blood cells, neurons, etc. The field of biology that studies how stem cells become differentiated cells is called **developmental biology**.

The second kind of cells are found in adults and can turn themselves only into a few kinds of cells. They are useful when the tissue around them has been damaged by disease or injury. Then they multiply into a large number of cells, which differentiate into the required tissue cells. This is called **healing**.

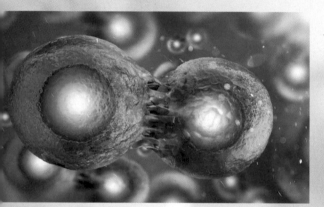

◀ *A stem cell divides itself into two. This is called mitosis*

Potential Applications of Human Stem Cells

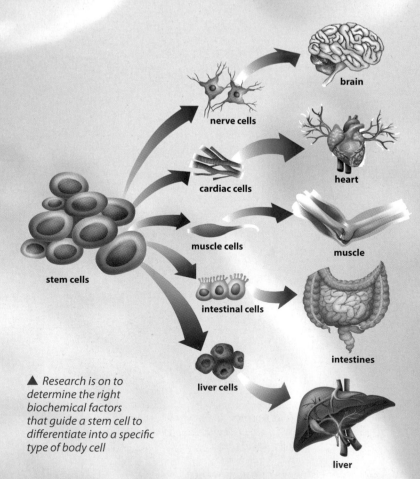

stem cells

nerve cells → brain

cardiac cells → heart

muscle cells → muscle

intestinal cells → intestines

liver cells → liver

▲ *Research is on to determine the right biochemical factors that guide a stem cell to differentiate into a specific type of body cell*

▲ *An embryo in its early stages, when organs have not developed. All cells in such a stage are stem cells*

Stem Cell Therapy

Some people have a genetic disorder that makes an organ or cell type fail (like thalassaemia), while others may suffer from organ failure. The thought behind stem cell therapy is to inject patients with stem cells programmed to differentiate into the required kind of cell and restore the organ.

Embryonic Stem Cells (ESCs)

The cells of an **embryo** in its early stages are all pluripotent stem cells, that is, they can give rise to any type of tissue in the body. As the embryo grows, they turn into different kinds of multipotent stem cells, which can give rise to a limited number of differentiated cells. During in vitro fertilisation, many embryos are made in the laboratory by fertilising egg cells with sperm cells (that's why we call babies conceived through this method test tube babies). Only one or two of these go on to become a baby, while the rest are discarded. Scientists figured that these embryos could instead be used as a source of stem cells for therapy. They can be made to multiply in the laboratory through cell culture and then differentiate into the required kind of cell. Genetic engineering is used to switch on the genes (programming) that lead the cell down the path of differentiation into a neuron, or a blood cell, or a liver cell, and so on.

▲ *Human embryonic stem cells are used in research to find out how they differentiate into other kinds of cells*

Induced Pluripotent Stem Cells (iPSCs)

Today, scientists have figured out how to 'induce' a differentiated cell to turn the clock back and become a pluripotent stem cell again. This can then be made to differentiate into a specific kind of cell. This avoids the trouble of immune rejection. It also avoids the ethical issue of destroying embryos.

▶ *Induced Pluripotent Stem Cells avoid the ethical dilemma of using embryonic stem cells*

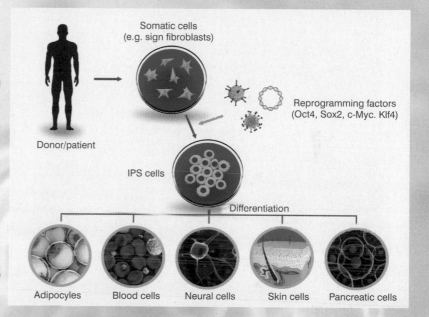

Somatic cells (e.g. sign fibroblasts)

Reprogramming factors (Oct4, Sox2, c-Myc. Klf4)

Donor/patient

IPS cells

Differentiation

Adipocyles | Blood cells | Neural cells | Skin cells | Pancreatic cells

▲ *Sudan, the last male Northern White Rhinoceros, died on 19 March 2018. The only hope for this species is through the use of stem cells or in vitro fertilisation*

Stem Cells in Conservation

Scientists are experimenting with stem cell technologies to revive species that are near extinction. By creating pluripotent stem cells, they hope that one day embryos of endangered animals and plants can be generated. If the embryo succeeds in growing into a live organism, there is a faint chance of the revival of these species.

☀ Isn't It Amazing!

Your umbilical cord, which connected you to your mother when you were a foetus inside her, has blood that is full of stem cells. Doctors now suggest that you save some of this, to be stored in a stem cell bank under freezing conditions (cryopreservation), to be thawed and used when you need stem cells later in life.

▲ *Cryopreservation helps store stem cells by mixing them with biologically safe antifreeze agents and storing them in liquid nitrogen*

Cloning

A clone is like a twin of yourself—except that it is made from your own cells. Viruses, bacteria, fungi, and many kinds of plants, as well as animals, clone themselves all the time. This is known as asexual reproduction. But human cloning has remained a dream. Imagine if you could clone yourself. Your clone may get into mischief of all kinds, while you take all the punishment! Thus, it is illegal in most countries.

Nevertheless, cloning can be used for medical purposes by cloning organs from stem cells. It is now being tried out in agriculture and animal husbandry as well.

⊛ Incredible Individuals

Sir Ian Wilmut and Keith Campbell cloned Dolly, a sheep. They made the important discovery that you could clone almost any kind of nucleus, as long as you injected it into a recipient cell at the right stage of development. These cells have the right proteins that help the DNA to multiply. Before that, it was believed that you could only clone an embryonic nucleus. Sir Ian also developed many ways of cryopreservation of embryos.

🔍 Twins

Did you know that identical twins are born from the same embryo? In the earliest stages of life, an embryo is made of stem cells that repeatedly split to make a ball of cells. Sometimes the cells split and separate completely. Each of these cells then goes on to make complete babies, so the two babies born are **identical twins**. On the other hand, **fraternal twins** are born from separate embryos. Their genetic make-up is not identical.

DNA Cloning

This is a process of genetic engineering in which a gene from one source organism is 'cloned' into another one. A copy is made of the gene and inserted into a circular DNA molecule called a plasmid, which is then inserted into the new organism.

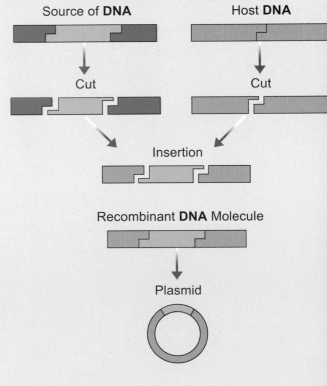

DNA Cloning

Source of **DNA** Host **DNA**

Cut Cut

Insertion

Recombinant **DNA** Molecule

Plasmid

◀ *Twins develop small genetic differences between them as they grow older*

The Story of Dolly

Most people think the first cloned animal was Dolly, the sheep, in 1996, but clones had been made long before. The first was actually a salamander, cloned by breaking an embryo into two, to make artificial twins. The idea of cloning was born when scientists found out that a nucleus from an embryonic cell could be transferred into another cell whose nucleus has been removed. If the cell developed into an organism, it would be the clone of the animal whose nucleus was taken. The first animals to be cloned like this were frogs, in 1952.

But the real promise of cloning came in 1996, when a nucleus was taken from an adult cell and transferred into an embryo cell. This cell was implanted into a **surrogate** mother, who ultimately gave birth to the baby. This is how Dolly (1996–2003) was born. Many other animals have been cloned since, but many were born with **birth defects**.

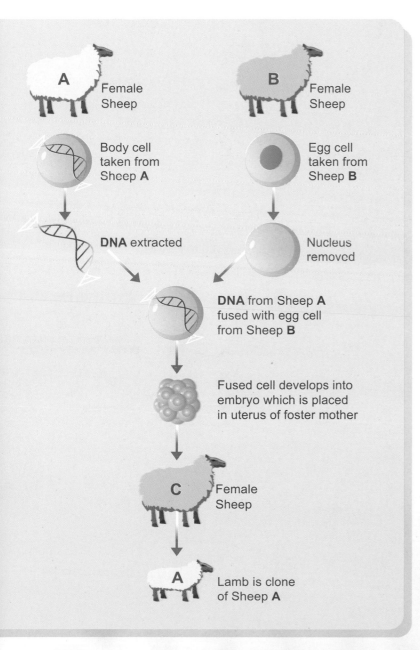

A — Female Sheep
B — Female Sheep

Body cell taken from Sheep **A**
Egg cell taken from Sheep **B**

DNA extracted
Nucleus removed

DNA from Sheep **A** fused with egg cell from Sheep **B**

Fused cell develops into embryo which is placed in uterus of foster mother

C — Female Sheep

A — Lamb is clone of Sheep **A**

▲ The ability to clone adult cells has opened up many possibilities in research aimed towards curing genetic disease

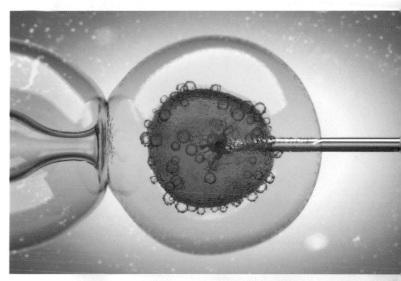

▲ A microscopic glass needle is used to inject a nucleus into an embryonic cell

Therapeutic Cloning

Some scientists have proposed the idea of cloning human cells to make a replacement organ in a laboratory, which would be tremendously helpful in case someone's kidneys or liver fail. In the case of a genetic ailment, the cloned organ can be genetically modified to avoid the ailment, giving you a healthy organ. However, any kind of human cloning is currently prohibited in most countries.

Apocalypse

In the movie *The Day After Tomorrow*, the Earth freezes over. In *Armageddon*, our planet is in danger from an asteroid about to crash into it. In *Independence Day* and *War of the Worlds*, the characters fight off alien invasions. Many movies have imagined the end of the world. Yet, did you know that our planet faces two real threats? Nuclear war and climate change. Both emerged as unforeseen consequences of scientific advances in the 19th and 20th centuries. Do you wonder whether anything we invent in our time will lead to a disaster in the future?

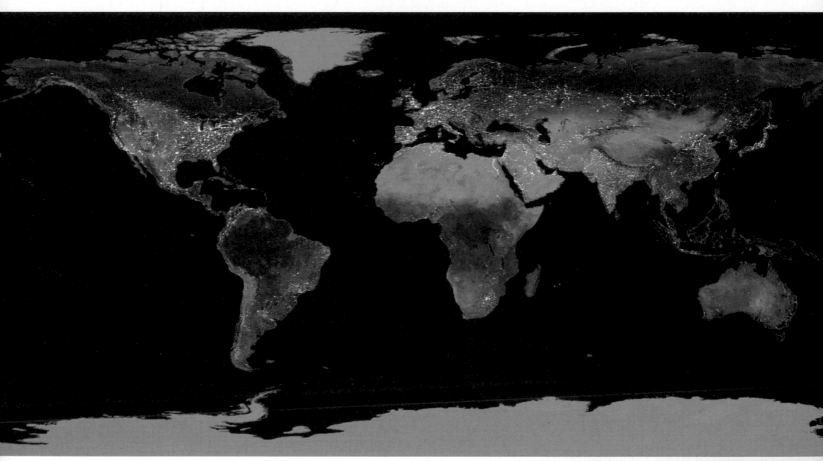

▲ *In red: the regions predicted to disappear if the seas rose by six metres*

☻ Incredible Individuals

Linus Pauling (1901–94) won two Nobel Prizes, for Chemistry (1954) and Peace (1964). He said that his wife Ava Pauling should have received the Nobel Prize for Peace, for she motivated him to think of the use of science for good causes and to campaign against nuclear weapons. The couple gave public speeches, petitioned governments, and wrote books on the dangers of nuclear weapons.

▲ *Linus Pauling was one of the people who helped bring about the Comprehensive Nuclear-Test-Ban Treaty*

Global Warming

Climate scientists have comprehensively shown that CO_2 levels are rising as we continue to burn fossil fuels. This gas is in turn heating our planet, causing glaciers and ice caps at the poles to melt. As they melt, the water flows into the oceans, raising sea levels all over the world. Also, because water expands with heat, the sea levels will rise even further. Scientists predict that if the ice sheets of Greenland melt, the level of the sea will rise by six metres (20 feet). That is enough to permanently flood Bangladesh, Belgium, the Netherlands, and much of Florida and Louisiana in USA. If the ice in Antarctica also melts completely, the sea will rise by 10.5 metres (34 feet). How much land would that drown?

It doesn't stop there. Global warming will increase evaporation of water, leading to loss of groundwater in many places. This will cause drought in many places, leading to crops and domesticated animals dying, and forcing people to migrate in search of water. Water vapour is also a powerful **greenhouse gas**, so the planet will only warm faster, disrupting clouds and causing more droughts in an endless cycle.

▶ *Many parts of Africa and Asia would be vulnerable to droughts as global temperatures rise*

Nuclear Winter

The apocalypse could come suddenly too, if a nuclear war broke out. Today, nine countries hold nuclear weapons—China, France, India, North Korea, Pakistan, Russia, UK, USA, and Israel. They are not all on friendly terms with each other, so it is possible that one wrong decision could lead to a nuclear war. What would happen then?

Take just one nuclear bomb going off. To start, the gamma rays from the explosion would wipe out most life in the area, and the accompanying electromagnetic pulse would shut down all electronics in a certain radius. Those who escape alive will have terrible **mutations**. The heat of the explosion would trigger wildfires and cause gas pipes to explode. The heat would also make the nitrogen and oxygen in the air react to form nitrogen oxides, which would destroy the ozone layer. The dust clouds created by the bomb would block out the Sun, and plant life would die, making animals die of starvation. There's more, but we think you get the idea.

▼ *Unless we act in time, a giant disaster is just the push of a button away*

Cleaning the Planet

Plastics are a part of almost everything we do today—the toys we play with, the pipes that supply water to our homes, the bags we carry our books in, the PET jars we store food in, and even the raincoats we wear to stay dry. Sadly, unlike materials like metals and wood, plastics remain on our planet for millions of years once we have thrown them away. There are two ways in which science can tackle this problem: by creating biomaterials and genetically engineering bacteria to eat plastic. Yet, the foolproof solution is in our hands: Reduce, Reuse, Recycle. Most plastics can be easily melted and remoulded, if they are segregated correctly.

Biomaterials

Many scientists are working to replace regular plastics with materials that will disintegrate easily on their own in the presence of light or by the action of bacteria. Other scientists are experimenting with materials made from natural sources such as starch, cellulose, and wheat gluten. These are hardy and can withstand the pressures of daily life, but once discarded, they will degrade into simple chemicals such as carbon dioxide and water.

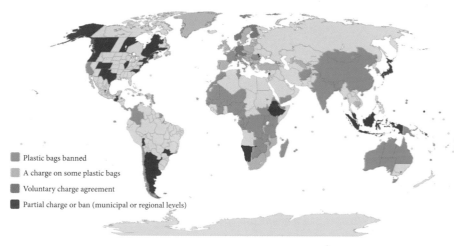

Plastic bags banned
A charge on some plastic bags
Voluntary charge agreement
Partial charge or ban (municipal or regional levels)

▲ *A map of countries with a partial or complete ban on plastic bags. (This image has been adapted from a picture by Elekh under the Creative Commons Attribution-Share Alike 3.0 Unported license)*

Plastic-eating Bacteria

Bacteria can make food out of anything. The species *Ideonella sakaiensis* can live off of polyethylene terephthalate, which is used for making plastic bottles. Biotechnologists are looking to see if they can engineer other bacteria to do the same, by transferring genes from *Ideonella sakaiensis* to other bacteria.

◀ *Scientists are looking for bacteria and archaea that can break down plastic into CO_2*

Carbon Sequestration

Over the last century, we have burned an enormous amount of fossil fuels (coal, petroleum, and natural gas) to generate electricity, heat our homes, and power our vehicles. All of these have generated carbon dioxide (CO_2), which scientists say is leading to global warming. There are different ways that engineers have proposed to remove carbon dioxide from the atmosphere, to reduce the **greenhouse effect**:

- **ARTIFICIAL TREES** are filters soaked in sodium hydroxide ($NaOH.H_2O$) that absorb CO_2 from the air and turn it to soda ash (Na_2CO_3).

$$2NaOH.H_2O + CO_2 \rightarrow Na_2CO_3 + 3H_2O$$

- **SCRUBBING TOWERS** suck up the air with huge turbines. The air is passed through a solution of sodium or calcium hydroxide ($NaOH$ or $Ca(OH)_2$) which absorbs carbon dioxide.

- **CARBON BURIAL** is a method to bury CO_2 captured from the air. It is pumped into underground reservoirs, like those which were once full of petroleum.

- **OCEAN FERTILISATION** is a method by which plankton and algae of the ocean can capture carbon. So encouraging their growth by adding fertilisers to the sea will help them convert atmospheric CO_2 into food.

There are many more methods. However, for any of them to work, they need to be implemented on a planet-wide scale. This will require countries and companies to work together and invest huge sums of money.

▲ Reducing our use of plastic, Reusing what we have, and scientifically Recycling plastic helps stop pollution

▲ The progress of a country is at times measured by the amount of sulphuric acid it uses

In Real Life

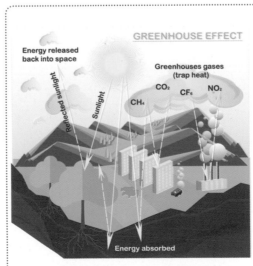

GREENHOUSE EFFECT

Energy released back into space

Reflected sunlight

Sunlight

Greenhouses gases (trap heat)

CO_2 CF_6 NO_2

CH_4

Energy absorbed

▲ Alongside carbon dioxide, nitrogen dioxide (NO_2) and methane (CH_4) also cause the greenhouse effect

Have you seen a greenhouse? It's a place where tropical plants can be grown in cool climates by artificially raising the temperature. The plants give off carbon dioxide, which absorbs a lot of heat from the Sun and stops it from radiating away. When the same happens on the scale of our planet, global warming occurs.

Science and Ethics

Scientists have long grappled with ethics, which is the knowledge of what is good and what is bad. As the famous nuclear physicist Richard Feynman said, "Scientific knowledge is an enabling power to do either good or bad—but it does not carry instructions on how to use it."

We don't have clear answers to questions that come up with the advancement of science. Sometimes, we have to think of the pros and cons: whether doing good for humanity in general (researching on embryonic stem cells) justifies the harm of one individual (the embryo being destroyed, which is, genetically, human). At other times, we have to think of whether alternatives that sound better are practical. For example, many scientists argue that organic food alone cannot sustain the human population; GM (Genetic Modification of) crops are needed. At other times, we need to think about whether we can sacrifice the present for the future, for example, scaling back our lifestyles and using lesser fossil fuels.

▲ GM crops have vexed a lot of people, for some think it is unethical to plant crops that may contaminate non-GM crops

🔍 Cloning & Genetic Engineering

Cloning, genetic engineering and the use of embryonic stem cells raise many ethical questions:

- Would a clone of another human have the same rights, or would it be a slave to the original human? Would the clone be a different person legally?
- If your clone commits a crime, would only the clone be responsible, or would you be responsible too?
- Is it right to make a genetically modified human? What if they develop an illness or complications because of the modification?
- Is it right to destroy an embryo to harvest its embryonic stem cells to heal others?

▲ We still do not know whether human cloning will be a dream come true or a nightmare

💡 Isn't It Amazing!

On 16 September 1987, many countries came together to sign the Montreal Protocol, an international treaty that aimed to end the use of Chlorofluorocarbons (CFCs). These chemicals, widely used as refrigerants, made a hole in the ozone layer that protects us from UV radiation. Many countries have followed the terms of the treaty and reduced the use of CFCs, allowing the ozone layer to recover.

The treaty is a model for how international cooperation can help overcome big problems, especially climate change.

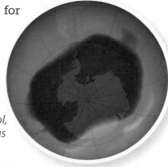

▶ After the Montreal Protocol, the hole in the ozone layer has been healing with time

Artificial Intelligence

Artificial Intelligence has raised many ethical questions too. Legal experts worry whether AI can have the power of life and death over us. Should a hospital's AI turn off a patient's ventilator, if the data indicates that they may not be able to recover ever? Should a self-driven car be programmed to save its rider's life in all cases, even if it may kill someone else on the road? Should a robot with its own intelligence be able to disobey its master if given an unethical command, such as being asked to murder a rival?

▲ Would it be ethical to let an AI-based credit card stop people from overspending?

Incredible Individuals

Born in 2003, Greta Thunberg of Sweden is leading a worldwide campaign for climate change action. She leads the 'school strike movement', which suggests that children must skip school every Friday to make their parents understand the need to act immediately to stop climate change.

▲ Greta Thunberg was nominated for the Nobel Prize for Peace in 2019

Climate Change

Barring some **climate sceptics**, most people agree that the Earth's climate is changing due to global warming and that we should stop it. But should the rich countries in Europe, North America, and Australia, who have burned more fossil fuels (which means they have a larger carbon footprint), take more responsibility than emerging and developing countries in Africa, South America, and Asia? Or, should everyone pay equally?

▼ Poor countries have argued that stopping climate change by reducing industrial growth cannot come at the cost of their citizens' right to a better life

LIGHT & ENERGY

LIGHTING UP THE WORLD

Light is what helps us see. It helps us distinguish objects, identify their shapes and colours, and note their movement. The biggest source of light is the Sun. Since Earth's rotation causes day and night, when sunlight reaches our part of the Earth, we experience daytime; and when we rotate away from the Sun, we experience nighttime.

The light of the Sun comes from nuclear reactions deep inside it. There are also other kinds of light, for instance, the lights we switch on at night. These devices give us light generated from electricity. When you light a candle, the light comes from the burning of the wick in air, which is a chemical reaction. The light of fireflies comes from another kind of reaction. The hot iron in an oven gives off light as a glow.

All of these things are different forms of energy—nuclear, electric, chemical, and thermal. Light, too, is energy. But what is energy? How is it measured? Can we make it? Can we destroy it? These are the questions that physicists ask themselves every day.

Energy is what makes our Universe the happening place it is. All the energy in our solar system came from the Sun, and continues to do so even today. Some of that energy was used over four billion years ago to create the rocky planet that we call home. Deep inside the Earth, nuclear reactions make the core extremely hot and form the forces responsible for the Earth's rotation around its axis. Meanwhile, on the surface, plants take the energy from sunlight and turn it into **chemical energy** that is stored in food. When we eat the food, the energy gets transferred and is used to keep our bodies warm and provide us with the ability to run or walk or do any other activity. In the case of bats, birds, and some insects, it gives them the ability to fly. Also, much of the heat that we derive from burning coal, gas, or wood is still the energy that was produced by the Sun and trapped by ancient plants millions of years ago.

So, let's explore the fascinating world of energy and light in the next few pages.

▶ *The Sun is the source of all energy on our planet, directly or indirectly*

Photons

Sunrise: when a tiny bit of Earth comes face to face with the Sun, as our planet rotates. Birds begin to chirp, and alarms begin to go off in our homes. Everything is filled with light and a new day begins. But did you ever wonder what light really is? How does it travel so fast? How does it get to be all around us? And why are we so helpless without it?

For a very long time, people believed that light was an element of the Universe because all the light they had came from fire of some sort. For example, they saw the Sun, which gives us light during the day, as a great fireball, while the light they received at night came from lamps or logs of burning wood. Over time, scientists did experiments and theorised that light was some form of wave, that moved through an invisible substance (called ether) in space, just as waves move on the surface of the sea. Later, various experiments highlighted that light is actually made of tiny particles. These particles are called photons and have no weight at all, but have energy that can be measured. Today, several scientists believe that light is both a wave and a particle at the same time. This is called wave-particle duality.

◀ *Nuclear fusion reactions deep inside stars are the source of all the photons in our Universe*

The Speed of Light

The speed of photons travelling in a vacuum is 299,792 kilometres per second. As photons are massless, nothing heavier can travel faster than them. However, light does slow down when it enters a gas, liquid, or solid, where it interacts with the electrons of the material. The speed of light is 225,000 kilometres per second in water and 200,000 kilometres per second in glass.

▲ *We can see objects because particles of light called 'photons' are reflected off them and enter our eyes, where they are captured by special 'vision' cells*

Incredible Individuals

At college, Max Planck wanted to choose physics, but his professor told him that it would be futile as all the major discoveries had been made. Planck went on to study physics anyway, and ended up changing it forever with the quantum theory.

Quantum Theory

In 1900, the German scientist Max Planck suggested that all energy existed in fixed units called quanta. The more quanta of energy a substance has, the more energy it possesses, either as electricity, heat, light, or magnetism. For example, each quantum of electrical energy is called an electron. The more electrons a wire has, the more current it carries.

For his theory, Planck won the Nobel Prize in Physics in 1918. But what about other forms of energy such as light? In 1905, the Swiss scientist Albert Einstein suggested that light, too, is made of tiny quanta (now called photons). The more photons in a beam of light, the brighter it is. He theorised that not just energy, but even radiation itself was **quantised** in the same way.

Today, an entire field of physics called quantum theory studies how quanta of various kinds of energy behave, particularly photons. But not all photons are the same, for their energy depends on their frequency.

▲ Our modern understanding of light comes from Albert Einstein (second from left) and Max Planck (centre)

Wavelength and Frequency

Each photon 'oscillates' a number of times per second, even as it is moving forward in a beam of light. That means it travels some distance towards the left, returns to the centre, and then moves an equal distance to the right before coming back again to the centre and starting all over again. Imagine a ball tied on a string swinging sideways while you are walking forward. This vibration is called its frequency.

The frequency decides its **wavelength**, that is, the length it will travel forward for the duration of one complete vibration. The higher the frequency, the more energy the photon has, but its wavelength is shorter.

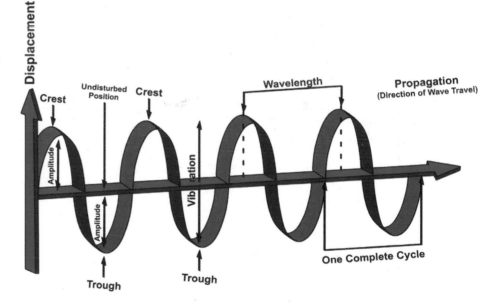

▲ Photons move as waves with a wavelength that decreases with energy

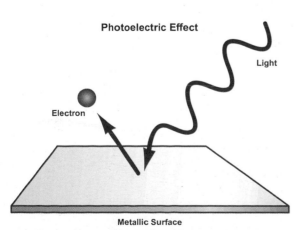

Photoelectric Effect

Light

Electron

Metallic Surface

The photoelectric effect is the emission of electrons or other free carriers when light is shone onto a material

▲ The photoelectric effect led to the discovery that light is made of photons

Photoelectric Effect

Many physicists knew that some materials, such as rubidium and caesium, discharge electrons when exposed to light, though they did not know why it happens. This is called the photoelectric effect. In 1905, Albert Einstein suggested that it could be possible only if light was made of something similar to electrons, but without an **electric charge**. He proposed that light is made up of photons, which are packets of energy. This theory not only solved the mystery of the photoelectric effect, but also won Einstein the Noble Prize in 1921.

Electromagnetism

Did you know that light is only one kind of wave? It belongs to a whole class of energy particles known as the electromagnetic (EM) spectrum. This contains all kinds of waves; from those whose wavelengths are in thousands of metres to those whose wavelengths are one-quadrillionth of a metre.

Electromagnetism happens when an electric charge moves through space, creating a magnetic field at right angles to it. This phenomenon was discovered by Michael Faraday and James Clerk Maxwell. When a charged particle moves as a wave, it sets up a waving magnetic field at a right angle to it. As a result, light was also seen to be an electromagnetic wave. Following this, Planck and Einstein established that the unit of electromagnetism was a photon.

Electric field
Magnetic field

▲ *Electromagnetic waves are made of two distinct fields, electric and magnetic.*

Visible Light

In quantum theory, the photon is a unit of **electromagnetic energy**, and not just light. The photons that we can see with our naked eyes are called visible light. Their wavelengths range from 380 to 750 nanometres (a nanometre is one-billionth of a metre).

Why can we see these photons? Actually, we cannot see the photons themselves, but we can see the object from where these photons originate. Our eyes have special rod cells and cone cells that are sensitive to different wavelengths of light. Each of these cells respond to a certain wavelength of light that hits it. When light falls on these cells, a tiny current passes from the cell to the optical nerve. The nerve collects the information from each cell and passes it to the brain, creating a picture in your head. The brain converts each wavelength of light into a different '**colour**'. This is what you 'see'. In reality, light has no natural colour. All these colours are the same in everyone's head, so all of us can agree that the sky is blue and the Moon is white.

In Real Life

Some people lack some kinds of cells in their eyes, or have other genetic trouble, because of which they cannot see colour or differences in colour. Doctors call this **colour blindness**.

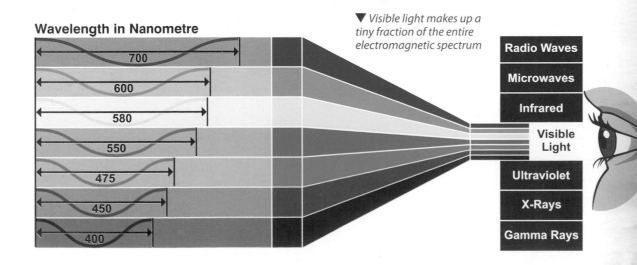

Wavelength in Nanometre

700
600
580
550
475
450
400

▼ *Visible light makes up a tiny fraction of the entire electromagnetic spectrum*

Radio Waves
Microwaves
Infrared
Visible Light
Ultraviolet
X-Rays
Gamma Rays

◀ *A magnetic scrap lifter*

 # Other Waves

Our eyes cannot see most of the electromagnetic waves that exist in the Universe. But we can detect them in other ways, usually using a radio antenna or other specially made **detectors**. The photons whose wavelength is smaller than visible light make up ultraviolet (UV) light. Honeybees have cone cells, which they use to see UV photons. Photons with wavelengths smaller than UV rays are called **X-rays**, and those with even smaller wavelengths are called **gamma rays**. These photons have a lot of energy in them. When they hit an atom, they can remove electrons from it and turn it into a positively charged ion. Therefore, together they are called **ionising radiation**.

Waves with lengths higher than visible light are called **infrared (IR) waves**. They are used in night vision glasses. Waves with longer wavelengths than IR waves are **radio waves**. They don't have enough energy to remove electrons from atoms, so they are called **non-ionising radiation**.

Isn't It Amazing!

Ozone (triatomic oxygen or O^3) is a molecule that can absorb most ultraviolet radiation. It forms a covering above our atmosphere called the ozone layer, and stops UV rays from reaching us.

Sun

UV-C
UV-B
UV-A

Ozone layer

◀ *Holes in the ozone layer expose people to harmful UV rays from space*

UV protection by the ozone layer

Electromagnetic Spectrum

Radiation type	Radio	Microwave	Infrared	Visible	Ultraviolet	X-ray	Gamma ray
Wavelenght (m)	10^3	10^{-2}	10^{-5}	0.5×10^{-6}	10^{-8}	10^{-10}	10^{-12}
Approximate Scale of Wavelenght	Buildings	Humans	Honey bee	Needle point	Protozoans	Molecules	Atoms	Atomic nuclei

Frequency (Hz)

▲ *Photons with shorter wavelengths than visible light have higher energy, and those with longer wavelengths have lesser energy*

Energy

There are two laws that govern energy existing in the Universe. One of them, the Law of Conservation of Energy, says that energy can neither be destroyed nor created but can only be converted from one form to another. The other is the Law of Relativity, discovered by Albert Einstein, which dictates that energy can be converted into matter (and matter into energy). This is what happens deep inside the Sun, where four hydrogen atoms merge into one atom of helium and some of the matter is turned into energy in the form of photons of very high frequency. Scientists call this nuclear fusion.

◀ *In a roller coaster, electric energy is converted to potential energy as the cars ride up. When the cars slide down, the potential energy is converted to kinetic energy under the influence of gravity*

🔍 Types of Energy

The Sun is the source of all the energy on our planet. Some of it is direct, like the light and heat that we get in daytime. Most of it is indirect, as we read earlier. But how many forms of energy are there, and how are they converted into each other?

Mechanical: This energy is visible in the movement of objects. We use this to do most of the work we want—from washing clothes in a machine, to running a blender or driving a car. There are two kinds of mechanical energy: kinetic energy that is present in moving things, and potential energy that is stored until needed. Sound is also a form of mechanical energy, which travels in the form of **mechanical waves** in the air.

Gravitational: This energy is stored in the gravitational fields of stars and planets, which makes them move around each other. It is also the energy that is released from objects that are falling to the Earth, such as water in a dam or apple from a tree.

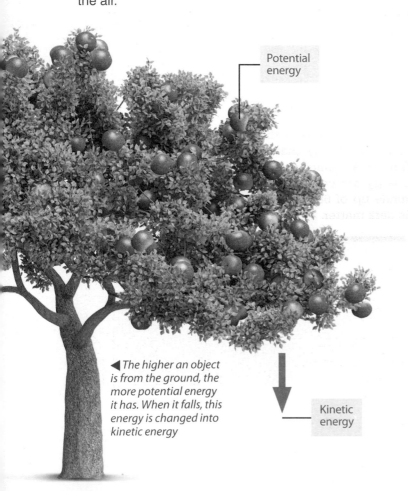

Potential energy

Kinetic energy

◀ *The higher an object is from the ground, the more potential energy it has. When it falls, this energy is changed into kinetic energy*

👤 In Real Life

Several power plants convert energy three times to make electricity:
1. From nuclear or chemical energy into **heat energy** to turn water into steam.
2. From heat energy into mechanical energy of a rotating turbine.
3. From mechanical energy into electrical energy by electromagnetism.

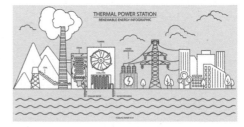

▲ *A lot of energy is lost to air as it is converted from one form to another in a power plant*

Electromagnetic: This energy is present in moving electric or magnetic fields, whether in a wire (electricity) or moving through space (radiation).

◀ *In an electric cell, chemical energy is converted to electromagnetic energy*

Thermal (Heat): This energy is stored in the vibrational movement of atoms, so it is really a form of mechanical energy, but at the atomic level. When a material is heated, the atoms vibrate faster and push each other away. This makes the material expand. When the material loses heat, the atoms vibrate less and therefore come closer. This is called contraction.

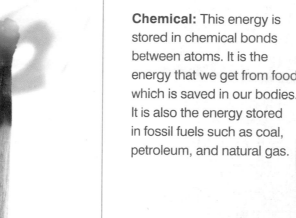

▶ *A matchstick converts the chemical energy stored in its head into thermal energy when it is struck*

Chemical: This energy is stored in chemical bonds between atoms. It is the energy that we get from food which is saved in our bodies. It is also the energy stored in fossil fuels such as coal, petroleum, and natural gas.

▶ *Our muscles convert the chemical energy stored in food into the kinetic energy that we need to walk, run, or swim*

Nuclear: This energy exists in the nuclei of atoms. When an atom is split into two in a nuclear reactor, this energy is released.

⚡ Isn't It Amazing!

Our Universe is a giant sphere, which is expanding. The galaxies at the edge are accelerating away from each other faster than those at the centre. Explaining this phenomenon, scientists proposed that there might be other forms of energy that we know nothing about. Since we cannot measure them, these forms of energy are called dark energy. Our Universe is made up of 68% of dark energy and about 27% is dark matter.

▲ *Dark energy might push galaxies away from each other but it does not seem to affect anything on Earth*

Radiation

Why can energy be converted from one form to another?
Most of it has to do with photons. When photons of certain wavelengths hit certain kinds of atoms, such as metals or semiconductors, they knock off electrons. This is seen in our lives in two very different ways:

1. Light from the Sun is turned into electricity in a photovoltaic cell. If you connect such cells to an electrical circuit, you can get an electric current.

2. Radio waves can move electrons which are loosely bound to metal surfaces to create a small current which is proportional to their wavelength. This principle is used in making antennas for radios.

When photons hit most other kinds of atoms, the energy of the photon is absorbed. The atom becomes excited and vibrates faster, thus becoming 'hot'.

When a nucleus explodes (fission), it releases its energy in photons. When a substance burns, it releases some energy as heat (vibrating molecules) and some as light (photons), and that's why you see a flame. Both of these kinds of energy are called radiation.

◄ *Electric devices work by converting electrical energy into other forms*

 ## Incandescence

Have you seen iron glow when it is heated in a forge? That's because iron, like other metals, emits light when heated at an extremely high temperature. The atoms absorb the energy from heat and then give it out as photons. This is called incandescence. In an incandescent lamp, electricity is used to create heat in a metal filament.

▲ *Incandescent lamps are either filled with inert gas or vacuumed to prevent the filament from corroding*

Fluorescence

In certain materials, when photons fall on their atoms, the electrons in the atoms absorb the photons. Such materials are called phosphors. The electrons then become 'excited', but after some time they release the extra energy and return to their normal state. This released energy is emitted as another photon, but this photon has a lower frequency (higher wavelength) and therefore lesser energy than the original. This is called fluorescence. It is seen best when materials absorb UV light and emit visible light.

In a fluorescent lamp, electricity makes an incandescent filament emit UV light. This falls on a phosphor coating that lines the inner side of the bulb. The phosphor absorbs the UV light and emits bright white light.

▲ Both incandescent and fluorescent lights are now being replaced by LED lights

Radio Waves

Radio waves are used for communication all over the world. These are waves of long wavelengths having low energy. They are emitted from a transmitter based on Earth which converts electrical signals into electromagnetic waves. These waves are received by satellites in space, which then transmit them back to Earth at a different wavelength. Some radio waves don't need satellites but are instead reflected by ions present in the ionosphere, part of the upper atmosphere.

In Real Life

Some types of metals absorb light in the X-ray spectrum (0.01 to 10 nanometre wavelengths) and emit it in the spectrum of visible light. Each metal has specific wavelengths at which it emits light, this is called its emission spectrum. This property can be used to find out what metals a material is made of.

Gamma Rays

Gamma rays are photons of extremely high energy. These are emitted during nuclear reactions and are highly dangerous. They remove electrons from every atom in their path, turning them into ions. Nevertheless, they can be used in irradiation, a procedure in which they are used to kill infectious bacteria or cancer cells.

◀ Gamma rays are also emitted by black holes and stars known as quasars

Optics

Did you know that the person you see in the mirror is not you but a slightly modified version of you? Because the right hand of the person in the mirror is actually your left hand and your right hand is your reflection's left hand; this is called a lateral inversion. But before we race on to that, let us understand something about reflection, refraction, and diffraction, which make up a fascinating field called Optics. This is a field whose scientific history begins with Isaac Newton, though, unlike his study of gravity, there were no apples harmed in the process.

Reflection

We've read earlier that light behaves both as a particle as well as a wave (pages 4–5). Well, if it behaves like a particle, then it should bounce like a ball when it hits a hard surface. That's exactly what happens when light is reflected on a mirror or a shiny surface. Shine is a property of metals that have loose electrons. These electrons keep photons from passing into the metal and reflect them instead. At whatever angle the photons hit the reflector, they travel away from it at the same angle. That's why when you turn a mirror, the reflection seems to move away by an opposite angle.

Absorption

Surfaces that are not very shiny, such as a cotton cloth, garden soil, and so on, will absorb light. Some photons of incoming light give up their energy to the electrons of the material they hit. You know that the energy of a photon depends on its wavelength. Each material absorbs photons of a certain wavelength and reflects the rest. The wavelength of photons reflected gives you the colour of the absorbing object. So, an object is blue if it absorbs photons of all colours but blue (that is, the range of light waves with wavelengths between 450 and 495 nanometres).

▲ *Your mirror switches your sides, so your right hand is the mirror image's left*

▼ *The sea looks blue because it transmits most wavelengths except blue, which it reflects*

Isn't It Amazing!

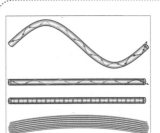

If light enters a tube whose inner surface is mirrored, the light will undergo multiple reflections until it comes out at the other end of the tube. This is called total internal reflection. This is the idea behind optical fibres, which convert computer signals (such as an email you wrote) into light rays of different wavelengths. The signals can travel at the speed of light to reach the destination.

◄ *Total internal reflection in optical fibre cables*

Transmission

Some objects, such as water and glass, neither reflect light nor absorb it. They transmit the light instead and are hence called transparent. Some objects, such as frosted glass, absorb some light and transmit the rest. These are called translucent. Objects that do not transmit any light at all are called opaque.

▼ *Water (left) is transparent, while lemonade (right) is translucent*

▼ *Refraction makes a pencil look out of shape under water*

▼ *Soap bubbles diffract white light into its many colours*

In Real Life

Stellar spectroscopy is the study of the spectra of starlight, that uses a special machine that looks at the wavelengths of lights coming from a star. While the spectrum of any star emits most of the wavelengths of visible light, it shows some black lines, which correspond to the light the star has absorbed (called its absorption spectrum). These lines, called Fraunhofer lines, first observed in 1802, tell you what elements the star is made of.

▲ *The depth of the lines indicate temperature, and the wavelength shifts point to motion of the composite gases*

Refraction

When you get into the bathtub, do you wonder why your body suddenly looks out of shape? Or why things look bigger or smaller when you look through mum's or dad's glasses? That's because water and glass bend light. When light travelling through air enters a denser medium, it loses speed, as the photons encounter resistance from the material's electrons. The speed of light in water is three-fourths its speed in air. This also causes a change in the angle of light which physicists call refraction. Refraction is used to build contact lenses that correct eyesight.

Diffraction

Ever blown soap bubbles and seen rainbow colours when light shines on them? That's because the bubbles diffract light. Diffraction happens when white light (that is light of all wavelengths) is refracted by a medium (like glass or water). As the photons slow down, they travel at different speeds according to their energy, so they bend at different angles. This means that photons of different wavelengths (colours) get separated.

Different crystalline solids will diffract light in different patterns. These patterns of diffraction are used by scientists to figure out the chemical composition of a substance.

Reflection

According to an ancient Greek legend, Medusa was a monster who could turn you to stone if you looked at her. Perseus was a Greek hero who was sent to kill her while she was asleep. To avoid looking at her, he used a mirrored shield to get closer to her and defeat her. As this legend is about 4,000 years old, we know that mirrors were known as far back as then.

Mirrors are one way in which humans use the science of optics (how light behaves with different media). Two other devices that have been with us since ancient times are the lens and the prism. Here we will look at how these devices work. Sometimes these are directly useful, while other times they are part of other devices like **telescopes** and cameras, which combine many lenses and prisms.

▲ *An example of an ancient Chinese bronze mirror. The front would have been polished metal, and the back would have beautiful carvings*

Mirrors

A mirror is a surface that reflects light. Most mirrors known to us are made of glass, covered on one side by a coat of fine aluminium or silver dust. Other mirrors, used for astronomy, are often made of polished metal surfaces. Mirrors come in three types:

1. Planar: These are the most common ones, including dressing mirrors. The image in the mirror is laterally inverted, that is, right becomes left and left becomes right.

2. Concave: The mirror is bowl-shaped, with the silvering on the outside. These mirrors are used to reflect incident light onto a single point (the focal point). They make an image look bigger, so dentists use them to examine your teeth.

3. Convex: This mirror is also bowl-shaped, with the silvering on the inside. They make an image look smaller, so they can be used to condense a large field into a smaller space. That's why they are used in rear-view mirrors of cars.

▼ *In a planar mirror, your left hand becomes your right hand, and vice versa*

▼ *Concave mirrors expand a small picture*

▼ *Convex mirrors shrink a big picture*

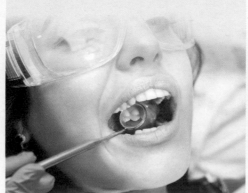

Reflection by Mirrors

Here are some more things you should know about mirrors. The incident ray is the ray of light falling on the mirror, while the reflected ray is the ray of light that bounces off a mirror. The angle at which the ray of light meets the mirror is called the incident angle. You can try it yourself: Shine a flashlight onto a mirror in a dark room. As you change the angle at which the light meets the mirror, the angle of the reflected beam will change equally. This is called the angle of reflection.

Newtonian Telescope

While it was Galileo who invented the telescope, most telescopes today use a design made by Isaac Newton. The Newtonian telescope uses a concave mirror to focus the light coming from faraway stars onto a smaller flat mirror that then reflects the image into an eyepiece. The eyepiece may have lenses of different magnifications that allow you to see or photograph the star or other celestial bodies that you want to observe. These telescopes are very easy to build and are popular among astronomers.

▼ How a Newtonian telescope works

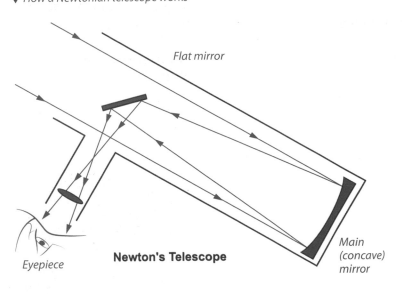

Flat mirror

Newton's Telescope

Eyepiece

Main (concave) mirror

⭐ Incredible Individuals

Archimedes, the ancient Greek scientist, is said to have used concave mirrors to defeat the invading Romans in the Battle of Syracuse in Italy (212 BCE). Some reports say that he used the mirror to focus the light of the Sun into an intense beam that burned the Roman ships. However, it is more likely that he used the blinding flashes of light to distract the soldiers instead.

◀ A statue of Archimedes holding a concave mirror in modern Syracuse

👤 In Real Life

In the Medieval Period, mirror-making was very expensive. The kings of France and Persia had halls of mirrors built in their palaces to show how rich they were. The walls of these halls are covered with mirrors of all kinds.

▲ The Hall of Mirrors, Golestan Place, Tehran

💡 Isn't It Amazing!

Charles Messier identified a list of 110 interesting objects in the sky, including galaxies, star clusters, and nebulae, during the late 18th century. Young astronomers use these objects to learn how to use a telescope.

◀ The Messier Marathon happens every year on a new moon night in March, when astronomers try to observe all 110 Messier Objects

Lenses and Prisms

A lens is a block of glass through which light is made to pass. Lenses can be concave or convex, though the latter is the most common. They use the power of refraction to make light either converge at a point (convex lenses) or diverge (concave lenses). A lens affects the view of an object behind it. Convex lenses are used in many instruments to focus light onto a point that needs to be lighted up, as well as in contact lenses and eyeglasses which help long-sighted people see better. In a camera, a **convex lens** shrinks the wide world into a small space. Concave lenses are used in flashlights and projectors to increase the area that can be lighted, and also in spectacles which help short-sighted people see better. In a movie projector, the **concave lens** does the reverse of the camera.

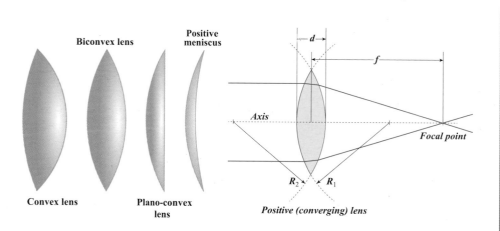

Convex & Concave Lenses

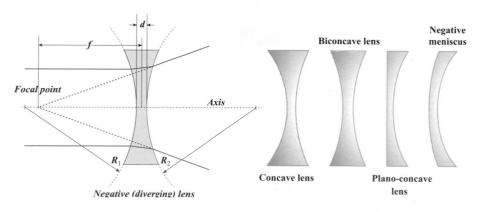

▲ Convex lenses focus light onto a focal point while concave lenses expand the area the light can cover

Isn't It Amazing!

There is a lens in your eye too. It is made of transparent proteins and is known as the crystalline lens. But unlike a glass lens, the thickness of the eye lens can be increased or decreased, allowing you to focus on a faraway object or a near one. In some people, the ability of the lens becomes limited, due to which they need to wear glasses of the correct **power**.

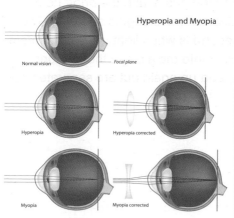

▲ Long-sightedness (far-sightedness or hyperopia) is corrected by convex lenses, while short-sightedness (near-sightedness or myopia) is corrected by concave lenses

Microscopes

The simplest microscope is a magnifying glass. It is a lens that is convex on both sides (**biconvex**), which projects light onto an object. As the light is reflected from the object, it comes back to your eyes in the form of an **image** which looks larger than it actually is. This is called **optical magnification**. If the image appears ten times larger than the object, it is said to be magnified 10 times.

▶ *A magnifying glass is also called a simple microscope*

In a compound microscope, the idea is taken further by using more than one lens. A condenser lens collects light from outside (either sunlight or an electric light) and focuses it onto the object in the slide. As the light passes through the object, it falls on the first convex lens, which scientists call the 'objective'. This lens focuses the image onto the second lens, called the 'eyepiece'. This adds more magnification before the image reaches your eye. The thickness of the objective lens determines its **optical resolution**. High resolution means that the distance between the two objects the microscope can 'see' as separate ones is really small. Anything below the resolution will appear unclear. If the eyepiece magnification is more than that of the objective, you get empty magnification, that is, the image is larger but not better resolved.

◀ *Light from the condenser focused onto the objective lens of a microscope*

Prisms

A prism is a device that makes refraction happen twice. The first is when light waves enter from air into the prism, and the photons of different wavelengths separate. The second is when light leaves the prism back into the air, and the photons speed up again but are separated so much that they now exit as separate waves. Prisms are used together with light filters to get a beam of light of a single wavelength. They can also be used to turn a beam of light by an angle. This is the principle used in a submarine's **periscope**.

▶ *A submarine periscope works by bending light twice so that ships above water can be seen*

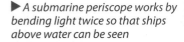

Changes of State

In Physics and Chemistry, a state or phase of matter is defined as the condition a substance is found in at any temperature or pressure. For example, at the atmospheric pressure of sea level, water is usually a liquid. If heated above 100°C, it boils and becomes a gas called steam. If steam is cooled below 100°C, it condenses back to water. This temperature is called the boiling/condensation point of water. If cooled below 0°C, water freezes and becomes a solid called ice. If ice is heated above this temperature, it melts. 0°C is therefore water's **freezing/melting point**. Sometimes, a solid turns directly to gas if heated fast enough. This is called sublimation.

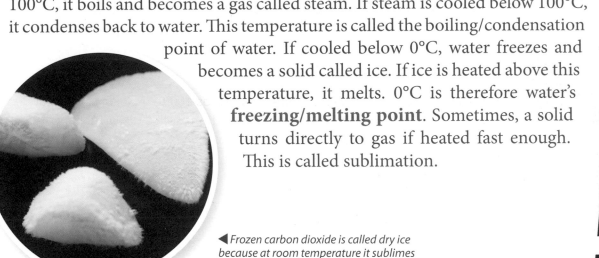

◀ Frozen carbon dioxide is called dry ice because at room temperature it sublimes directly from solid to gas

▼ Ice can be transparent or near opaque depending on the level of impurities in the water

🔍 What Happens in a Phase Transition?

Think of water. In ice, the H_2O molecules have no freedom to move, except to vibrate a tiny bit about themselves. As you heat the ice, the heat is converted to kinetic energy and the molecules vibrate faster. When heated past 0°C, a sudden change occurs. The ice molecules now break free of the forces holding them and begin to move about with greater freedom. Nevertheless, they remain attracted to each other by weak **van der Waals forces**. Therefore, water still has a fixed volume.

When water is heated past its boiling point, it turns into steam. Any meagre force holding the molecules together is now broken completely and each molecule is on its own. Its kinetic energy makes it shoot about faster. If the steam is released into the atmosphere, it will disperse completely, as you see in a pressure cooker.

If the temperature drops, the kinetic energy is lost as heat. The molecules move around much less. When cooled below 100°C, the water molecules stick to each other and turn into droplets, which then begin to form puddles. If you cool these puddles below freezing point, the molecules begin to line up in rows and columns, turning into crystals of ice.

▼ Water is the most common liquid on our planet

▼ While mostly visible, saturated or super-heated steam is invisible

Gas

Solid

Liquid

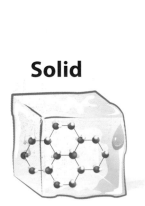

◀ Changes of state are accompanied by changes in the movement of atoms or molecules

States of Matter

🔍 Latent Heat

Water does not start boiling the moment it reaches 100°C. Instead, some heat is absorbed without a change in temperature. This is called the latent heat of vaporisation. This heat is needed to break the hydrogen bonds that form between water molecules. Many other substances have their own specific latent heat of vaporisation.

Ice does not melt immediately at 0°C either. Instead, it takes some heat to break all the bonds between the atoms that hold them in the regular crystal structure of rows and columns. This is called water's latent heat of fusion. All crystalline substances have their own latent heat of fusion.

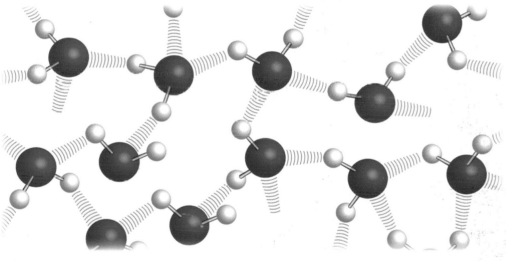

▲ All hydrogen bonds between water molecules must be broken before it can boil

🔍 Combustion

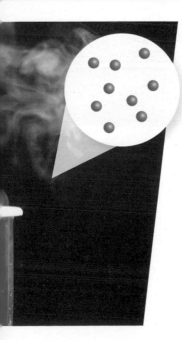

Not all things melt, boil, or sublime when heated. Some burst into flames instead. This is because when they are heated, they react with the oxygen in the air and undergo combustion. This is important for cooking oils, which need to be hot enough for frying, but not hot enough to start burning. The smoke point of an oil is the temperature at which it starts to smoke.

▶ Heating oil beyond its smoke point may cause it to burst into flames

Heat Transfer

Let's now turn our focus towards heat. Heat, as seen on page 9, is a form of energy that is stored in the movement of atoms and molecules. The hotter they are, the more kinetic energy they have. Because of this, heat can also travel and therefore make other things hot, because it moves from a place of high temperature to a place of lower temperature. If this did not happen, our Universe would be a cold dead place. Here we will look at how heat can be used to do a lot of our work.

▲ *Radiation is the method by which the Sun's heat is transmitted to our planet*

 ## Conduction

Ever wondered why a saucepan is stirred with a wooden spoon while cooking? That's because wood is a poor conductor of heat, that is, heat does not travel along the molecules of wood. On the other hand, it travels fast among the atoms of a metallic spoon, until the spoon becomes as hot as the sauce. This is called conduction of heat.

Metals have atoms arranged in neat rows and columns. When a metal atom gets heated, it begins to vibrate faster, converting heat into kinetic energy. As it vibrates, it crashes into the next atom, transferring some of the energy to it, so the next atom also begins to vibrate. In this way, all the atoms begin to vibrate, and the entire metal spoon becomes hot. Metals are therefore good conductors of heat. On the other hand, the molecules in wood are not arranged in a regular way at all and they all vibrate out of sync with each other. Hence, heat cannot travel in any one direction, and the spoon takes much longer to become hot.

Conduction

▲ *A wooden ladle helps you stir chocolate while it melts without burning your hand*

💡 Isn't It Amazing!

What happens if you put a flask with a shiny outer surface into one with a shiny inner surface and create a vacuum between them? There can be no heat transfer by conduction or convection, and the surfaces reflect the light, so radiation is also ruled out. This is the principle of the vacuum flask, which was invented by James Dewar.

Convection

Shell some peas and boil them in a saucepan. Do you notice that they bounce up and down as the water heats up? This is because of a form of heat transfer called convection, which occurs in liquids and gases. When water molecules are heated by the gas or electric coil at the bottom of the pan, they begin to move around faster and rise to the top. They push the colder water to the bottom, which then gets heated and moves up. This sets up a round motion in the water called a **convection current**. Convection currents allow for uniform heating and cooking of food in a pan or a steamer.

▲ *Convection currents in a boiler make peas jump up and fall down*

Radiation

Radiation transfers heat even in a vacuum through photons whose energy is very high. In an electric radiator, which is used in many homes to heat rooms during winter, the electrons moving through the machine collide with the atoms it is made of, making them eject photons. These photons hit the molecules in the air and heat them, thus heating the room. Radiation is also how the Earth receives heat from the Sun.

▼ *The three different kinds of heat transfer*

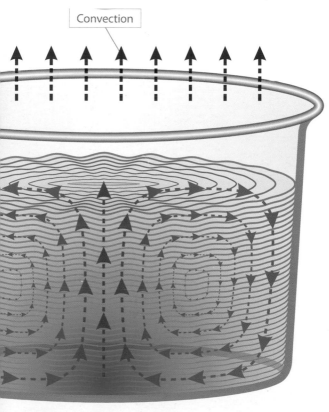

Convection

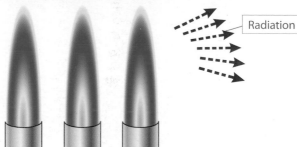

Radiation

▲ *Radiators heat rooms in winters by converting electricity into electromagnetic waves*

Energy and Work

In the 18th century, scientists realised that steam energy could be harnessed to do work. It is based on the principle that steam has a lot of kinetic energy when compressed, and that this energy can be harnessed to do useful work through a machine called an engine. Scientists tried to figure out how these engines could be made more **efficient**, so that they could get more work out of the energy put into them. In this process, the scientists discovered the science of **Thermodynamics**. But before we read further about this science, we need to learn a few definitions:

System: The set of molecules that one studies in thermodynamics. It can be a test tube full of liquid, or the whole Universe.

State: A description of a system that includes its temperature, pressure, amount of heat, and other physical properties.

Open System: A system which is open to the rest of the world, so both matter and energy can come in and go out. For example, water boiling in a vessel: energy goes from the stove to the water, but steam escapes into the air from the vessel.

Closed System: A system which can let energy come in and go out, but not matter. For example, a battery, which gives electric power and can be recharged, but whose contents don't leak. Air is a closed system, as is your body.

Isolated System: A system that does not let energy or matter come in or go out. The Universe is an isolated system (since nothing can escape it or enter it); a sealed vacuum flask is another. Since our Universe is an isolated system, there are only finite amounts of matter and energy that exist. No new matter or energy can be created, but they can be converted from one form to another.

Work: In Physics, work means the conversion of any form of energy into mechanical kinetic energy, which moves a device.

Energy: It is defined as the force in Newtons required to move an object by one metre. The unit of energy is Newton-metre, also called Joule.

Heat Engine: A machine that converts heat energy (or any other kind of energy) into mechanical work.

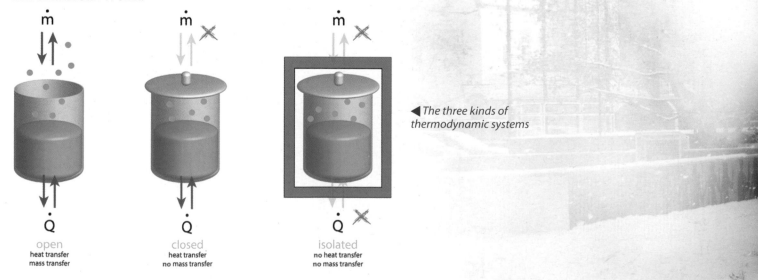

◄ *The three kinds of thermodynamic systems*

open
heat transfer
mass transfer

closed
heat transfer
no mass transfer

isolated
no heat transfer
no mass transfer

First Law of Thermodynamics

We've actually read this before as the Law of Conservation of Energy. In our practical world though, we think of the law in terms of using energy (symbol: Q) to drive work (W) in a machine. Some of that energy will remain unconverted and instead become part of the internal energy (ΔU) of the machine. Physicists show this in the form of an equation:

$$\Delta U = Q - W$$

A closed system that retains its internal energy is rare. Many engines give away the energy to the atmosphere in the form of waste energy. For a simple example, consider a kitchen blender making a smoothie. It converts incoming electric energy into the mechanical energy of the rotor blades. But some of the energy goes into heating the rotor blade. If you wash the blender immediately afterwards, the heat is lost.

▶ Although thermodynamics was originally about heat engines, it can be applied to any kind of energy used to do work

⊛ Incredible Individuals

You may have read that James Watt (1736–1819) was so fascinated by a kettle when he was a child that he went on to invent the steam engine. This story is not true. Watt did not invent the steam engine, but he did improve its design. He added a steam jacket that made sure that the heat of the engine was not lost; and a condenser that reduced the pressure of the steam, so that it would not make the engine explode.

◀ James Watt's improved steam engines powered the Industrial Revolution

▲ A steam engine converts the thermal energy of compressed steam into the kinetic energy that makes the wheels move

Second Law of Thermodynamics

According to the Second Law of Thermodynamics, an isolated system's entropy (the measure of molecular disorder of a system) will never decrease with time. When the forces between the atoms and molecules reduce, they have more freedom to move around, and the system becomes more random. For example, water left by itself will evaporate into the Universe. That is true even when the water is very cold, it will just be a lot slower.

Still, in many processes, this law does not really appear to hold. Otherwise, you would never get water to freeze—a process by which randomly floating liquid water molecules become arranged in a crystal of ice. But remember, when water is freezing, it has to lose heat to something else (usually air), which becomes more disordered in the process. Water and air together make the system.

▲ The Sun's entropy increases as it shines, and as it makes water evaporate, it makes the Earth's atmosphere's entropy rise too

Third Law of Thermodynamics

Entropy is the word used by scientists for the disorderliness of a system. It depends on the amount of pressure on the system, its temperature and other chemical properties. The Third Law says that if the temperature dropped to zero, such that there was no heat in the system at all, the entropy would also be zero. This is called Absolute Zero and physicists have worked it out to be -273.15°C. The system would become **infinitely ordered**, not just a solid, since even a solid's atoms or molecules have some freedom to vibrate. If this is hard to imagine, you're in good company; scientists have not yet achieved Absolute Zero practically, and cannot say what will happen at that temperature.

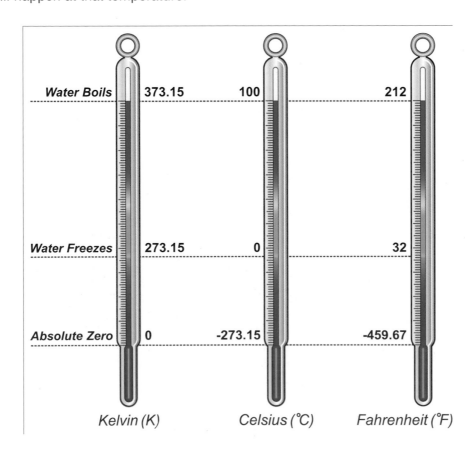

◀ At Absolute Zero, a system would freeze to infinite order, which no one has been able to achieve yet

In Real Life

For long, humans have dreamt of the perfect machine, which works without needing any energy, or converts all the energy perfectly into work, which can then be converted back into energy. But the first kind of machine will violate the First Law of Thermodynamics, because any machine (including our bodies) needs energy to do work. The second kind of machine will violate the Second Law, because such perfect conversion is impossible.

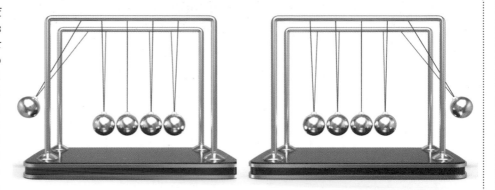

▲ *In theory, this would be a perpetual motion machine, as the energy of the first ball would make the last one move and rise. The last ball would then come down and in the same manner make the first ball rise again. But friction and gravity would soon bring the balls to rest instead of allowing continuous movement*

From Big Bang to Heat Death

According to the Second Law, the Universe should expand as it gets more disordered, and it does. According to the Third Law, at Absolute Zero, the Universe would have no entropy, so it would shrink to a point with no dimension (length, width, or height) at all. So, if the two are put together, we know how the Universe was born, and how it will die. The birth of the Universe is called the Big Bang. Its temperature was infinite, but its volume was zero. Therefore, it was infinitely dense. But since the Universe follows the Second Law, it began to expand very quickly as the temperature dropped, and it has been doing so for the last 13.8 billion years. What next? As it keeps expanding, the atoms and molecules will keep flying apart till the Universe becomes infinitely rare—so wide and deep and long that no atom would ever collide with another. Its entropy would become the maximum possible, but the Universe would have died. This is called a Heat Death. Lucky for us, it's billions of years away.

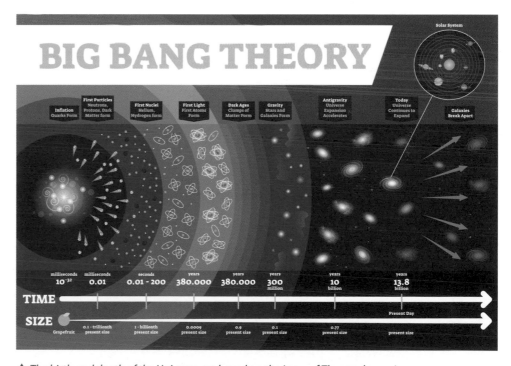

▲ *The birth and death of the Universe are based on the Laws of Thermodynamics*

Incredible Individuals

Anders Celsius (1701–1744) is most famous for inventing the scale used in thermometers, now known as the Celsius scale. He originally set 0 degree as the temperature at which water boils, and 100 degrees as the temperature at which it freezes. Carl Linnaeus reversed the scale to what it is today.

Colour Mixing & Colorimetry

Artists have long known that if you mix two colours, you get a third one. After Isaac Newton discovered that white light was made of different colours, two scientists, Thomas Young and Hermann Helmholtz developed the Trichromatic Colour Vision theory. They noticed that the human eye is most receptive to three colours—red, blue, and green. These are now called primary colours. The colours you get by mixing any two of these are called secondary colours; if you mix all three you get white. Since then, artists and engineers have worked on getting all the colours from these three, and today we have the science of **colour theory**.

Additive Mixing

Additive mixing of colours is used for light rays and transmitted colours. This is the principle that works in electronic screens, in your TV, computer, mobile phone, or gaming console. The screen is divided into millions of tiny pixels, each of which is made of three light-emitting diodes (LEDs), which emit red, green, or blue light when electricity passes through them. The digital signal that reaches each pixel of your screen tells it how much of the three colours to emit. For example, say a pixel is told to emit red and blue in equal proportions. The light waves of red and blue fall on the cone cells that are sensitive to those colours, and the brain reads the two signals together. You 'see' a magenta signal at that pixel. The other secondary colours are cyan (blue + green) and yellow (red + green). This is called RGB colour mixing.

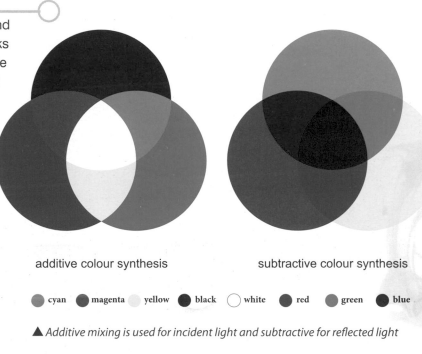

additive colour synthesis   subtractive colour synthesis

● cyan   ● magenta   yellow   ● black   ○ white   ● red   ● green   ● blue

▲ *Additive mixing is used for incident light and subtractive for reflected light*

In Real Life

The colour wheel was invented by Isaac Newton to show how white light was made of different colours. If you rotate it really fast, the colours cancel each other out as they reach your eye, and you see a white disc. Newton's wheel uses red, blue, and yellow as the primary colours.

▶ *The colour opposite each primary colour is its complimentary colour*

YELLOW
primary

YELLOW GREEN
tertiary

YELLOW ORANGE
tertiary

GREEN
secondary

ORANGE
secondary

BLUE GREEN
tertiary

RED
ORANGE
tertiary

BLUE
primary

RED
primary

BLUE VIOLET
tertiary

RED VIOLET
tertiary

VIOLET
secondary

PRIMARY
YELLOW
RED
BLUE

SECONDARY
ORANGE
VIOLET
GREEN

TERTIARY
YELLOW ORANGE
RED ORANGE
RED VIOLET
BLUE VIOLET
BLUE GREEN
YELLOW GREEN

Subtractive Mixing

Additive mixing works only for incident light. If you mix the colours as paint though, you will end up with black! That's because paints and pigments are made of materials that absorb light of all wavelengths except the ones of their 'colour'. If you mix them, you end up with a mix that absorbs everything. Instead, like the artists and engineers who work in colour printing, you have to use a different scheme known as CMYK (cyan, magenta, yellow, and key). You mix pigments in such a way that the mix reflects only the colour you want. Here the primary and secondary colours of the RGB scheme switch places. If you print a picture with cyan and magenta in equal proportions, you get blue. CMYK, nevertheless, uses a black ink separately (called key), to get a darker shade.

▲ *Colour cartridges in printers have pigments that mix cyan, magenta, yellow, and black*

💡 Isn't It Amazing!

A number of studies have shown that male humans cannot distinguish as many colours as female humans. The wavelength also matters: men will see yellow where women see orange, and blue-green to women is blue to men.

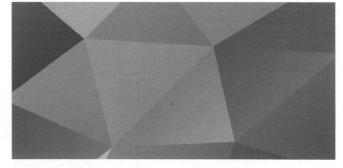

▲ *How many shades of pink can you make out?*

Putting Light to Work

▲ *Polarized sunglasses have polarizing filters in them which reduce the amount of light entering your eyes*

When a light wave is moving, you know that the photons vibrate creating a magnetic field. But all the photons do not vibrate in the same direction. This is called unpolarised light. However, when light passes through some materials, only the photons that vibrate in a certain direction are transmitted and the rest are absorbed. This light is now called polarised light. It has many uses; one of them being in photography to get clearer pictures, by using a polaroid lens.

Colour Filters

A **colour filter** is a prism or a lens that reflects photons of certain wavelengths and transmits others. The atmosphere acts as a giant light filter, which filters out light of short wavelength. In the morning and evening, as the sunrays fall on us obliquely, the light has to pass through more air. The long wavelength photons (red-orange) pass but the blue ones don't, making the Sun look red.

Other filters are made of coloured glass and crystals for different uses. They help create a beam of light of almost a single wavelength (called monochrome light), which has many uses, especially in lasers. Light filters are used in spectrometry, fluorescence microscopy, and many other fields, often alongside a polarizing filter.

◀ *Colour filters are used to create monochromatic light*

Colorimetry

Colorimetry is a technique used by chemists to find out the concentration of a coloured substance in a solution. It works on the principle that the substance will transmit all the photons that match its colour and absorb the rest. If you use a light beam of a colour complimentary to the substance, the more amount of the substance there is, the more photons it will absorb. By measuring the intensity (number of photons per second) of the transmitted light, you can find out the amount of substance present in the solution. This is usually done by using a photovoltaic cell, in which the photons attack electrons and set off a small current.

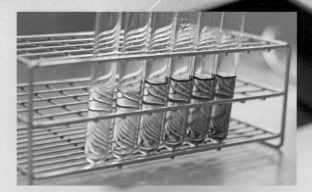

▲ *Colorimeters measure concentration of coloured substances without destroying them*

🔍 Lasers

Lasers were invented by Theodore Maiman (1927–2007) in 1960. A laser is a beam of monochrome, polarised light that has photons of very high energy. They are made by striking photons onto a charged material. The photons take up the energy of the electrons in the material, producing a stronger beam of light. By doing this repeatedly, the energy of the photons can be amplified to several thousand times.

The energy of a laser is enough to burn things, so lasers are used for cutting and welding materials very precisely, especially in the electronics industry. Lower-energy lasers are used to burn cancer cells and in surgery as very high-precision knives. LASIK surgery is an application of lasers used to reshape the cornea to improve vision, eliminating the need for glasses or contact lenses.

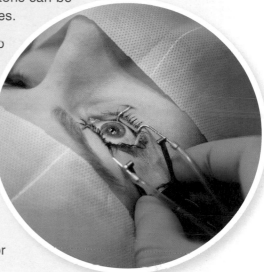

▲ *While LASIK technology is improving, there are enough risks involved with using lasers in the eye that make people cautious*

⭐ Incredible Individuals

Lasers are usually delivered in **pulses**, rather than continuous waves. A high-energy laser pulse could not be amplified beyond a point without damaging the equipment. Donna Strickland, a Canadian physicist, solved this problem. She reduced the energy but increased pulse time, and then amplified the pulse to high levels of energy. Finally, this high-energy pulse was reduced to a smaller-sized pulse of even higher energy. For this, she received the Nobel Prize in 2018.

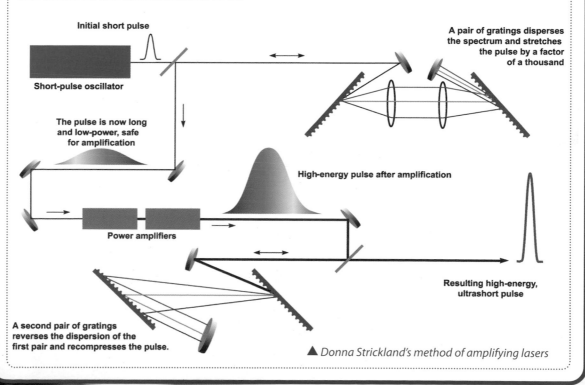

Initial short pulse

Short-pulse oscillator

A pair of gratings disperses the spectrum and stretches the pulse by a factor of a thousand

The pulse is now long and low-power, safe for amplification

High-energy pulse after amplification

Power amplifiers

A second pair of gratings reverses the dispersion of the first pair and recompresses the pulse.

Resulting high-energy, ultrashort pulse

▲ *Donna Strickland's method of amplifying lasers*

Optical Illusions

An optical illusion is something that fools your eye into seeing something that isn't quite there. You would think this is only for conjurers and tricksters, but it is part of a huge industry that we love: the movies! Did you know that a '**motion picture**' is actually a giant visual illusion? That's because our eyes are digital in nature. They see the world in snapshots, with about twelve '**frames**' every second. If a series of still pictures run faster than that in front of our eyes, we think they are moving. Most motion pictures are shot at about 24 frames per second (FPS), so you see a smooth movement. Largely, they can be divided into three classes: physical, physiological, and cognitive illusions; with each having the 4 types discussed below.

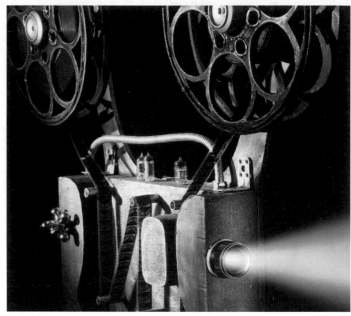

▲ *In the old days, a film projector would run 24 or more frames of a camera film over a concave lens to 'show' the film*

🔍 Other Optical Illusions

Apart from the movies, the illusions we have fun with can be classified into four types:

Ambiguities: These are illusions that make us see the same image in more than one way. The drawing of a cube is one: is it facing downwards or upwards? These illusions work by tricking the retinas of your eyes into seeing two different pictures, which the brain must then resolve.

Distortions: These make us see imaginary angles and curves. They make use of how the brain creates 3-dimensional (3D, also **stereoscopic**) vision by combining the images from the two eyes.

Paradoxes: These also fool our stereoscopic vision into seeing what is physically impossible. The artist M.C. Escher made many drawings of illusions like these.

Fictions: These make us see things when there aren't any. They make use of the fact that our brains don't record every detail of what we see, but only the boundaries between colours, and they mentally make up the rest.

ⓥ Incredible Individuals

Charles-Émile Reynaud (1844–1918) was a painter, photographer, engineer, and industrial designer, who made one of the world's first animated movies. He invented the praxinoscope, the precursor to the modern projector. It had a series of pictures on a turntable; if you cranked it fast enough, you could see motion.

◄ *Reynaud's Praxinoscope works on the principle that the human eye sees more than 12 FPS as motion*

💡 Isn't It Amazing!

Why do you need 3D glasses to watch a 3D movie? That's because they create an elaborate illusion of depth in a flat image. The movie is made of two separate images, that you can resolve only by separate cyan and red filters on your glasses. The two images reach your brain, where they are merged to form a 3D image.

ALPHABET
STEREO ANAG
3D LYPH
DESIGN
FONT

ABCDEFGHIJKLMN
OPQRSTUVWXYZ
0123456789.?!

▲ *The two colour filters separate the two images, which reunite in the brain to form a 3D image*

🔍 Forced Perspective

Our eyes receive information about the world onto a flat surface (the retina). The brain has to figure out the distance of objects from this flat image, so it uses the relative sizes of images. Faraway objects look small because the brain is saying to itself that if it looks small when it should look bigger, it must be far. Some kinds of illusions make use of this. This is called forced perspective.

▼ *Is the castle really sitting on the birdbath?*

💡 Isn't It Amazing!

Pareidolia is our brain's tendency to perceive a meaningful image in a random visual pattern. In the African Savanna where humans evolved, the ability to spot a lion's or an enemy's face in the grass meant life or death.

▲ *Do you see a double fire hydrant or a big-eyed face?*

LIVING THINGS

LIFE AND EVOLUTION

Living things are all the organisms that are, or once were, alive. From the wondrous microscopic bacteria to the great blue whales gliding in our oceans, from the terrifying dinosaurs who roamed our planet millions of years ago to the beautiful butterflies that flit in our gardens, all of this life came to be by a wonderful process called **evolution**. First suggested by Charles Darwin and Alfred Russell Wallace, this idea says that all creatures try to make more of themselves (reproduction) and try to fit as well as possible into their environment (adaptation). Some succeed more than others and leave behind more animals and plants of their kind. Others fail and go extinct. But when the climate changes or food becomes scarce or a new predator evolves, those who can change themselves survive. Those who cannot, like the dinosaurs, become extinct. This is called **natural selection**. In this book, we will explore the wonderful world of microbes, plants, and animals.

▼ Fish swimming around a coral reef. They are both living things

Our Diverse World

Our planet is divided into many climatic zones. Each of these zones has its own weather. The microbes, plants, and animals that grow in these zones are adapted to it. The plants and animals that naturally occur in large numbers in any **habitat** are called biomes. Many of the living beings in them are **endemic**, which means that they cannot live anywhere else. But many other beings can regularly come and go between these zones. These are called migratory.

🔍 Polar Zone

This is the icy world of polar bears (in the Arctic) and penguins (in Antarctica), but almost no plants grow here. This snowy world, called **tundra**, receives very little sunlight and remains in the dark for six months of the year.

◀ The white, furry coat of polar bears helps them retain heat and also acts as a camouflage

Arctic Ocean

🔍 Subpolar Zone

The **taiga** region lies in Canada and Russia, full of great pine trees, grizzly bears, and white wolves. In the Southern Hemisphere, it is made of the Southern Ocean, where the humpback whales roam.

◀ Humpback whales hunt in groups by making 'nets' of bubbles in which they trap small fish

Atlantic Ocean

🔍 Temperate Zone

The temperate zone lies across Europe, China, North America and the southern tip of Argentina. It has long winters and short summers and is home to many animals and plants. Parts of it are forested, while the others make giant grasslands called the prairies in America, and steppes in Russia.

▲ Wheat, which grows mostly in the temperate zone, is the staple food of nearly a billion people

Pacific Ocean

▲ Major biomes around the world

🔍 Mediterranean Zone

The Mediterranean zone is a small climatic zone found around the Mediterranean Sea, as well as parts of Australia, and California.

⊙ Incredible Individuals

Starting in 1954, the famous TV presenter David Attenborough recorded many programmes about the incredible diversity of life, helping promote awareness of ecological science and environmental conservation.

In Real Life

The Mariana Trench is Earth's deepest point. At 11,034 meters, it is too deep and dark to support much life. However, data suggests that microbial life does exist. Its deepest point is called the Challenger Deep, only four people have ever been to this frigid depth.

◀ Volcanoes on the seafloor provide heat and nutrients for microbes to thrive

▲ Camels store food and water in their humps to adapt to long journeys in the desert

Desert Zone

Deserts are found in all continents, often far from the sea, where there is little rain. Few plants grow in the desert, but they are adapted to the scarcity of water.

Mountain Zone

The mountain biome is found on tall mountains, like the Himalayas and Andes. The animals and plants here have adapted to thin air and cold weather.

Tropical Zone

The tropical zone is the richest in the world in terms of plants, animals and microbes. The **rainforests** of the Amazon, Central Africa, and the Malay Archipelago lie within the tropical zone. It also includes the grasslands called **savanna**.

▲ The tropical rainforests have the largest share of Earth's biodiversity

The Ocean

The ocean has many **pelagic** biomes of its own, depending on how deep the water is. The deeper you go, the less oxygen there is, and the more the pressure of the seawater above you.

Most marine beings live within a depth of 200 metres in the **epipelagic zone**. This includes all the major fish species that human beings eat. It is made of estuaries, where rivers meet the sea, coral reefs that host hundreds of marine species and the open ocean. The **mesopelagic zone** has many kinds of sharks and jellyfish. As you go into the **bathypelagic zone**, sunlight begins to fade. Then in the **abyssopelagic zone**, it is completely dark. Marine animals that live here make their own light, like the angler fish.

ic Ocean

Pacific Ocean

Indian Ocean

	Polar
	Subpolar
	Temperate
	Mediterranean
	Desert
	Mountain
	Tropical

▼ This diagram gives the various pelagic zones of the ocean

ocean surface – 0 m

Epipelagic zone

about 200 m

Mesopelagic zone

about 1 000 m

Bathypelagic zone

about 4 000 m

Abyssopelagic zone

ocean floor

Hadopelagic zone

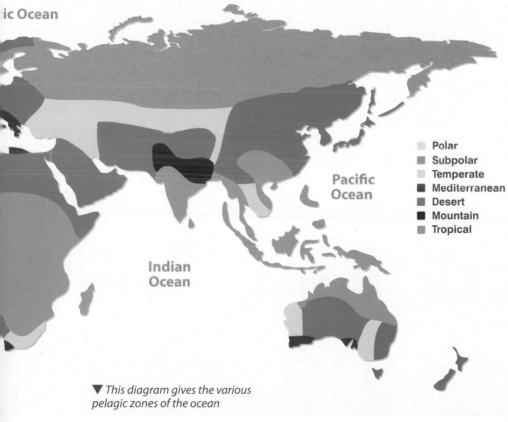

The Goldilocks Planet

Our planet Earth has been called the Goldilocks planet. It is 'just right' for life to flourish. It is neither too close to the Sun to be too hot, nor too far from it to be too cold. It has enough gravity so that the atmosphere that encircles Earth does not blow away.

 ## Atmosphere

Our planet's atmosphere traps enough heat from the Sun so that the water on Earth is mostly in liquid state. A little hotter and most of the water would be vapour; a little colder and it would be ice. Liquid water creates the oceans where **marine beings** first evolved.

The atmosphere also has enough oxygen in it to allow terrestrial beings (beings that live on land and breathe air) to evolve. Radioactivity from within the Earth keeps its interiors liquid, which allows for volcanism, which brings fresh minerals to the surface. No other planet in our solar system has all these together.

 ## Habitable Zone

Can there be life on other planets that revolve around a star far away from us? After studying the Earth, scientists have come up with the idea of the **habitable zone**, which has the right temperature, the right amount of light, and other conditions for life to thrive on any planet that is within it.

The habitable zone of our Sun is between 0.9–1.5 times the distance from the Earth to the Sun. But does such a planet exist elsewhere? In 2014, astronomers discovered Kepler-186f, an Earth-sized planet that revolves around a star 500 light years away from us, which is in the habitable zone of its sun.

▼ *The atmosphere traps enough heat from the Sun for life to prosper; no less and no more*

▼ *The habitable zone of a solar system depends on the size of its star*

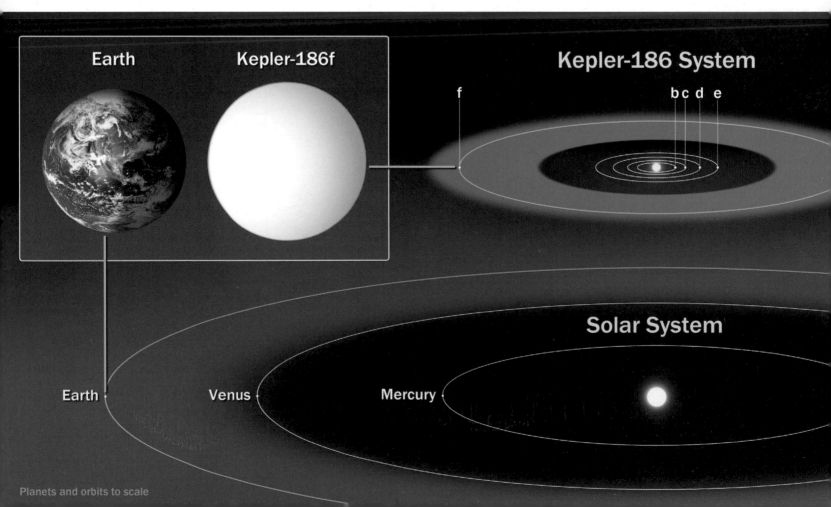

Earth
Kepler-186f

Kepler-186 System

f   b c d e

Solar System

Earth   Venus   Mercury

Planets and orbits to scale

Incredible Individuals

Charles Darwin was the first (with Alfred Russell Wallace) to suggest the Theory of Evolution. He began his career as a naturalist on board the British ship *HMS Beagle*, which sailed around the world collecting specimens of animals and plants. One of these visits was to the Galapagos Islands in the Pacific Ocean, where Darwin saw many different kinds of finches, which looked the same but had different kinds of beaks. This set him thinking, and he finally wrote his thoughts in a book that changed the world: *The Origin of Species*.

▲ *Darwin began his research at the age of 22, but published it only after 28 years in 1859*

The Moon

The Moon is in the habitable zone. So why does it not have life? That is because the Moon is **tidally locked** to Earth, so that one side is always facing us. This makes the temperatures extreme on the dark and light sides of the Moon. Also, the Moon's gravity is too weak to tie down its atmosphere. The Moon's atmosphere is extremely thin, containing gases like sodium and potassium which are absent from the Earth's atmosphere.

▶ *There is a misconception that wolves howl at the Moon. That is untrue. Wolves howl at each other. The Moon just happens to be there!*

Urey-Miller Experiment

Scientists think that life may have started on Earth not when it had plenty of oxygen, but when its atmosphere was comprised of gases like methane, ammonia, and hydrogen. The scientists Harold Urey and Stanley Miller tried an experiment, mixing these gases with water and running electricity through them. A week later, Miller and Urey found amino acids in the mix, the building blocks of life.

In Real Life

The Movile Cave in Romania is pitch dark. It has an atmosphere made of poisonous gases, and has been cut off from the rest of the world for millions of years. Yet many unique species of animals live in it, feeding on the bacteria that make food from the poisonous gases. Scientists think it may be how life might evolve on other planets.

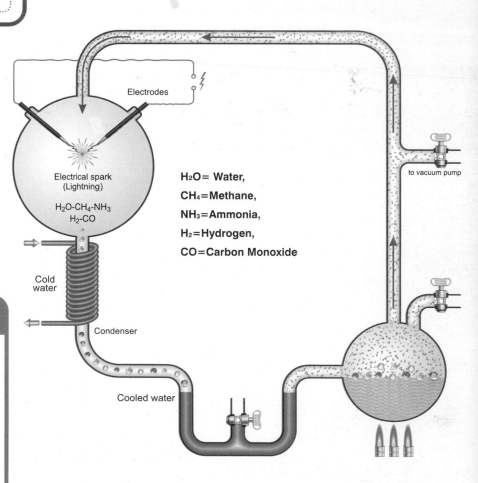

Electrodes

Electrical spark (Lightning)

H_2O-CH_4-NH_3
H_2-CO

to vacuum pump

H_2O = Water,
CH_4 = Methane,
NH_3 = Ammonia,
H_2 = Hydrogen,
CO = Carbon Monoxide

Cold water

Condenser

Cooled water

▲ *A diagram of the Urey-Miller experiment*

Classifying Living Things

Two discoveries revolutionised the way scientists look at the living world. The first discovery, made in 1859, was called the Theory of Evolution. The second discovery, made in the early 20th century, claimed that all living things on our planet have the same **genetic code**. That meant that all life on this planet descended from a single ancestor, who may have lived over 3.5 billion years ago (or earlier).

Early Classification

Earlier, scientists would classify living organisms based on how similar they look to each other (for example, lions, tigers and cats all belong to one family). Now they use the study of DNA taken from these organisms. The science of classifying life is called taxonomy.

The Three Domains

DNA is present in all life forms and carries the recipe for making that being. Minor changes in the sequence of the DNA can lead to major differences in how the living being turns out, and that is how life evolves. This system of taxonomy divides all beings into three domains—Bacteria, Archaea, and Eukaryota. The last one includes all the **multicellular organisms** of the planet, including animals, fungi, and plants.

▲ *Before DNA, biologists used the appearance of living beings to classify them*

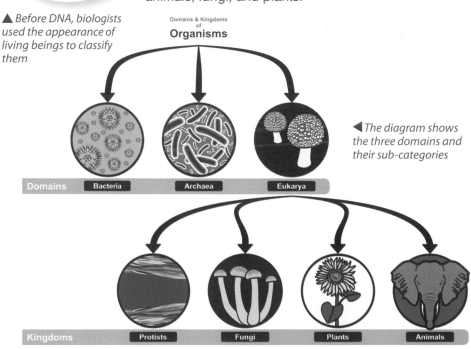

Domains & Kingdoms of
Organisms

◄ *The diagram shows the three domains and their sub-categories*

Domains | Bacteria | Archaea | Eukarya

Kingdoms | Protists | Fungi | Plants | Animals

Bacteria

Spirochetes

G
pos

Proteobacteria

Cyanobacteria

Planctomyces

Bacteroides
Cytophaga

Thermotoga

Aquifex

Hierarchical Taxa

A **taxon** is a unit of classification (plural: taxa). Different taxa are arranged in ranks to form a hierarchy.

Domain: It is the highest level of classification. There are only three domains, in which humans are eukaryotes of the Eukarya domain.

Kingdom: It is the division of a domain. Until 1990, these were the highest level of classification. Unicellular prokaryotes were thought to make one kingdom, called Protista, but now scientists have found that the differences are too vast, so many taxa have their own kingdoms.

▲ *Despite their differences, all dogs belong to the same species, Canis lupus*

Phylum: This is the basic division of a kingdom. Some phyla (plural) may be bunched together to form sub-kingdoms. Earlier, **zoologists** divided them into vertebrates and invertebrates depending on whether they had a backbone or not. This is no more considered scientific, but it is still a useful classification.

Class: This is the division of a phylum, for example, the class Insecta or class Mammalia. Animals within a class share many similarities.

Order: Classes are divided into orders, which club animals that are similar. For example, the order Primates includes all animals that can climb trees, have colour vision and grasping hands, like monkeys, lemurs and apes.

▲ *All cats belong to the family Felidae*

Family: This is a group of really similar animals within a class, like cats (Felidae) or big apes (Hominidae).

Genus: Usually, all animals grouped in a genus look quite similar to each other, except for really minor differences. For example, lions and tigers are both grouped within the genus *Panthera*. Often, they can breed with each other. The genus and species name of an animal make up a living being's scientific name.

Species: This is the final unit. All the animals in a species should be able to breed with each other. For all of our differences, we human beings form one species in one genus—*Homo sapiens.*

Archaea   Eukaryota

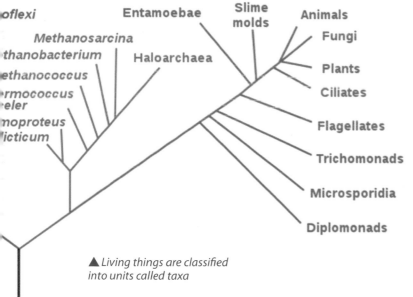

▲ *Living things are classified into units called taxa*

► *All human beings, no matter their ancestry, belong to one species: Homo sapiens*

Bacteria and Archaea

Bacteria and Archaea make up two of the three domains of the world, but they are quite simple to understand. They are both single-celled beings, made of a hard **cell wall**, a softer **cell membrane**, and a liquid matrix filled with proteins (cytoplasm) inside it. The **cytoplasm** is made of lots of enzymes that carry out many chemical reactions that keep them alive. The DNA of Bacteria and Archaea is not enclosed in a nucleus, so they are called **prokaryotes**.

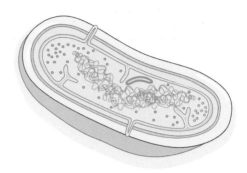

▲ *The main difference between Bacteria and Archaea is in the biochemistry of their cells*

Where in the World?

Bacteria and Archaea live everywhere except the coldest environments. They live in ponds and lakes, in the soil, in rotting food, in the ocean, and even inside you! The ones that live inside you are of two types. The first kind are called pathogens and they cause diseases. The other kind are **symbionts** that help you digest food, make vitamins, and keep pathogens out.

Extremophiles

Many species of Bacteria and Archaea can live in environments which are dangerous for other organisms. These are called extremophiles. Many of them have been studied by microbiologists as they can provide valuable drugs and chemicals for industrial uses.

◄ *The Morning Glory hot spring in Yellowstone National Park. Its amazing colour comes from the thermophilic microbes growing in it*

Isn't It Amazing!

Bacteria can feed on anything. The species *Ideonella sakaensis* can live off polyethylene terephthalate, which is used for making plastic bottles.

▲ *Scientists are looking for Bacteria and Archaea that can break down plastic into CO_2*

Name	Grow in
Acidophiles	acidic soil or water of pH 1–5
Alkaliphiles	alkaline soil or water of pH above 9
Halophile	soil or water with high amounts of salt
Thermophiles	water whose temperature is between 60–80°C
Hyperthermophiles	at temperatures above 80°C
Psychrophiles	at temperatures of 15°C or lower (but will freeze below 0°C)
Piezophiles or Barophiles	at high hydrostatic pressure, like the bottom of the ocean
Oligotrophes	soil or water poor in nutrients
Endolithic microbes	rock or minerals
Xerophiles	soils that have very little water

Fungi

Fungi make up a kingdom by themselves and grow everywhere. Mushrooms, truffles, yeast, and moulds are all fungi. They grow mostly in the soil, but also in spoiled food, stagnant water, and other places.

How to Find Fungi

You can identify fungi easily by their net-like body, called **mycelium**. Sticking out from the mycelia are tiny pin-like bodies called **sporangia**. These contain spores, which are the 'seeds' of fungi. They travel in the air and settle in new places where the fungus can grow. Fungal spores can withstand heat, dryness and even pesticides. But you also need fungi, especially yeast, to make bread, wine and many kinds of cheese.

◄ *Bread turns mouldy because of the growth of Penicillium or Aspergillus fungi*

Classification of Fungi

Fungi are divided into seven phyla on the basis of DNA studies:

- **Chytridiomycota:** Aquatic fungi
- **Neocallimastigomycota:** Fungi found in the intestines of cows, horses and deer
- **Blastocladiomycota:** Parasitic fungi, especially on fruits
- **Microsporidia:** Unicellular fungi parasitic on other unicellular life forms
- **Glomeromycota:** Fungi that symbiotically live with plant roots (**mycorrhiza**)
- **Ascomycota:** Parasitic fungi of plants, including truffles, yeasts, and many antibiotic-making fungi
- **Basidiomycota:** Parasitic fungi of plants that cause rust. This phyla also comprises of **mushrooms**

Incredible Individuals

Fungi live in places where they are regularly attacked by bacteria. They protect themselves by releasing chemicals into the environment, which prevent bacteria from growing. The first of these was discovered by Alexander Fleming. He saw that a fungus called Penicillium had killed the bacterial cultures he had preserved in petri dishes. He soon found the chemical that was doing this and named it Penicillin. Ever since then, scientists have discovered hundreds of such chemicals from fungi, which we call antibiotics.

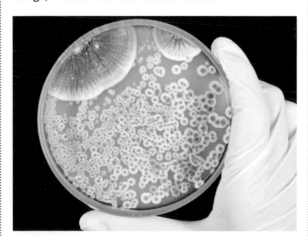

▲ *The species Penicillium roqueforti is used to make blue cheese*

▲ *Toadstools that grow in a circle are called fairy rings*

Toadstools

Toadstool is a common word for mushrooms that are poisonous, but there's no way to tell which ones are poisonous unless you are an expert.

Inside a Plant

When you think of a plant, you usually think of something that has green leaves and brightly-coloured flowers. This is an angiosperm, the most successful group of plants. But did you know that plants also include algae, moss, ferns, grasses and herbs, alongside shrubs and trees?

Kingdom Plantae

Algae form a kingdom of their own, while the rest are members of kingdom Plantae. Many plant species were wiped out during **mass extinction**; so, many of the plants we see evolved just a few million years ago. A typical 'plant' has roots, stems, leaves, and flowers—but many of the simpler plants are not organised this way.

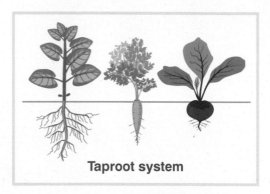

Taproot system

Fibrous root system

Root

The roots of a plant anchor it to the ground and pull in water and minerals from the soil. Different kinds of plants have different roots. Most monocots and 'lower plants' have **fibrous roots**, which emerge from the level of the ground and go underground in different directions. Most dicots have **taproots**, which have a main root that gives off branches. Many root vegetables are made of taproots that have been modified by evolution to store starch, so that the plant can 'winter over' to the next season, i.e. be able to survive underground in winter without **photosynthesis**.

◄ *Onions and potatoes also grow underground, but they are modified stems, not roots*

▶ *Trees have three important organs; roots, leaves, and the stem—which may have branches*

▲ *Lawn grass with a well-developed fibrous root system*

▲ *Water travels by capillary action from the roots to the leaves, where it combines with CO_2 to form glucose by photosynthesis*

Stem

The stem is the part of the plant that grows above the ground. In most plants, it is soft and green, but in trees it grows to become wide and woody as a thick bark made of lots of dead cells. The main job of the stem is to carry water from the roots to the leaves and flowers. It does so through two sets of tubes called the xylem and phloem. The xylem carries water upwards through capillary action, while the phloem carries minerals. Plant stems are divided into long intervals called internodes, separated by nodes. The nodes are the place from which the branches and leaves grow.

Leaf

Leaves are the most complex organs of a plant. The upper surface of a leaf is made of a waterproof cuticle and a protective layer called palisade mesophyll. The lower part has tiny openings called stomata (singular: stoma) through which the plant 'breathes in' carbon dioxide during daytime. The veins of the leaf bring water from the roots. Carbon dioxide reacts with water in the spongy mesophyll to make glucose by photosynthesis.

All plant cells contain a chemical called **chlorophyll**, which is required to make glucose. Chlorophyll traps energy from sunlight and passes it on to the leaf's enzymes for photosynthesis. It is chlorophyll that gives plants their green colour.

ANATOMY OF A LEAF

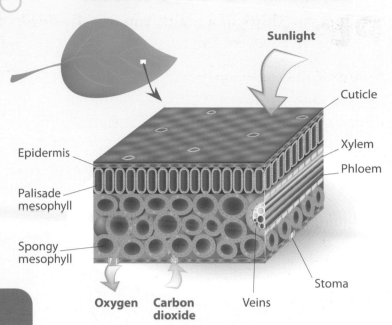

Sunlight

Cuticle

Epidermis

Xylem

Phloem

Palisade mesophyll

Spongy mesophyll

Oxygen   Carbon dioxide   Veins   Stoma

▲ At night, photosynthesis stops, and the plants use the food to grow, releasing CO$_2$ again. That is why it is said that you should not sit under trees at night

In Real Life

The world's tallest tree is a giant sequoia in USA named General Sherman. Its xylem is therefore the world's longest natural column of water.

▶ General Sherman is 84 metres tall

Isn't It Amazing!

Did you know that lichens are made of two kingdoms cooperating with each other to make a living together? There are many different types of lichens, but each is made of a fungus and an alga (singular form of algae). This is called symbiosis.

▲ The lichen's alga makes food for the fungus, while the fungus takes in water and minerals for the alga

Algae, Bryophytes, and Pteridophytes

Some plants evolved from single-celled organisms. They are known for their ability to make their own food by the process of photosynthesis. They reproduce in two ways—by making asexual spores in one generation, and male and female sexual gametes in the next generation. Although they have left behind very few fossils, we know that they might have evolved over 500 million years ago.

In Real Life

Sargasso is a kind of alga that grows while floating on seawater. There is so much of it in the Atlantic Ocean between Bermuda and Florida that the area is called the Sargasso Sea.

▲ *The algae in the Sargasso Sea capture much of the plastic waste we release into the oceans*

 ## Algae

Algae make up many kingdoms of their own and are found in all parts of the world. They may be single-celled or made of many cells clumped together as filaments or sheets. Algal blooms form on ponds and lakes which may be polluted with sewage or faecal matter. The Red Sea gets its name from frequent blooms of red algae. They often appear as shiny sheets on the surface and are called pond scum.

 ## Bryophytes

These include the liverworts, hornworts mosses, and other plants that often grow where no other plants grow. They have a simple body structure without stems or leaves or roots. Instead, they have tissue called rhizoids that go underground to absorb water and minerals.

▲ *Bryophytes grow in difficult terrains like walls and rocks*

 ## Pteridophytes

Ferns, club mosses, spike mosses, quillworts, horsetails, and whisks make up the **pteridophytes**. They evolved over 400 years ago and dominated Earth before the evolution of the higher plants (the **gymnosperms** and angiosperms). They have two forms. Long-living, larger-sized sporophytes make **asexual spores**, which grow up to make smaller, short-lived **gametophytes**. These make male and female gametes that merge to give rise to a new sporophyte. This is called alternation of generations.

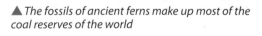

▲ *The fossils of ancient ferns make up most of the coal reserves of the world*

▼ *Algae are a very diverse group of organisms. Many sea organisms depend on them for food*

▶ *Algae that grow in the sea are called kelp or seaweed and are used in making dishes such as sushi*

Gymnosperms

The scientific word 'gymnosperm' means 'naked seed'. The seeds of a gymnosperm are not enclosed in a fruit. On the other hand, angiosperms have seeds which are enclosed in fruits.

Where Do They Grow?

Some gymnosperms (like pines and firs) grow in the temperate regions of the world, making up the great pine forests of Canada and Russia. Other gymnosperms, like cycads, grow in the tropics. Plants that shed all their leaves either in summer or winter are called deciduous. On the other hand, gymnosperms are called **evergreen** because new leaves grow as old ones fall off.

◀ Evergreen trees like pines keep their leaves in winter too

Pine Reproduction

▲ Squirrels play an important role in dispersing pine seeds

Pine seeds grow on a special branch called a cone. Therefore, pine trees are called conifers. Cones may be male (bearing pollen) or female (bearing eggs). The pollen is carried by wind to the eggs of other pine trees. Pollen and eggs join to become one cell called the **embryo**; this is called **fertilisation**. The embryo grows to become a pine seed over 2–3 years. Squirrels and other animals that eat the cones carry the seeds with them and drop them in a new place. Scientists call this **germination**.

▲ Pine seeds are used in desserts and other dishes

💡 Isn't It Amazing!

Over 250 million years ago, plants of the order Ginkgoales were spread throughout the Earth but became extinct soon after. However, one species survived the apocalypse—Ginkgo biloba—and it still grows in temple gardens in China and Japan.

▲ Ginkgo fossil compared to a fresh ginkgo leaf. Ginkgo is called a living fossil

Pine Pollen and Ice Ages

Palynology is the study of pollen from soil. The deeper the soil, the older it is, because new soil is deposited on top as dust every year. Scientists use pollen to find out how Earth's climate was in the past, and what plants grew then. As pine trees grow in cold climates, if you see their pollen from soil samples in the tropics, it tells you that there was an ice age in the past.

Pine pollen under a microscope ▶

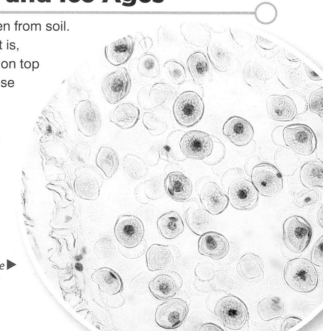

Angiosperms

When we think of plants, we really think of the angiosperms, which botanists call flowering plants. They make 80 per cent of all plants on our planet today. They can be divided into two types—dicots and monocots. Dicots include all the plants with pretty flowers like roses, dahlias, and chrysanthemums. They also include plants which give us most of our fruits and vegetables like mangoes, oranges, carrots, and tomatoes. Monocots include grasses and most of our crop plants like rice, wheat, corn, barley, oats, millets, and more.

▲ *There are about 3,00,000 species of angiosperms worldwide, most in the tropics*

Dicots vs Monocots

Take a dicot seed, like a bean, and you can split it into two. Each of these halves is called a cotyledon. Monocots only have one cotyledon. Monocots and dicots also have other differences.

Monocots	Dicots
They have 3 petals and sepals.	They have 4–5 petals and sepals.
Leaf veins are parallel.	Leaf veins are branched.
Xylem and phloem are scattered in the stem.	Xylem and phloem form a ring.
They have fibrous roots.	They have taproots.
They are rarely branched.	Most dicots are branched.

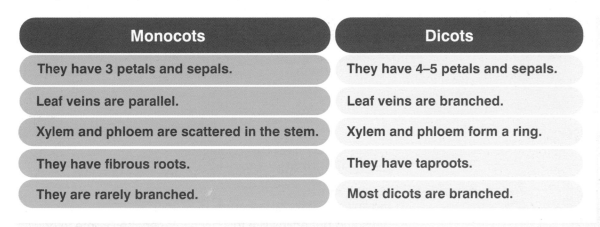

▲ *Monocots and dicots provide us with almost everything we eat*

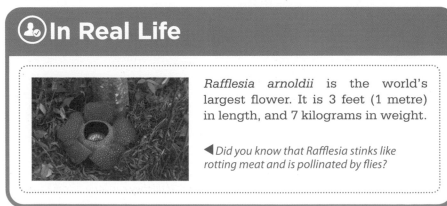

In Real Life

Rafflesia arnoldii is the world's largest flower. It is 3 feet (1 metre) in length, and 7 kilograms in weight.

◀ *Did you know that Rafflesia stinks like rotting meat and is pollinated by flies?*

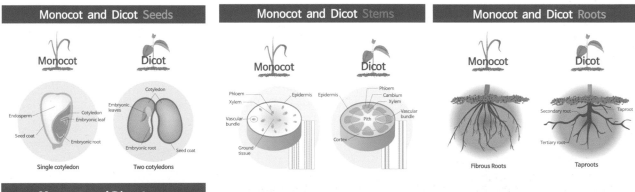

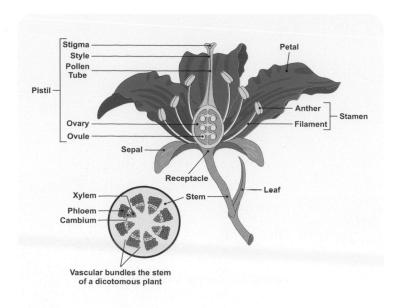

▲ *Parts of a flower*

 ## Flower

Did you know that a flower is not one organ, but four? The outermost parts—sepals (green) and petals (coloured)—help to protect the flower, and also attract insects and birds. The inner parts are the male organ androecium, which makes pollen, and the female organ gynoecium, which makes the egg. Pollination happens when pollen from one flower reaches the egg of another flower, often on a different plant.

Pollination

Different plants have different ways of getting their pollen to another flower. Some have bright flowers, and at the deep end of the flower is a small pool of sugary liquid called nectar. Insects like bees and butterflies like this nectar. When they come to drink it, the pollen sticks all over their bodies. When they go to another flower, the pollen is picked up by that flower. Other plants have small flowers, and their pollen is picked up by the wind.

◀ *Yellow flowers attract honeybees and bumblebees, while red flowers attract small birds*

 ## Seed Dispersal

After pollination, the egg of the flower turns into a seed, while the remaining parts fall away. In some plants, the seed is enclosed in a fleshy fruit (like berries), while in some it is inside a papery pod (like peas), and in others, it is inside a wooden nut (like walnuts).

Plants that make fruits and nuts depend on animals that eat them and throw away the seed, which makes a new plant if it finds new ground. Plants that make pods wait till the pod dries, which then cracks open with a bang, flinging the seeds many metres or yards away.

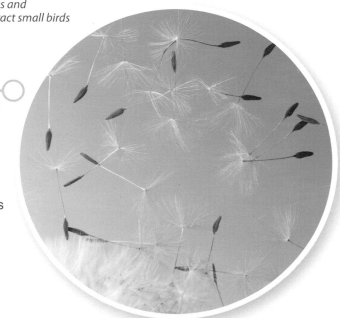

▶ *Dandelion seeds have feathery stems that help them float away in the wind till they can land on new ground*

Inside an Invertebrate

Most biologists divide the animal kingdom into invertebrates and vertebrates. Although advances in taxonomy have shown that this is not a scientific way to classify animals, it is still useful for many reasons. Invertebrates are animals that do not have a hard skeleton, or have their bodies organised into complex organ systems. Vertebrates are abundantly seen in the fossil record of the planet because they leave behind bones that can become fossils. Invertebrates are made of soft tissue, which decays after death, leaving behind no trace of the animal.

▲ *Invertebrate bodies are made of many segments. In many species, a single segment can regrow the rest of the animal*

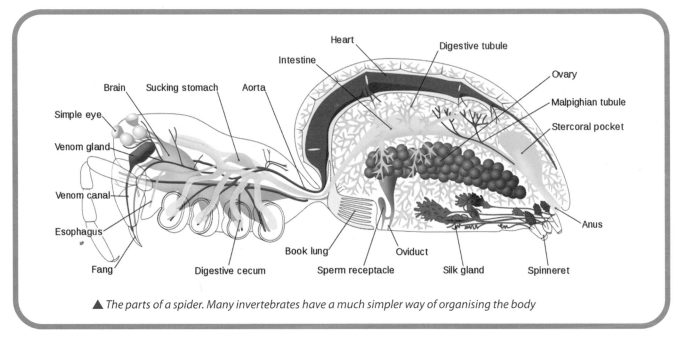

▲ *The parts of a spider. Many invertebrates have a much simpler way of organising the body*

Anatomy

Invertebrate anatomy differs very starkly from that of vertebrates. Here we will discuss the anatomy of Arthropods (insects, spiders, and crustaceans), which make up the largest and most diverse phylum of the animal kingdom.

Many invertebrates cannot swallow their food like we do. Instead, they squirt digestive enzymes onto the food (which may be rotting fruit, insects, or other animals), and suck in the digested juice. Invertebrates breathe in many ways. Animals like spiders have book lungs, while others have spiracles or gills. These take in air directly through the tissues.

Invertebrate blood is called haemolymph, and carries food absorbed from their intestines to the rest of the tissues. Most (except Arthropods and Molluscs) lack a brain and spinal cord; instead, a neural net made of ganglia controls their senses and movements. Many invertebrates have sophisticated sensory organs, such as compound eyes, antennae (for smell and touch), and taste buds on their feet.

◀ *Spiders spit digestive enzymes onto their prey and suck in the remains*

In Real Life

The nervous system of the squid is made of nerve cells that have axons with wide diameters. These were used by Alan Hodgkin and Andrew Huxley to work out how the nerves conduct messages, for which they received the Nobel Prize in 1963.

▲ *A squid's axon can be up to 1mm in diameter—50 times that of a crab, and 1,000 times that of a human*

Classification

The classification of invertebrates is now based on DNA sequencing. However, earlier it was based on comparing various features such as body cavity, the number of appendages, the symmetry of the body etc. Today, biologists recognise 34 phyla of invertebrates.

The simplest are called Parazoa—those that are barely like animals, including sponges and placozoans. These are made of cells of the same type, not organised into tissues. Next come the Coelenterates, which include animals like jellyfish. These have very basic tissues. Following these are a number of phyla together called Helminths—including flatworms, roundworms, and rotifers.

Annelids are a phylum of worms made of segmented bodies, like earthworms. The adaptive benefit of these is that each segment can function entirely on its own, even if the animal is cut in two. Annelids gave rise to Arthropods, which are the most abundant phylum of animals today, and Molluscs, which include both shelled animals like snails and oysters, and shell-less animals like squids and octopi. After them come the Echinoderms which include starfish, sea urchins, and sea cucumbers.

▲ *Jellyfish are among the oldest animal species, having lived for over 500 million years*

◀ *Beetles are the most diverse group of invertebrates, with over 83,000 species*

Invertebrates
Animals without backbone

Worms	Arthropods	Cnidarians	Echinoderms	Mollusks	Sponges
They are animals with soft, tube-shaped bodies and a distinct head	They have legs and some have wings	They have a central opening surrounded by tentacles	Their bodies are covered in spikes or spines	Soft-bodies with external or internal shells	They are the simplest invertebrates
Some worms live inside other animals, others live in the water or on land	They live on land, in the water and in the air	They live in water	They live in water	Some live on land and others live in water	They live in water
They eat living organisms such as nematode, protozoan, rotifer, bacteria, fungi	They eat fungi, worms, or other arthropods	They take in food and eliminate waste through the central opening	They have a central opening for taking in food	They have a muscular foot that allows them to move and hunt for food	They filter food from the water that surrounds them

▲ *Scientifically, the kingdom Animalia is divided into 35 phyla, of which invertebrates make up 34*

▲ *Gastropods with shells are called snails, while those without shells are called slugs*

💡 Isn't It Amazing!

Unlike vertebrates, the intestines of invertebrates, especially insects, have an acidic environment. The bacterium *Bacillus thuringiensis* makes a protein that turns into crystals in this environment. These crystals plug the intestine and the insect starves. This gene has been transferred by genetic engineers into plants like cotton to make them resistant to pests.

▶ *Bt Cotton, a genetically engineered form of cotton, is resistant to insects*

Parazoa and Radiata

The phyla on this page represent the very beginning of the animal kingdom. Some are no more than a bunch of cells clumped together to feed and protect themselves. In other phyla, we see tissues beginning to emerge. In these animals, cells have different jobs, like some ingest food while others protect from predators, and so on. They reproduce asexually, which means they can simply split into two halves, each of which makes a new organism.

▲ *Sponges emerged on Earth over 541 million years ago*

Porifera and Placozoa

The Porifera and Placozoa are two phyla which are together called Parazoa, which means 'nearly animals'. The Porifera (sponges) are little more than a sheet of cells rolled into a tube. Water passes into the opening of the tube (osculum), and filters through the body. The cells grab and eat up bacteria and other one-celled organisms as they pass. This is called filter-feeding. Only one genus makes up the phylum Placozoa and it is the *Trichoplax*, which looks like floating dandruff.

▶ *The scientific name of jellyfish is Medusa, since it resembles the Gorgon of Greek mythology*

Coelenterates

These are animals that look like blobs floating in the water, but they have nerve cells and muscle cells. There is an outer sheet of cells called the ectoderm which protects the body, and an inner sheet called the endoderm which digests food. The nerve cells make up a network called the nerve net. Some cells are arranged into long tentacles, at the end of which are stinging cells which inject venom into their prey.

In Real Life

The Portugese Man o' War resembles a jellyfish, but it is a siphonophore. A colonial organism made of small creatures called zooids, that make up a gas-filled float that travels the waters. Despite its strong venom, the Bluebottle fish *(Nomeus gronovii)* lives among the tentacles. It takes care not to get stung, but has adapted to survive in its chosen home.

▼ *Portuguese Man o' War*

Helminths and Annelids

The Helminths and Annelids are phyla which have a range of lifestyles. They might live on the sea bed or underground. They also show the evolution of organs, body cavities, and different methods of reproduction.

Acoelomates

Acoelomates are animals that do not have a body cavity, so they are called flatworms. They have no blood or gills, so they breathe through their skin. Some, like tapeworms, are parasitic, while others live on the sea floor.

▶ *The bright colours of this flatworm act as a warning to predators that it is poisonous*

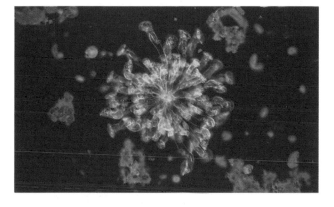

Pseudocoelomates

Pseudocoelomates are a group of tiny animals that are found almost everywhere. They have nerves but not a nervous system, and a digestive system not attached to the body by muscles. They include Nematoda (roundworms) and Rotifera (wheeled animals).

◀ *Rotifers make up most of the zooplankton that whales and other filter-feeders eat*

Coelomates

Coelomates are those who have a true body cavity in which all their organs are present. The inner part of the cavity is made of the digestive system and the outer part by the skin. Earthworms, insects, fish, and human beings are all coelomates. The phyla Annelida (earthworms) and Arthropoda also have a segmented body plan.

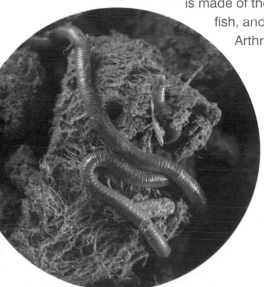

◀ *Earthworms eat and excrete their whole bodyweight in a day*

💡 Isn't It Amazing!

As they eat, earthworms enrich the soil with phosphorus and nitrogen, help water reach deep within the soil, and help the soil particles stick better to each other. Many farmers introduce earthworms to make soil fertile. This is called vermicomposting.

▲ *The presence of earthworms in soil indicates that it is fertile*

Reproduction

If both males and females are required to make a baby, the animal (or plant) is called sexual. Some animals and plants can reproduce by breaking off a part of their body—they are called asexual. Earthworms are hermaphrodites, that is, both male and female organs are present in the same animal.

Protostome Coelomates

Protostome is a word that scientists use to describe animals whose first body opening during their development becomes their mouth. They consist of many phyla, many of which were common over 500 million years ago but are now rare. However, two of them make up the most common animals on land and sea—Arthropods and Molluscs.

▲ *The phyla Tardigrada, Brachiopoda, and Bryozoa are made of tiny animals together called zooplankton*

 ## Arthropoda

Arthropods are the most abundant animals on land. The word 'arthropod' means 'jointed feet'. All the animals belonging to this group have jointed legs. They include:

- **Chelicerata:** Over 77,000 species including horseshoe crabs, spiders and sea-spiders
- **Crustacea:** Over 52,000 species including crabs, shrimp, prawns and krill
- **Myriapoda:** Over 13,000 species including centipedes and millipedes
- **Insecta:** Over 1 million species

Insecta are further divided into different groups of species.

▲ *Phylum Arthropoda includes 84 per cent of animals that live on land*

Species	Examples
Zygentoma	Silverfish
Archaeognatha	Jumping bristletails
Ephemeroptera	Mayflies
Odonata	Dragonflies
Plecoptera	Stoneflies
Blattodea	Cockroaches
Notoptera	Gladiator bugs
Phasmatoptera	Stick insects
Orthoptera	Grasshoppers
Dermaptera	Earwigs
Phthiraptera	Lice
Thysanoptera	Thrips
Hemiptera	True bugs
Homoptera	Cicadas
Megaloptera	Alderflies
Neuroptera	Lacewings
Mecoptera	Scorpionflies
Trichoptera	Caddisflies
Lepidoptera	Butterflies
Coleoptera	Beetles
Hymenoptera	Ants, bees and wasps
Diptera	True flies
Siphonaptera	Fleas

⊛ Incredible Individuals

Bees, ants, wasps, and termites are eusocial insects, that is, they are social insects amongst which some exist only to help their family, led by the queen. In bees, the workers have a unique dance language by which they tell other bees where to find nectar and pollen, which is what they eat. Karl von Frisch spent his lifetime trying to work out this fascinating language. He managed to translate for us the meaning of the waggle dance, where bees move and make the figure 8 to tell each other where the food is. He won the Nobel Prize for Physiology or Medicine for this research.

▶ *A worker who has found food will 'dance' to tell others where to look for it and how much food there is*

 ## Molluscs

Barring land snails, all animals of this phylum live in the sea. They are divided into shelled and shell-less animals. Those without shells come under the classes Aplacophora, Polyplacophora and Monoplacophora. Clams, mussels, oysters, scallops, shipworms, and cockles all make up class Bivalvia, which have two shells each. Limpets, snails, and slugs make up class Gastropoda, which have coiled shells. But the most notable is class Cephalopoda (nautiluses, cuttlefishes, squids and octopuses), famous for their long tentacles, ink glands, and movement by shooting jets of water.

▲ *Squid and cuttlefish grow to be among the largest invertebrates in the world*

Deuterostome Coelomates

Deuterostome is a word that scientists use to describe animals whose first body opening during development becomes their anus (the second one becomes the mouth). These were rare over 500 million years ago, but are now common, including Chaetognatha (arrow worms), Echinodermata (starfish), Hemichordata (acorn worms), and Chordata (fish, amphibians, reptiles, birds, and mammals).

◄ *The acorn worm, representative of the Hemichordates*

▼ *If a starfish loses a limb, the severed limb can become a whole new body, making a new starfish*

Echinoderms

▲ *Echinoderms are named for their spiny (echino) skins (derma), from the Greek language*

This phylum with 7,000 species includes starfish, brittle stars, sea urchins and sea cucumbers. Animals of this phylum do not move about much. Unlike other animals which have a left side and a right side (bilateral symmetry), they have radial symmetry, so they can have up to five sides. They are covered with a thick exoskeleton, so many fossils of this phylum have survived from ancient times.

Protochordates

These animals are a bridge between invertebrates and the animals that finally evolved into vertebrates. They include the Hemichordata—which are worm-like animals that breathe through gills, and the Urochordata—which have a notochord, a rod-like organ made of cartilage that forms a simple endoskeleton. But as they grow up, the animals lose their heads and notochord and develop a tunic around their body, through which they filter plankton to eat.

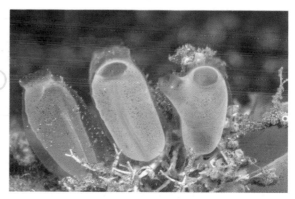

▲ *Tunicates show reverse development in the animal kingdom*

Cephalochordates

The Cephalochordata are members of phylum Chordata, but they do not have a backbone that encloses the spinal cord, so they are still considered to be invertebrates. Instead of a backbone, they have a notochord and muscles attached to them, but no circulatory system or heart.

Giving Birth

Except for mammals, all animals are oviparous, which means that they lay eggs to reproduce. Their eggs may be naked or covered with a thick shell made of calcium carbonate. The baby grows within the egg, and when it is ready to come out, the egg breaks. The baby is ready to come out when all its organs have fully developed. On the other hand, mammals are viviparous. It means that the baby develops inside its mother, who gives birth when she and the baby are fully ready. Some animals keep the eggs within the body until they hatch, like seahorses. These are called ovoviviparous.

Inside a Vertebrate

Vertebrates are what we think of when we say 'animal'. Elephants, ostriches, crocodiles, frogs, salmon, and sharks are all vertebrates. They deserve the title, for although they come late in the fossil record (just a few hundred million years ago), today they have become the most dominant animal life forms on the planet. They live almost everywhere, from the bottom of the oceans to the tops of mountains, from the ice sheets of Greenland to the raging desert of the Sahara. Yet, in spite of their diversity, their bodies are remarkably similar on the inside.

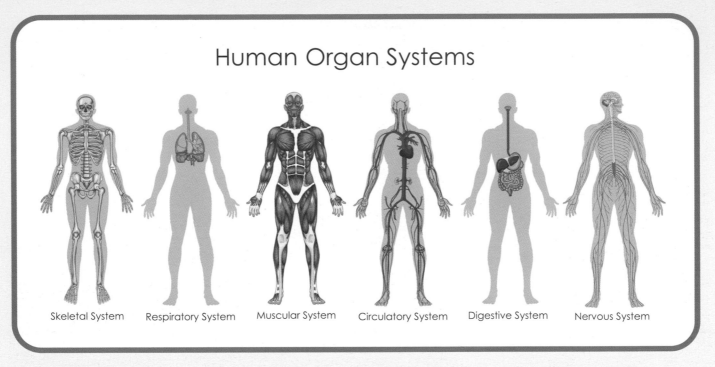

Human Organ Systems

Skeletal System   Respiratory System   Muscular System   Circulatory System   Digestive System   Nervous System

▲ *The name 'vertebrate' comes from the bones of the backbone (vertebra) that are common to all in this phylum*

Anatomy

All vertebrates are made of organ systems, in which different organs link up to form a functional part of the animal. Many organ systems have continued from our invertebrate ancestors but have become more complex. The digestive system and the nervous system are examples of this. The digestive system has many glands and has an alkaline environment, while the nervous system has a large brain and a prominent spinal cord.

Others have evolved anew, like the respiratory system and the skeletal system. Invertebrates depend on an exoskeleton to give them shape, while vertebrates are made of a new type of organ called the bone, to which the muscles attach. The respiratory system does not carry air directly to the tissues but depends on a new molecule called haemoglobin, which evolved with the vertebrates.

The circulatory system and the muscular system are a mix of old and new organ systems. The circulatory system does not just transport food, but also carries oxygen to the tissues from the gills or lungs. The muscular system is also more sophisticated, with the emergence of voluntary and involuntary muscles.

▲ *An elephant's spine is very unique. Instead of smooth, round spinal disks, they have sharp bony protrusions that extend upwards from their spine*

◄ *Fishes, amphibians, reptiles, birds and mammals are all vertebrates*

Heart

What makes vertebrates so successful? Some biologists say it is the evolution of the circulatory system that could now carry oxygen to the tissues, and a heart that keeps beating throughout life. As a regular supply of oxygen feeds the tissues, the animals get more energy to catch more food, and make more babies.

▲ Crocodiles are the only reptiles with four-chambered hearts

▶ A sea turtle has a backbone which is connected to its shell so the shell can never come off

Classification

Vertebrates are classified into two large groups. One group includes cold-blooded animals or poikilotherms, which cannot control their body temperature. The other group includes warm-blooded animals or homoiotherms, which can control their body temperature. The former group includes fish, amphibians, and reptiles, while the latter includes birds and mammals. Ever since they evolved, fish have dominated the seas, and the Age of the Fish is still ongoing there.

On land, the reptiles were the most dominant beings, culminating in the Age of Dinosaurs. Sadly, when a comet crashed into Earth 65 million years ago, it raised a dust cloud all over Earth so thick that it blocked the Sun and thousands of species became extinct, including many plants and dinosaurs. A new kind of animal became dominant on land and its age still continues. It is the Age of Mammals.

★ Incredible Individuals

Galen was a Roman doctor who studied the anatomy of animals by dissecting them. As dissecting human beings was not allowed by the Roman government, he dissected barbary apes instead, believing that their anatomy was very similar to ours.

▲ Galen, along with Hippocrates and Avicenna, is one of the three fathers of modern medicine

▼ Vertebrates are the most successful phyla of animals after Arthropods

▲ Did you know that birds descended from dinosaurs?

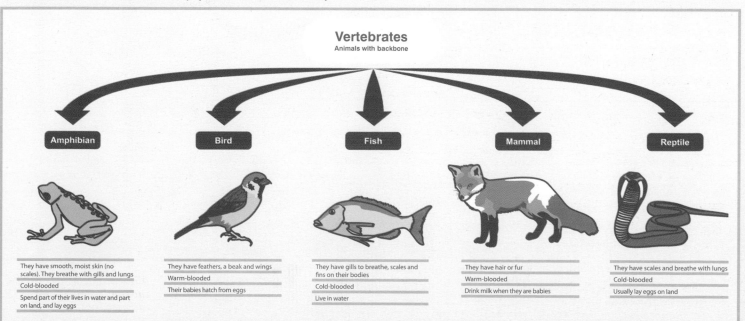

Vertebrates
Animals with backbone

Amphibian	Bird	Fish	Mammal	Reptile
They have smooth, moist skin (no scales). They breathe with gills and lungs	They have feathers, a beak and wings	They have gills to breathe, scales and fins on their bodies	They have hair or fur	They have scales and breathe with lungs
Cold-blooded	Warm-blooded	Cold-blooded	Warm-blooded	Cold-blooded
Spend part of their lives in water and part on land, and lay eggs	Their babies hatch from eggs	Live in water	Drink milk when they are babies	Usually lay eggs on land

Poikilotherms

Poikilotherm is a word used by scientists to describe animals who cannot control their body temperature. Though they are also called cold-blooded animals, their body temperature depends on the environment they are in. Because of this, most poikilotherms live in the tropics and warmer climates. Others that live in colder climates have various adaptations. For example, fish in Antarctic waters have special proteins that stop their blood from freezing. Others adapt by going into **hibernation**, during which they burrow themselves deep underground to save body heat, as the temperatures come close to freezing.

Jawless Fish (Agnatha)

This group includes lampreys and hagfishes. These animals do not have jaws, but a circular mouth instead.

Cartilaginous Fish (Chondrichthyes)

This class has 940 species including sharks, skates, stingrays, and sawfishes. Their skeletons are made entirely of cartilage, not bone.

▶ *Did you know that sharks' teeth never stop growing throughout their lives?*

▲ *Many fish live in coral reefs, which gives them safe places to lay eggs and spawn*

Bony Fish (Osteichthyes)

These make up 33,000 of the 34,000 known species of fish. They include everything from salmon and seahorses, to eels and goldfish. Fish do not lay fertilised eggs like all other chordates. Instead, the female lays unfertilised eggs in a secure place (like under a rock), and the male 'spawns' over them. In seahorses, the female lays eggs in a special pouch that the male has, and the eggs develop in it till they hatch.

Amphibians

The word 'amphibian' is of Greek origin and means 'double life'. That is true of class Amphibia, for they are almost different creatures on land and in water. The living orders of class Amphibia are Gymnophiona (snake-like caecilians, of which 170 species are known), Anura (frogs and toads, with over 5,400 species recorded) and Caudata (salamanders and newts, with over 550 species). They live mostly in the tropics and in various other habitats including rainforest trees, deserts, ponds, and rivers. They can breathe underwater through their skin, and on land through lungs.

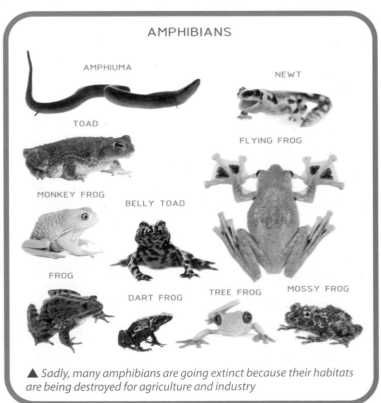

AMPHIBIANS

AMPHIUMA

NEWT

TOAD

FLYING FROG

MONKEY FROG

BELLY TOAD

FROG

DART FROG

TREE FROG

MOSSY FROG

▲ *Sadly, many amphibians are going extinct because their habitats are being destroyed for agriculture and industry*

Reptiles

Class Reptilia is made of four living orders: order Testudinidae (tortoises, terrapins and turtles), order Crocodilia (crocodiles, alligators and caimans), order Sphenodontidae (tuataras), and order Squamata (lizards and snakes). It also has many extinct orders which make some of the world's most famous fossils—the dinosaurs, which include true dinosaurs, ichthyosaurs, archosaurs, pterodactyls, plesiosaurs, and mesosaurs.

Crocodiles have four-chambered hearts, which separate deoxygenated blood from oxygenated blood, while the rest have only three-chambered hearts. This makes them less sluggish than the rest.

▲ Reptiles range in size from 14mm (Nano-chameleon) to 8m (Saltwater Crocodile)

Dinosaurs

Dinosaurs can be divided into two main groups according to the shape of their hips: Saurischia (lizard-hips) and Ornithischia (bird-hips). Ornithischia includes Cerapoda (such as the genus *Triceratops*) and Thyreophora (such as the genus *Stegosaurus*). Saurischia were made of Sauropodomorpha, which includes the genus *Brontosaurus*, and Theropoda, which includes the famous *Tyrannosaurus rex* and the only surviving dinosaurs—birds.

▲ People once thought that dinosaurs were sluggish and cold-blooded

☀ Isn't It Amazing!

Some scientists think that *Argentinosaurus* may have been the world's largest dinosaur, though no complete skeletons have been found. If confirmed, it would be the world's largest terrestrial animal, weighing 100 tonnes.

★ Incredible Individuals

Mary Anning (1799–1847) discovered many of the world's famous fossils near the seaside town of Lyme Regis. She discovered ichthyosaurs, plesiosaurs, pterodactyls, and many others. But she got no credit for her discoveries, which instead went to male scientists.

▼ The tongue-twister 'She sells seashells on the seashore' was written in honour of Mary Anning

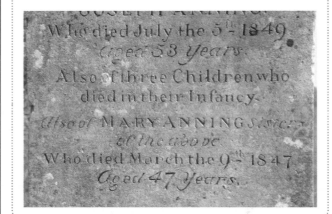

▲ Argentinosaurus is still half as big as the world's largest animal ever—the blue whale

Homoiotherms

The vertebrates who can control their body temperature are divided into two large classes. These are the birds (or aves) and the mammals. Mammals are in turn of three kinds—the egg-layers, the pouch-holders, and the true mammals. The common feature of all mammals is the mammary gland, which produces milk for their children. All other animals must find their own food from the day they are born, although in many species their parents will bring it to them for the first few months.

◀ *Modern research says that all birds evolved from a group of dinosaurs called the theropods*

Order	Examples
Passeriformes	Songbirds
Apodiformes	Hummingbirds
Piciformes	Woodpeckers
Charadriiformes	Gulls
Pteroclidiformes	Sandgrouse
Psittaciformes	Parrots
Columbiformes	Doves
Falconiformes	Raptors
Galliformes	Fowl
Gruiformes	Cranes
Procellariiformes	Albatrosses
Coraciiformes	Kingfishers
Strigiformes	Owls
Musophagiformes	Turacos
Cuculiformes	Cuckoos
Anseriformes	Waterfowl
Ciconiiformes	Storks
Caprimulgiformes	Nightjars
Pelecaniformes	Pelicans
Tinamiformes	Tinamous
Trogoniformes	Trogons
Podicipediformes	Grebes
Sphenisciformes	Penguins
Gaviiformes	Loons
Coliiformes	Mousebirds
Struthioniformes	Ostriches

Birds

Birds of a feather flock together, goes the old saying. For birds, this is quite literally true, as feathers (and beaks) are the common feature of all birds. Feathers help birds stay warm, not get wet, and, of course, to fly. Flightless birds like ostriches, emus, and kiwis make up the Palaeognathae, while the rest make up the Neognathae. There are over 9,000 species in 26 orders, of which songbirds (order Passeriformes) make 59 per cent of all birds.

Mammals

The 5,000 species of class Mammalia can be broadly divided into three types. Monotremes are the only mammals that lay eggs, and are found only in Australia. **Marsupials** include kangaroos, wallabies, koalas, and opossums. These mammals are found in Australia and South America. The placental or true mammals make up the rest, from the tiniest rodents and bats, to the largest elephants and whales. The females of

▲ *Marsupials give birth to live babies but carry them in a pouch (the marsupium) outside their bodies*

these species carry their babies inside their bodies in an amniotic sac. The baby is fed from the placenta and the umbilical cord, through which food, vitamins, minerals, and antibodies from the mother's blood enters the baby's blood. When the baby is finally ready to come into the world, the placenta breaks. The umbilical cord soon falls off, leaving a small mark called the navel or belly button. Rodents make up 42 per cent of all mammals, followed by bats, who make up 20 per cent.

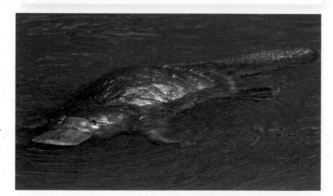

▲ *Platypus were discovered in the 18th century by European explorers, but experts in Europe thought these were frauds, made of the body parts of various animals.*

Order	Examples
Tachyglossa	Echidnas
Platypoda	Platypus
Diprotodontia	Kangaroos
Dasyuromorphia	Carnivorous marsupials
Peramelemorphia	Bilbies
Notoryctemorphia	Marsupial moles
Microbiotheria	Monito del monte
Didelphimorphia	Opossums
Paucituberculata	Shrew-opossums
Rodentia	Rodents
Chiroptera	Bats
Soricomorpha	Shrews
Afrosoricida	Tenrecs
Erinaceomorpha	Hedgehogs
Primates	Monkeys
Artiodactyla	Cattle
Cetacea	Whales
Perissodactyla	Rhinos
Hyracoidea	Hyraxes
Sirenia	Manatees
Proboscidea	Elephants
Tubulidentata	Aardvark
Carnivora	Cats
Lagomorpha	Rabbits
Cingulata	Armadillos
Pilosa	Anteaters
Scandentia	Tree-shrews
Macroscelidea	Elephant-shrews
Pholidota	Pangolins

In Real Life

You know that the blue whale is the world's largest mammal, but which is the smallest? It is the bumblebee bat of Thailand, which grows to only 33 mm.

▼ Did you know that female blue whales are larger than males?

Incredible Individuals

The famous biologists Jane Goodall, Dianne Fossey, and Biruté Galdikas were picked by Louis Leakey to study chimpanzees, gorillas, and orangutans to better understand how human beings evolved.

▶ Jane Goodall has been working with chimpanzees for over 60 years, and her discovery that they make and use tools was groundbreaking

▲ Orangutans, gorillas, chimpanzees, and human beings are together called the great apes

Habitats

Habitat is the scientific word for the immediate environment in which a living organism can survive and reproduce. It includes the climate, food, terrain, predators, and the social group of males and females of its own species. Every organism is said to be adapted to its habitat, otherwise it will be driven extinct by other organisms that are better adapted. Look at this table and guess which animal we are talking about:

Habitat	Adaptation
Flat terrain with trees here and there	Walking on two flat feet with hands that can grip
A diet of fruits, roots, eggs and small animals	Teeth with small canines and square molars
A tropical climate that does not get too cold	Skin with hair but not fur, rich in melanin
Tool use and climbing	Opposable thumbs with power grip
Hunting	Binocular, colour vision
Throwing	Strong biceps and triceps
Complex social organisation	Large brain

All of this points to a primate whose natural habitat is the savanna of East Africa—human beings! Indeed, without cultural adaptations like making tools and wearing clothes, human beings cannot live in any other habitat naturally.

◀ *Olduvai Gorge, Tanzania, where our species is believed to have evolved*

Ecological Niche

The habitat to which each organism is fully adapted is called its ecological niche. Human beings have adapted themselves to a number of ecological niches, so they can live in Tibet, the Netherlands, Patagonia, Tanzania, and more. But most plants and animals can only live in one niche. For example, butterflies can only live in places where the weather is not too cold and lots of angiosperms grow because they live off the nectar of flowers; while the albatross makes the open sky its niche, where it can fly for days together.

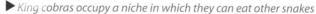
▶ *King cobras occupy a niche in which they can eat other snakes*

In Real Life

Many people have reported seeing an ancient animal (like a dinosaur, a water snake, or a dragon) in the Loch Ness in Scotland. But we know from studies of the habitat that nothing so large could live and breed there.

◀ *Loch Ness is too small to have enough food and resting space for a creature like the supposed Loch Ness Monster*

Island Biogeography

The theory of island biogeography says that if a species of a small animal got isolated on an island, it could grow to a bigger size since it escapes its predators. On the other hand, a species of a big animal will get smaller because it does not get enough to eat.

Isn't It Amazing!

Not many people thought that the theory of island biogeography applied to human beings until the discovery of the bones of an extinct species of humans on the island of Flores, Indonesia in 2003.

▲ *Under 4 feet high, Homo floresiensis remains were nicknamed hobbits*

Parasitism and Commensalism

Parasitism is a niche in which one organism lives off another (the host) without the other benefitting at all. Many disease-causing bacteria, fungi, leeches, lampreys, and even plants are parasitic. Commensals are similar to parasites but do not cause harm to their hosts.

▲ *Banyan trees start out as parasites of other trees, before growing their own roots*

Symbiosis

Symbiosis is a niche in which two organisms grow together and benefit each other. Lichens are an example of this. Another example is the bacteria in your large intestine. They give you vitamins, and you keep them safe.

Extinction

Biological extinction happens when too few members of a species are left for them to make enough babies for a sustainable population. Physical extinction occurs when the last individual of the species dies.

▶ *The dodo, native to Mauritius, went extinct after the Dutch landed on the island and killed most of the birds*

▼ *Some ants live symbiotically with aphids. They keep them safe in exchange for a sugary drink the aphids make*

Word Check

Chemistry

Antacid: A chemical that counters the action of acid in the stomach.

Beta Particle: A weightless, negatively charged subatomic particle.

Centrifuge: A machine used to separate undissolved solids from a liquid by spinning.

Chemical Energy: The energy stored in the form of a chemical bond between the atoms of a molecule.

Chemical Reaction: An exchange of electrons between two elements or compounds.

Damp: A material that reduces the rate of chemical reactions, especially burning.

Fertiliser: A chemical that is added to soil to provide additional nutrients to plants.

Fossil Fuel: Fuel made from the remains of plants and animals that died millions of years ago.

Hydroxyl Ion: An ion made of an oxygen atom and a hydrogen atom, with a net negative charge, that is made by alkalis.

Ingot: A block of pure metal.

Interstellar Gas: Gas that exists in space and is not part of stars or the atmosphere of planets.

Kiln: A special kind of oven in which ceramics are hardened.

Monomer: An organic compound that can react with its own molecules to form a polymer.

Nitre: A common name for potassium nitrate, used in making explosives.

Nuclear Fusion: A nuclear reaction in which the nuclei of atoms merge to form new elements.

Nuclear Reaction: A reaction by which the nuclei of atoms give out energy by splitting apart.

Oil Rig: A facility for pumping out petroleum from the seabed.

Oil Well: A facility for pumping out petroleum from the ground.

Orbital: The space in which an electron revolves around the nucleus of its atom.

Ore: A mineral from which metal can be extracted on a large scale.

Pascal: The unit for measuring pressure, defined as one Newton of force applied over an area of one square metre.

Patina: Corrosion of a metal that leaves a coloured compound on its surface.

Period: A row of the periodic table in which all elements have a common outer shell.

Photosynthesis: The creation of glucose in living organisms from water and carbon dioxide, which stores energy from sunlight.

Polymer: A chemical made of repeating units of a simpler compound called a monomer.

Proteins: Compounds made by linking together different kinds of amino acids in a long chain.

Radioactivity or Radioactive Decay: The process by which a giant nucleus gives out an alpha or beta particle.

Reactivity: The ease with which an element or compound reacts with other chemicals.

Respiration: The breakdown of glucose in living organisms to water and carbon dioxide, which releases energy.

Rust: Corrosion of iron in damp air that leaves brown iron oxide on its surface.

Salt: A compound formed by the reaction of an acid with a base.

Saturated: An organic compound in which each carbon atom is bound to four different atoms.

Solvent: A substance that dissolves another substance.

Supersaturation: A solution which has crossed the maximum amount a substance will dissolve in it.

Tarnish: Corrosion of silver that leaves black silver sulphide on its surface.

Unsaturated: An organic compound in which at least two carbon atoms are bound to each other by two or three covalent bonds.

Valency: The number of electrons an atom can spare for chemical reactions.

Viscosity: The resistance a substance offers to flowing.

Electricity & Electronics

Anode: The part of a cell that generates anions (gives off electrons).

Anode reaction: The chemical reaction in a cell that gives off electrons.

Application: A set of programmes that helps a computer to do a certain task.

Cathode: The part of a cell that generates cations (needs electrons).

Cathode reaction: The chemical reaction in a cell that takes up electrons.

Chip: A tiny plate of semiconducting material onto which an integrated circuit is printed.

Computer language: A set of codes in which computer algorithms can be written.

Conduction: The passage of electricity through a material.

Current: The movement of electrons across an electric potential.

Current electricity: Electricity that moves across an electric potential.

Diamagnetic: Materials that cannot be magnetised at all.

Diaphragm: A thin membrane that vibrates when sound waves fall on it.

Dielectric: A substance that does not allow current to pass.

Diode: An electronic device that allows current to pass in one direction only.

Electric charge: An excess or lack of electrons in a material. It is measured in Coulombs.

Electric motor: A device that converts electrical energy into mechanical energy through induction.

Electricity grid: A network of electric cables and power plants that supplies power to a city or country.

Electrode: A device that conducts electricity into a circuit (anode), or away from it (cathode).

Electromagnetism: An electric field created by a moving magnet, or a magnetic field created by a moving electron.

Ferromagnetic: Materials that can be magnetised permanently.

Gate current : An additional current in a transistor that increases or decreases its conductivity.

Hardware: The physical parts that make up a computer or other smart devices.

Induction generator: A device that produces electricity by magnetic induction.

Magnetism: A condition in some metals in which the electrons move in the same direction.

Memory chip: A semiconductor chip used for saving data in magnetic form.

Miniaturisation: The process by which digital sensors and displays are made smaller to reflect the analogue world.

N-dope: A non-metallic dope added to a semiconductor to make it relatively negatively charged.

Nuclear reaction: A reaction by which the nuclei of atoms give out energy by splitting apart.

Operating system: The set of programmes that are needed to run a computer smoothly.

P-dope: A metallic dope added to a semiconductor to make it relatively positively charged.

P-n junction: A diode made by putting together small crystals of p-doped and n-doped semiconductors together.

Parallel circuit: A circuit in which various devices are connected parallel to each other.

Paramagnetic: Materials that can be magnetised for a short while

Pixel: The digital unit of space used to convert analogue images into digital ones.

Quantum Theory: The fundamental theory of physics that electromagnetic forces are made of discrete particles that may be charged (e.g. electrons) or not (e.g. photons).

Semiconductor: A material that allows only some electricity to pass through it.

Series circuit: A circuit in which various devices are connected one after another.

Software: The operating system and applications used in a computer or smartphone.

Static electricity: Electricity that is created by a build-up of charge.

Subscriber Identity Module (SIM): A silicon chip that carries a code identifying a user, which is added to the mobile signal during each call.

Super hot water: Water that has been heated above 100°C, but has not turned to steam because of extreme pressure.

Turbine: A device rotated by flowing liquid or gas.

Volcanism: Release of energy, mostly as heat, from within the earth.

Force and Movement

Adhesion: The forces that pull atoms or molecules of two substances together.

Angular Velocity: The velocity with which an object traverses an arc of a circle.

Buoyancy: The force exerted by a fluid resisting the force of gravity.

Coefficient of Kinetic Friction: A measure of how much force will be needed to overcome friction between two substances moving in opposite directions.

Coefficient of Static Friction: A measure of how much force will be needed to overcome friction between two substances resting on each other.

Dark Matter: Matter whose particles are not organised into atoms, so they cannot interact with photons.

Density: The mass of an object in a unit volume.

Displacement: The difference between the initial and final locations of an object.

Drag: Friction caused by an object moving through a fluid.

Efficiency: The fraction of the input energy that a system delivers as work.

Energy: The ability of a system to do work.

Experiences: The effect of an external force upon an object.

External Work: The work done by a system on the environment.

Friction: The resistance offered to motion by electromagnetic attraction between objects.

Friction Force: The force needed to overcome friction.

Geocentric Theory: The theory that the Earth is at the centre of the Solar System.

Gradient: The ratio of the rise of a plane and its horizontal length.

Gravitational Waves: Disturbances in space-time caused by the movement of astronomical bodies.

Heliocentric Theory: The theory that the Sun is at the centre of the Solar System.

Inertia: An object's innate resistance to a force acting on it.

Internal Work: The work done within a system.

Jet: A fast-moving fluid which generates thrust because of its velocity.

Kinetic Energy: The energy a system possesses because of its motion.

Lattice: The pattern of arrangements of atoms, ions or molecules in a crystalline solid.

Lift: A force exerted by a fluid at right angles to an object moving through it.

Light Matter: Matter whose particles are organised into nuclei, electrons, and atoms, which can interact with photons.

Mass: The amount of inertia in a system at rest, proportional to the number of particles in it.

Mechanics: The science of motion and forces.

Momentum: The amount of inertia in a body due to its mass and velocity.

Normal Force: The force exerted by a solid resisting a substance pushing against it.

Orbital Period: The time taken by an object to go around another object (for instance, a planet around the Sun or a satellite around a planet).

Order of Magnitude: The approximation of a measure in units of ten: tens, hundreds, thousands, etc.

Potential Energy: The energy available in a system for conversion to work.

Possession: The physical attributes innate to an object.

Propagation: The forward movement of an oscillating particle.

Relative Density: The ratio of the density of a substance to the density of a reference substance.

Revolution: Circular motion of an object about another object.

Rotation: Circular motion of an object around its own axis.

Scalar: A physical measure with magnitude but no direction.

Specific Gravity: The ratio of the density of a substance to the density of water.

Strain: The resistance a solid offers when pulled.

Thrust: The reaction force offered by the ground when something pushes against it.

Van der Waals Force: The attraction between atoms and molecules of a substance due to minor electric charges on them (electric dipole).

Vector: A physical measure with magnitude and direction.

Velocity: The rate at which a body moves in one direction.

Wave: The path of a moving, oscillating particle.

Weight: The force on a body because of its mass and the Earth's gravitational pull.

Future Science and Technology

Artificial Intelligence: Intelligence demonstrated by a machine, not a living organism.

Association: A method of learning in which one event is linked to another.

Automaton (plural Automata): A machine that does its work without a human operator. All robots are automata.

Birth Defects: Handicaps in the body or its functions due to errors in development.

Blockchain: A set of digital databases in which each unit of data is called a block. New units are added to the end of each database like a chain of blocks.

Carbon Sequestration: The removal of carbon dioxide from the atmosphere to stop global warming.

Climate Sceptic: A person who does not believe that climate change is being caused by human actions.

Cloning: The science of creating an identical copy of a living organism.

Creative Destruction: The replacement of low-skilled jobs by higher skilled jobs due to progress made by technology.

Data Centre: A place where data from various parts of a city is saved.

Deductive Reasoning: A decision based on current circumstances as well as memory.

Designer Baby: A human whose genome has been modified artificially to eliminate disease traits or to enhance intelligence, strength, etc.

Developmental Biology: The science that studies how an organism develops from a single cell, and how differentiation of tissues happens.

Differentiation: The process by which stem cells turn themselves into other kinds of cells.

Embryo: The earliest stage of a developing organism.

Encryption Key: A computer code that is used to identify the user and make their transactions secret.

Ethics: The knowledge of absolute rights and wrongs and how to determine them.

Fraternal Twins: Siblings born at the same time who are not genetically identical.

Gene Editing: A genetic engineering method to replace 'bad' mutant DNA with 'good' DNA.

Genetic Disease: A disease caused by changes in a person's DNA, because of which their bodies don't work correctly.

Genetic Engineering: Modification of DNA to improve crops or fight diseases.

Global Warming: A rise in the average temperature of the Earth because of the accumulation of carbon dioxide.

Gravity Assist: The speeding up of a spacecraft as it is attracted by the gravity of a planet. Also called the slingshot effect.

Greenhouse Effect: Heating of air caused by the absorption of the Sun's heat by greenhouse gases.

Greenhouse Gas: A gas, like carbon dioxide or nitrogen dioxide, that absorbs heat from the Sun, which would otherwise have been lost by radiation.

Healing: The body's way of repairing wounded tissue by getting stem cells to turn themselves into necessary cells.

Identical Twins: Siblings who are genetically identical.

Inductive Reasoning: A decision based on the memory of past actions.

Instinct: Automatic behaviour by an organism not based on memory.

Insulin: A biochemical produced by our bodies that makes sure that sugar from our food reaches our cells.

Language: A set of sounds whose meanings are shared by a group of people, organised into words and sentences.

Mutation: A change in a person's DNA.

Rote: A method of learning by repeating the thing to be learned till it is memorised.

Solar Wind: A 'wind' made of hydrogen ions that are emitted from the Sun.

Surrogate: A female mammal who is pregnant with a baby that is not hers.

Synapses: Junctions between nerve cells.

Trait: The physical and behavioural characters of an individual that depend on their genes.

Visual Recognition: The ability of a machine to recognise things in front of them, by comparing them to images stored in their memory.

Light and Energy

Biconvex Lens: A lens in which both surfaces are curved outwards, as in a magnifying glass.

Chemical Energy: This is the energy stored in chemical bonds between atoms.

Colour: The way your brain distinguishes each wavelength of visible light.

Colour Blindness: The inability of some humans to distinguish light of certain wavelengths.

Colour Theory: The theory that all colours can be derived by mixing the three primary colours.

Combustion: The reaction of some substances with oxygen when they are heated.

Concave Lens: A lens in which one or both surfaces are curved inwards.

Convection Current: The circular movement of atoms or molecules in a liquid or gas caused by the heating of one side.

Convex Lens: A lens in which one or both surfaces are curved outwards.

Detector: An electronic device that creates a current when an electromagnetic wave falls on it.

Efficiency: The ability of an engine to convert the maximum input energy into work.

Electric Charge: A property of matter that makes it react to an electromagnetic field.

Electromagnetic Energy: The energy of a moving electric charge or magnetic field.

Electromagnetic Spectrum: The range of all wavelengths of photons, including gamma-rays, X-rays, ultraviolet light, visible light, infra-red waves, microwaves and radio waves.

Frame: A single still picture in a motion picture reel.

Freezing/Melting Point: The temperature at which a liquid becomes solid while losing energy, and a solid becomes liquid while gaining energy.

Gamma Rays: Very high energy electromagnetic waves with wavelengths smaller than X-rays, emitted from nuclear reactions.

Heat Energy: This is the energy stored in the movement of atoms.

Image: The representation of an object formed by reflection from a mirror or refraction from a lens or prism.

Infinite Order: The state of matter at Absolute Zero, where the atoms or molecules have zero freedom to vibrate.

Infrared (IR) Waves: Low energy electromagnetic waves with wavelengths smaller than visible light but longer than microwaves.

Ionising Radiation: Electronic waves that can remove electrons when they hit an atom and turn them into positively charged ions.

Lens: A block of glass through which light is made to pass to refract it.

Mechanical Energy: The energy that we see in the movement of objects.

Mechanical Waves: Non-electromagnetic waves made by the movement of atoms and molecules.

Melting: The phenomenon by which a solid becomes liquid.

Microscope: A device to make a tiny thing look much larger than it is.

Mirror: A surface that reflects light.

Motion Picture: An optical illusion that tricks the eye into perceiving motion by showing still pictures at a very fast rate.

Non-ionising Radiation: Electronic waves that cannot remove electrons when they hit an atom.

Optical Magnification: The ratio of the size of an image to the size of the object creating it.

Optical Resolution: The smallest distance between two objects that can make them appear as separate images through a lens.

Periscope: A device to make an image of an object that cannot be seen directly.

Power: A numerical value that indicates how far a person's eye's focal point is from their retina. Power zero indicates perfect vision.

Pulse: An electromagnetic wave delivered for a very small period of time, used in radios and lasers.

Quantised: The property of all energy to be made of tiny units called quanta

Radio Waves: Very low energy electromagnetic waves with wavelengths longer than microwaves.

Stereoscopic or 3D Vision: The ability of the brain to perceive the depth of the image by combining the images of the retinas of both eyes.

Subtractive or CMYK Colour Mixing: Obtaining reflected colours by mixing two or more secondary colours.

Telescope: A device to magnify the image of an object that is very far away.

Thermodynamics: The science of understanding how energy can be converted to work.

Van der Waals Forces: Weak forces that hold the atoms or molecules of a substance together in liquid state.

Wavelength: The distance a photon moves while completing a single vibration.

X-rays: High energy electromagnetic waves with wavelengths smaller than ultraviolet light but more than gamma rays.

Living Things

Abyssopelagic zone: The layer of the ocean 4,000 metres and below up to the ocean floor.

Antibiotics: The chemicals made by fungi to protect themselves from bacteria.

Asexual spore: A reproductive cell made by fungi and some plants without sexual reproduction.

Bathypelagic zone: The layer of the ocean that starts from 1,000 metres from the surface and extends to 4,000 metres below the surface.

Cell membrane: It is the outer covering of a cell.

Cell wall: It is an extra covering outside the cell membrane.

Chlorophyll: It is a chemical that is present in all green plants that makes photosynthesis possible.

Climatic zones: It is a region of the Earth, including the land and the ocean, where the climate is the same.

Cytoplasm: It is the jelly that makes up most of the cell. It has water, proteins, fats and organelles in it.

Embryo: The youngest stage in the life of a multicellular organism.

Endemic: Any living organism that grows in only one place and nowhere else.

Epipelagic zone: The layer of the ocean that starts from the surface and extends to 200 metres.

Evergreen: Plants which never shed all their leaves at the same time.

Evolution: The process by which one species transforms into another, often over thousands of years.

Fertilisation: The process by which two sexual gametes unite to form an embryo.

Fibrous roots: They are threadlike roots that grow from the base of the stem.

Gametophyte: It is the generation of a pteridophyte that makes sexual gametes.

Genetic code: The set of rules by which information encoded in genetic material (DNA or RNA sequences) is translated into proteins (amino acid sequences) by living cells.

Germination: The process by which a seed or spore gives rise to a fungus or plant

Gymnosperm: It is a plant that makes naked seeds.

Habitable zone: It is the distance from a star where a planet can sustain life.

Habitat: It is the natural home or environment of any living organism.

Hibernation: The period in winter during which some animals sleep to preserve body heat.

Living fossil: An organism which was abundant in a previous era but is now reduced to a small number of individuals.

Marine beings: Any living thing that lives in the sea.

Marsupials: Animals that carry their babies in a pouch on their body.

Mass extinction: These were periods when many different life species suddenly went extinct.

Mesopelagic zone: The layer of the ocean that starts from 200 metres from the surface and reaches up to 100 metres from the surface.

Multicellular organism: A living thing made of more than one cell.

Mycelium: The main body of a fungus from which root-like rhizomes and fruiting bodies (sporangia) branch off.

Mycorrhiza: It is a symbiotic association between a fungus and the roots of a vascular host plant.

Natural selection: The process by which a living thing adapted to its conditions survives and reproduces, while others that cannot adapt go extinct.

Organism: It is the scientific name for any living thing.

Pelagic: It is any biome that is present in the ocean.

Photosynthesis: It is the process by which green plants make food from carbon dioxide and water in the presence of sunlight.

Prokaryote: It is any living thing whose cells do not have a nucleus.

Pteridophytes: It is a group of plants that has a vascular structure but produces no flowers or seeds.

Rainforests: They are dense forests in tropical areas which receive regular and heavy rainfall.

Savanna: It is a biome in the tropical climatic zone which has strong winds and warm temperatures, where grain can be cultivated.

Sporangia: The part of a fungus and some other living things where spores are made.

Symbiont: A living thing that lives closely with another species and protects it or makes food for it.

Taiga: A climatic zone which has very cold temperatures, marked by forests of coniferous trees.

Taproot: A primary root that grows vertically downward and gives off small lateral roots.

Taxon (plural: taxa): A group of any rank, such as a species, family or class, in the classification according to taxonomy.

Tidally locked: When a moon's rotation and revolution have the same period, it is said to be tidally locked to its planet.

Tundra: A climatic zone which has such cold temperatures that it is covered by huge icesheets.

Zoologist: A person who studies animals.

a: above, b: below/ bottom, c: centre, f: far, l: left, r: right, t: top, bg: background

Cover

Inside

Shutterstock: Front: Andrey Suslov; Pixfiction; Mega Pixel; bluebay; Alexander Kolomietz; NosorogUA; Mimka; Nerthuz; abramsdesign; Tatiana Popova; Bjoern Wylezich; Berents; Vladyslav Starozhylov; Phonlamai Photo **Back:** mipan; AlexLMX; zentilia; Vector FX; GalapagosPhoto; Gino Santa Maria; New Africa; lovelyday12;

Chemistry

Inside

Shutterstock: 3b/Romolo Tavani; 4&5c/Vector FX; 4b/Szasz-Fabian Ilka Erika; 5tr/everything possible; 5bg/pro500; 5br/amirage; 6&7 c/ollomy; 7bl/Nasky; 8tr/Fouad A. Saad; 8b/tony mills; 9tr/Marc Rossmann; 9cl/PHIL LENOIR; 9br/Standret; 10tl/Okrasiuk; 10cr/Serenethos; 10b/Dmitri Ma; 11tr/Steve Cymro; 11cr/Yuttasak Chuntarothai; 11bc/ Paul Hakimata Photography; 13tr/VectorMine; 14bl/Serj Malomuzh; 14&15c/Designua; 15tr/Theeraphong; 15br1/Alhovik; 15br/MilanB; 16cl/Crevis; 16br/VectorMine; 17tr/ ppart; 17br/ilozavr; 18cl/mipan; 18br/abramsdesign; 19cr/White Space Illustrations; 19br/Michal Ludwiczak; 20cl/udaix; 20bg/Alena Ohneva; 20cr/Kazakova Maryia; 21tr/ fujilovers; 21bl/danylyukk1; 22bc/YURY STROK; 22br/Chatchawal Kittirojana; 23tl1/StudioMolekuul; 23tl2/StudioMolekuul; 23tl3/StudioMolekuul; 23tl4/StudioMolekuul; 23tc1/ StudioMolekuul; 23tc2/StudioMolekuul; 23tc3/StudioMolekuul; 23tr1/StudioMolekuul; 23br2/StudioMolekuul; 23b/xpixel; 24cl/Lakeview Images; 24b/SAM THOMAS A; 25tl/ StudioMolekuul; 25cr/raigvi; 25b/svekloid; 26tr/Bjoern Wylezich; 26cl/spyarm; 26cr/Erkipauk; 26b/Andrey Lobachev; 27tr/Oleksandr_Delyk; 27cl/Kaarthikeyan.SM; 27cr/ Shestakov Dmytro; 28tr/Zerbor; 28b/Mohammad Fahmi Abu Bakar; 29tl/Mari-Leaf; 29tr/Josep Curto; 29cr1/StudioMolekuul; 29cr1/StudioMolekuul; 29bl/FeyginFoto; 29br/ Manusphoto; 30cr/MPanchenko; 30bl/Jurik Peter; 31tr/Rich Carey; 31cr/metamorworks; 31b/Orakunya

Wikimedia Commons: 5cr/File:Helium-Bohr.svg//wikimedia commons; 6br/File:Biographies of Scientific Men 167 Mendeleev.jpg/File:Biographies of Scientific Men.djvu, Public domain, via Wikimedia Commons/wikimedia commons; 12cl/udaix; 13br/File:Dalton John desk.jpg/Henry Roscoe (author), William Henry Worthington (engraver), and Joseph Allen (painter), Public domain, via Wikimedia Commons/wikimedia commons; 17cr///wikimedia commons; 18tl/File:Nuclear fusion.gif/Someone, CC BY-SA 3.0 <https://creativecommons.org/licenses/by-sa/3.0>, via Wikimedia Commons/wikimedia commons; 19bc/File:SeoulLights.jpg/Chitrapa at English Wikipedia, Public domain, via Wikimedia Commons/wikimedia commons; 20br/File:Carl Wilhelm Scheele.png/Ida Falander (1842—1927), Public domain, via Wikimedia Commons/wikimedia commons; 21bc/File:Priestley.jpg/English: Ellen Sharples (1769 - 1849)한국어: 엘렌 샤플즈 (1769 - 1849), Public domain, via Wikimedia Commons/wikimedia commons; 21br/File:Lavoisier 1877.png/Unknown authorUnknown author, Public domain, via Wikimedia Commons/wikimedia commons; 22cl/File:Diamond and graphite2.jpg/Diamond_and_graphite.jpg: User:Itubderivative work: Materialscientist, CC BY-SA 3.0 <http://creativecommons.org/licenses/by-sa/3.0/>, via Wikimedia Commons/wikimedia commons; 22tr/File:Electron shell 006 Carbon.svg/Pumbaa (original work Greg Robson), CC BY-SA 2.0 UK <https://creativecommons.org/licenses/by-sa/2.0/uk/deed.en>, via Wikimedia Commons/ wikimedia commons; 25bl/File:Pottenbakkersschijf.JPG/Oriel, Public domain, via Wikimedia Commons/wikimedia commons; 30br/Unknown authorUnknown author, Public domain, via Wikimedia Commons/Unknown authorUnknown author, Public domain, via Wikimedia Commons/wikimedia commons

Electricity & Electronics

Inside

Shutterstock: 3b/DAMRONG RATTANAPONG; 4tr/jafara; 4cr1/LIAL; 4cr2/bouybin; 4cr3/phRedy; 4br/mikeforemniakowski; 5tr/Khaled ElAdawy; 5cr/DGLimages; 5br/Shaiith; 5bl/LIAL; 6tr/fokusgood; 6cr/ShadeDesign; 6bl/MDL80; 6bl/ciqdem; 6&7c/gui jun peng; 7tr/zhengzaishuru; 7br/tornadoflight; 8t/cigdem; 8cl/Aleksandr Pobedimskiy; 8br/ Francescomoufotografo; 9cl/BlurryMe; 9br/zentilia; 10tr/13_Phunkod; 10bl/VectorShow; 10br/Zern Liew; 11tr/Designua; 11br/Sashkin; 11bl/Nor Gal; 12cl/Fouad A. Saad; 12&13c/Peter Braakmann; 12bc/Marusya Chaika; 13t/Olha1981; 13bl/jakit17; 14c/Fouad A. Saad; 14br/Photo smile; 14&15tc/mipan; 15tr/corbac40; 15cr/papa studio; 15br/Designua; 16&17t/NosorogUA; 16bl/Oleksandr Kostiuchenko; 16br/Cool Vector Maker; 17tr/VectorMine; 17br/tkyszk; 18b/julie deshaies; 18&19 bc/Glitterstudio; 19tr/ Designua; 19cl/Golubovy; 19br/Steve Collender; 20tr/Zurbagan; 20b/milan noga; 20&21c/Roman Yastrebinsky; 21tr/Macrovector; 21b/Vasyl Shulga; 22tr/Sergey Nivens; 22br/ ilove; 23tr/ImagineerInc; 23cr/Clayton Burne; 23br/vlabo; 24tl/Evgeny Zimin; 24br/Maksym Drozd; 25t/alexslb; 25tl/Fouad A. Saad; 25b/ktsdesign; 26tl/Everett Collection; 26cr/ raigvi; 26bl/siraphat; 27b/por_suwat; 28tr/BrAt82; 28l/StockImageFactory.com; 28br/Diego Schtutman; 29tl/Romolo Tavani; 29r/leisuretime70; 29bc1/tantawat; 30cr/Andrey Armyagov; 30&31b/lovelyday12; 31tr/Jetsadaphoto; 31cl/Puripat Lertpunyaroj; 31br/Breedfoto

Wikimedia Commons: 27tr/File:Ada Lovelace portrait.jpg/Alfred Edward Chalon, Public domain, via Wikimedia Commons/wikimedia commons; 27c/File:Diagram for the computation of Bernoulli numbers.jpg/Ada Lovelace, Public domain, via Wikimedia Commons/wikimedia commons; 29bc/File:Fibiger.gif/The photo is taken by the Danish photographer Thora Hallager (1821-1884), Public domain, via Wikimedia Commons/wikimedia commons; 30cl/File:Rachel Carson w.jpg/The original uploader was Cornischong at Luxembourgish Wikipedia., Public domain, via Wikimedia Commons/wikimedia commons

Force and Movement

Inside

Shutterstock: 3b/jeab05; 4&5tc/Khakimullin Aleksandr; 4cl/Mopic; 4cr/haryigit; 4bc/OSweetNature; 5cr/Nasimi Babaev; 5br/Lunja; 6tl/Sergey Nivens; 6cr/solarseven; 6&7 b/ petovarga; 7tr/Dragon Images; 7br/Gelia; 8tl/Prachaya Roekdeethaweesab; 8tr/koya979; 8bl/Sergiy Zavgorodny; 8br/Bakhur Nick; 9tr/magnetix; 9b/Falcon video; 10tr/Taras Kushnir; 10bl/Outer Space; 10br/VectorMine; 11tr/Master1305; 11b/Tom Wang; 12tr/JasminkaM; 12cl/Africa Studio; 12br/Malachy666; 13tr/VectorMine; 13bl/Nejron Photo; 13br/isarescheewin; 14c/Vitoriano Junior; 14br/Marusya Chaika; 14br/Marusya Chaika; 15tr/Jurik Peter; 15br/carlosramos1946; 16&17t/Mauricio Graiki; 16br/Rost9; 17cr/ Andrey VP; 18tr/Georgy Shafeev; 18bc/Coolakov_com; 18br/Decha Photography; ; 19t/gui jun peng; 19cr/Goskova Tatiana; 19br/jeab05; 20bl/udaix; 20br/Vdovichenko Denis; 21tr/Unkas Photo; 21tc/Heide Pinkall; 21cr/Dmitry_Tsvetkov; 21bc/OlegD; 21br/Vladyslav Starozhylov; 22tr/Crevis; 22br/apiguide; 23cr/Jim Barber; 23bl/Nieuwland Photography; ; 24bl/Sergey Bogdanov; 24br/Sergey Merkulov; 25tr/Sergey Merkulov; 25cl/ArtWell; 25br/Philip Lange; 25b/Arcansel; ; 26cl/EreborMountain; 26&27c/tratong; 27tl/verzellenberg; 27br/frank_peters; 28&29c/Sergey Nivens; 29tr/Dr. Norbert Lange; 30cl/AlexLMX; 31all/fosgen

Wikimedia Commons: 17br/File:Sir Isaac Newton by Sir Godfrey Kneller, Bt.jpg/Godfrey Kneller, Public domain, via Wikimedia Commons/wikimedia commons; 23tr/File:Uss_los_ angeles_airship_over_Manhattan/USN, Public domain, via Wikimedia Commons/wikimedia commons; 24tl/File:Musée des Arts et Métiers - Fardier de Cugnot (23725801128). jpg/Frédéric BISSON from Rouen, France, CC BY 2.0 <https://creativecommons.org/licenses/by/2.0>, via Wikimedia Commons/wikimedia commons; 25bc/900px- Berthabenzportrait/Bühler, Mannheim, Public domain, via Wikimedia Commons/wikimedia commons; 26tl/File:Gowy-icaro-prado.jpg/Jacob Peter Gowy, Public domain, via Wikimedia Commons/wikimedia commons; 26br/Mme._la_Baronne_de_Laroche,_aviatrice,_au_poste_de_direction_d'un_biplan_Voisin_(c._1910)/Library of Congress, Public domain, via Wikimedia Commons/wikimedia commons; 28br/662px-Cyrano_Mond//wikimedia commons; 31br/Grad_protractor/Wikinger from en.wiki, CC BY-SA 3.0 <http:// creativecommons.org/licenses/by-sa/3.0/>, via Wikimedia Commons/wikimedia commons;

Future Science and Technology

Inside

Shutterstock: 3b/Kite_rin; 4tl/Tschub; 4b/Prostock-studio; 5tl/Meletios Verras; 5cr/Dimarion; 5br/Momentum Fotograh; 6br/iconspro; 7cr/sutadimages; 7br/ozrimoz; 8bl/Yuganov Konstantin; 8cr/Viktoriia_M; 8&9c/Phonlamai Photo; 9t/New Africa; 9br/all_is_magic; 10tr/Andrey Suslov; 10cl/Africa Studio; 10&11c/Jenson; 11tr/MASTER VIDEO; 11cr/Volodymyr Horbovyy; 12bl/Bikeworldtravel; 12&13c/Zapp2Photo; 13tr/one photo; 14c and br/elenabsl; 15tr/MarinaGrigorivna; 15cl/sspopov; 15br/Alena Che; 16tr/Yaorusheng; 16bl/andrey_l; 16br/; 17cr/jamesteohart; 17bl/Trismegist san; 17br/Elisabeth Aardema; 18tr/Naeblys; 18cl/Vadim Sadovski; 18bc/vchal; 19tr/HelenField; 19cr/Pavel Chagochkin; 19b/Joseph Sohm; 20tl/Alf Ribeiro; 20cr/Soleil Nordic; 20br/MedstockPhotos; 21l/ImageFlow; 21cr/Nathan Devery; 22cl/Andrii Vodolazhskyi; 22bl/BlueRingMedia; 22&23 c/Anusorn Nakdee; 23tr/Juan Gaertner; 23cr/Steve Tum; 23cr/Meletios Verras; 23br/Elena Pavlovich; 24bl/KMW Photography; 24&25 c/Pattarawit Chompipat; 25cr/Suliman Razvan; 24&25b/Zaie; 26&27b/Zastolskiy Victor; 28bl/Teerasak Ladnongkhun; 28 & 29c/Bellovittorio; 29cr/Lakeview Images; 29bc/danylyukk1; 30tl/Marcin Balcerzak; 30bl/Aynur_sib; 31tl/Syda Productions; 31tr/Liv Oeian; 31b/Roschetzky Photography

Wikimedia Commons: 7tr/Unidentified U.S. Army photographer, Public domain, via Wikimedia Commons; 10bc/Work Projects Administration Federal Art Project, New York City, Public domain, via Wikimedia Commons; 11br/Rube Goldberg, Public domain, via Wikimedia Commons; 16br/File: Robert H Goddard 1963 Issue-8c.jpg/Bureau of Engraving and Printing, Public domain, via Wikimedia Commons/wikimdia commons; 18br/Voyager_Path.jpg: created by NASAderivative work: Rehua, Public domain, via Wikimedia Commons; 19b/Grombo, CC BY-SA 3.0 <http://creativecommons.org/licenses/by-sa/3.0/>, via Wikimedia Commons; 21br/Smithsonian Institution/Science Service; Restored by Adam Cuerden, Public domain, via Wikimedia Commons; 26c/NASA, Public domain, via Wikimedia Commons; 26br/Nobel Foundation, Public domain, via Wikimedia Commons; 27tr/By Melih Cevdet Teksen; 28cl/Elekhh, CC BY-SA 3.0 <https://creativecommons.org/licenses/by-sa/3.0>, via Wikimedia Commons; 30br/NASA, Public domain, via Wikimedia Commons; 31tr/Frankie Fouganthin, CC BY-SA 4.0 <https://creativecommons.org/licenses/by-sa/4.0>, via Wikimedia Commons

Light and Energy

Inside

Shutterstock: 3b/PopTika; 4tl/Color4260; 4br/Vasily Deyneka; 5cr/udaix; 5bl/udaix; 6tr/Fouad A. Saad; 6bl/udaix; 6&7c/Petar An; 7cr/Designua; 7br/Fancy Tapis; 7br/Roman Zaiets; 8bl/varuna; 8br/Racheal Grazias; 8br1/Olha1981; 9tc/haryigit; 9cl/Nattawat Kaewjirasit; 9cr/Anna Shepulova; 9bl/TTstudio; 9br/JaySi; 10tr/wk1003mike; 10bl/Dmytro Bochkov; 11tr/Mr.1; 11bl/Marc Ward; 12&13 tc/Roman Juchimcuk; 12bl/Fouad A. Saad; 12cr/RenataOs; 12br/Jorge A. Russell; 13cl/Pat_Hastings; 13bl/Studio 37; 14tr/sanyanwuji; 14bl/Africa Studio; 14bc/DenisProduction.com; 14br/tyrin; 14&15bg/lunopark; 15tc/Vladimir Korostyshevskiy; 15c/Maximus256; 15cr/Artography; 15bl/lisheng2121; 15br/Tragoolchitr Jittasaiyapan; 16tr/REDPIXEL.PL; 16bl/Milagli; 16br/Alila Medical Media; 17tr/Volodymyr Nikitenko; 17cl/Billion Photos; 17br/MAV Drone; 17cr/Fouad A. Saad; 18tl/Stella_E; 18bl/Designua; 18&19 tc/showcake; 18&19c/sl_photo; 18&19bc/Lesterman; 19tl/magnetix; 19cr/magnetix; 19br/Prarinya; 20tr/VladisChern; 20bl/Robyn Mackenzie; 20&21bc/Fouad A. Saad; 21tr/Edward Westmacott; 21br/feedbackstudio; 22bl/magnetix; 23tr/Africa Studio; 22&23 centre/Nils Z; 23br/Andy Lidstone; 24tr/stockelements; 24bc/Fouad A. Saad; 25tr/CD_works27; 25cr/VectorMine; 26cr/Peter Hermes Furian; 26br/aekikuis; 26&27c/Leigh Prather; 27cr/petrroudny43; 27cr/Proxima Studio; 27br/enterlinedesign; 29tl/Chase Clausen; 28cl/Fotovika; 28br/Kallayanee Naloka; 28&29c/gualtiero boffi; 29tr/Roman Zaiets; 30tr/RazoomGame; 30bl/Megan Betteridge; 30bc/hunthomas; 30br1/haroldguevara; 30br1/Yuriy Vlasenko; 31tr/MicroOne; 31b/arshambo; 31br/DG Stock

Wikimedia Commons: 5tr//Unknown authorUnknown author, Public domain, via Wikimedia Commons/wikimedia commons; 5bl/File:Photoelectric effect in a solid - diagram.svg/Ponor, CC BY-SA 4.0 <https://creativecommons.org/licenses/by-sa/4.0>, via Wikimedia Commons/wikimedia commons; 13tr/nl:Gebruiker:MaureenV, Public domain, via Wikimedia Commons; 15tc/File:Statua di Archimede, Siracusa.png/Stella, CC BY-SA 4.0 <https://creativecommons.org/licenses/by-sa/4.0>, via Wikimedia Commons/wikimedia commons; 23br/File:Watt James von Breda.jpg/Carl Frederik von Breda, Public domain, via Wikimedia Commons/wikimedia commons; 29br/File:Chirped pulse amplification.png//wikimedia commons; 31tl/File:Lanature1882 praxinoscope projection reynaud.png/Louis Poyet, Public domain, via Wikimedia Commons/wikimedia commons

Living Things

Inside

Shutterstock: 3b/Ethan Daniels; 4tc/Lamberrto; 4cl/Mogens Trolle; 4bc/Ivan Kruk; 4 & 5 c/Designua; 5tl/File:Mariana-trench.jpg/1840489pavan nd, CC BY-SA 4.0 <https://creativecommons.org/licenses/by-sa/4.0>, via Wikimedia Commons/Wikimedia commons; 5tc/Lee Bernard; 5cr/Sergey Uryadnikov; 5bl/EreborMountain; 6tr/Designua; 6tr/Designua; 7tl/Everett Collection; 7tr/sonsart; 7br/Fouad A. Saad; 8tl/ju_see; 8cl/udaix; 8bc/Eric Isselee; 9tl/Dora Zett; 9cr/Volodymyr Burdiak; 9bc/tratong; 9bc/Iakov Filimonov; 9br/Syda Productions; 10tr/Soleil Nordic; 10cl/Kenneth Keifer; 10bl/Teerasak Ladnongkhun; 11tl/hadkhanong; 11bl/Kallayanee Naloka; 11br/Matt Gibson; 12tl/Kazakova Maryia; 12bl/photowind; 12bc/Aldona Griskeviciene; 12 & 13c/rolandtopor; 13tr/Designua; 13bc/Jovana Pantovic; 13br/Matthew Connolly; 14tl/Alexandra Tyukavina; 14cl/Yarygin; 14cr/Elizaveta Galitckaia; 14br/Joshua Resnick; 14b/divedog; 15tl/nicostock; 15cl/Giedriius; 15cr/Kate Cuzko; 15bl/Breck P. Kent; 15br/Rattiya Thongdumhyu; 16tl/Dani Vincek; 16tc/StudioPortoSabbia; 16cl/Jakinnboaz; 16c/Jakinnboaz; 16cr/Jakinnboaz; 16bl/Jakinnboaz; 16bc/Anna ART; 17tl/Vector Flower Parts Diagram with stem cross section anatomy of plant morphology and its contents useful for school student stamen pistil petal sepal leaf receptacle root botany science education; 17tr/elesi; 17cl/baismartin; 17br/PRILL; 18 & 19tc/WIROJE PATHI; 18cl/Patrick Foto; 18bl/Vova Shevchuk; 18br/Jiang Zhongyan; 19tl/paulista; 19tr/Jirik V; 19c/udaix; 19cr/Picture Partners; 19bl/Georgy Dzyura; 19br/Andrea Anderegg; 20tl/Dennis Sabo; 20cr/H.Tanaka; 20b/IVANNE; 21tr/Gerald Robert Fischer; 21cl/Choksawatdikorn; 21bl/Witaya Proadtayakogool; 21br/unjiko; 22tl/3Dstock; 22tr/Protasov AN; 22cr/rtbilder; 22br/fenkieandreas; 23tl/Dieter Decroos; 23cl/P; 23c/John A. Anderson; 23cr/John A. Anderson; 24c/Vecton; 24br/Volodymyr Burdiak; 24br/Eric Isselee; 25tc/Naypong Studio; 25tc/Jao Cuyos; 25cr1/Nejron Photo; 25cr1/rawisoot; 25cr2/Bonnie Taylor Barry; 25b/udaix; 26cr/le bouil baptiste; 26cl/Vlad61; 26br/Rosa Jay; 27tl/Susan Schmitz; 27cr/DavidYoung; 27cl/Gluiki; 27br/Elisa Manzati; 28tl/Agustin J. Villarreal; 28bl/Martin Pelanek; 28cr/worldswildlifewonders; 29tr/Maria Spb; 29cr/Tinseltown; 25cl/Everett Collection; 29bl/PHOTO LOLA; 29bl/GUDKOV ANDREY; 29br1/GUDKOV ANDREY; 29br/Cookie Studio; 30cl/Yakov Oskanov; 30cr/Mufti Adi Utomo; 30bl/dnaveh; 31tl/E.G.Pors; 31tr/Mazur Travel; 31br/; 31b/Alexey Wraith;

Wikimedia Commons: 6bl/File:Kepler186f-ComparisonGraphic-20140417 improved.jpg/NASA Ames/SETI Institute/JPL-Caltech, Public domain, via Wikimedia Commons/wikimedia commons; 8 & 9c/1024px-Phylogenetic_tree.svg/This vector version: Eric Gaba (Sting, fr:Sting), Cherkash, Public domain, via Wikimedia Commons/wikimedia commons; 18tc/File:Spider internal anatomy-en.svg/!Original:John Henry ComstockVector: Pbroks13 (Ryan Wilson), CC BY 3.0 <https://creativecommons.org/licenses/by/3.0>, via Wikimedia Commons/wikimedia commons;